RAGS....TO BITCHES AND DOGS

Volume II

The Cherry Tree Years

By: Maria L A Parnell

ISBN No. 9781849144742

25 Years ago on 26th May 1988...I fell in love with my dream cottage, it's been a labour of love ever since. Fondly known as 'Money Tree Cottage,' it's name is Cherry Tree! We built a life here, we have lived, loved, luaghed and cried here....we had hoped to see out our days here....who knows what the future holds anymore but until then....here it is on the day we moved in.....and also 'Today' 25Yrs on........

Cherry Tree Cottage 1988 - 2012.... and still DIY'ing !!

RAGS....TO BITCHES AND DOGS

Volume II - The Cherry Tree Years is the sequel to my
first Book, The Pre-Dog Years.
It will transport you to the middle phase of my adult years and the
progress I made, or lack of it, in my life!
This Volume documents my adventures from around the age of 28
to 42 years of age...... *Cwtch up and prepare yourself to join me on
my adventures...!

* Cwtch...A Welsh word for 'Hugging/Cuddling/Snuggling up

Published By: CPI Group / Antony Rowe

Dedications

Dedicated first and foremost to my beautiful late Airedale, **Dexter**. The dog who changed my life!

Then to my wonderful Husband, **Byron** for all the years he has put up with me! For all the times he's called me a 'crazy crumpet' and for all the years he has stood by my side, shoulder to shoulder, back to back and fought every battle thrown at us. Byron, you really couldn't have known what you were taking on when you asked me to be your Wife.....my life was destined to be troublesome from the day I was born!

To my dearest, treasured and much loved friend **Carol Withers** for all that she brings to my life and means to me.

To all those beautiful and loving cats mainly rescued, and those who adopted us whether we liked it or not! They shared our life at the Cottage, enjoyed the sun on their backs, fields to wander through, mice to catch and generally led a life of bliss until either their calling came, illness or accident took them or they simply left home of their own accord.......**Chester, Maxwell, Thomas, Sophie, Basil, Macey, Rupert, Verity, Emily, Halshaw, Milly, Benson, Fat Barry, Harley, Mrs Polly** - god bless all your little paws as you swat butterflies on the Great Bridge. With the exception of Harley and Mrs Polly who reside in the lap of luxury with my dearest friend Carol Withers to date, April 2014.

Acknowledgements

Once again to the fabulous *Caroline Owen* for being the woman who reached out her arms to me over the internet on Face Book at a time in my life when I felt life was no longer for living....for me! For her insistence and kick up the butt in ensuring this book was written. Without her encouragement, these memories would remain just that, locked up in my brain eating away at my soul.

The writing of my Autobiography so far has been both cathartic and healing. To be able to put it all down sequentially on paper and close the book feels like finally being able to move on.

....And there is still Volume III to go!

To *Simon Rees* for his extremely talented photography work in creating the Book Covers for both Volumes to date. I am always amazed at Simon's ability to see 'within' an image for things that move the heart an soul. His Landscape shots often posted on Face Book are thrilling for me as he moves expertly, in my Layman's opinion, from still life to rolling mountain terrain, animal or floral shots. His ever faithful companion the delightful Sammy the Jack Russell Terrier is always at his side enjoying the adventures with his Dad.

To *Sammy*, for being a wonderful Doggy Model for my Book Covers, fame has not rushed to his head and I am sure he doesn't realise how 'paw'sum' he really is.....

For this Volume, my remit to Simon was to create a Book Cover that would boldly and simplistically describe the Title whilst encompassing the original theme of Volume I. Thus Sammy.... as I move toward the richness and love dogs have brought to my life and a Cherry Tree.... the Cottage and home that has sailed us through so many life battles and storms for the past 26 years!

And to **Karl MacWilliam** and his lovely wife, **Susannah**. Dexter's Breeders, these wonderful people not only provided us with a puppy that grew up to become the love of our lives but were also there when our hearts broke when he died. There can never be another Dexter, just as his Breeders are, he was unique and very special.

Foreword

Volume II has been a much more difficult reiteration for me of my life's adventures. During it's writing as the second volume of my Autobiography, I have needed to face many demons, relive many foul memories that on times have rendered me sobbing. This action in itself I see as being part of the healing process, to 'get it out' of my system, tell it as it was warts and all.

Looking back I can barely comprehend how I got through some of these experiences let alone understand how and why they happened. I do know however, that the vast knowledge and life learning I hold this present day comes from making those past mistakes and having learned from said experiences, you have to make the mistake in the first place to learn from it! I would also say that many of my experiences have been caused through no fault of my own.....but this doesn't mean I didn't learn anything from them.

It seems a shame that such wisdom comes to us all late in life, years and years of 'living' tucked under our belts. It is with this in mind that I really want this Book and my other writings to work for others.

Read my adventures not as a woe betide me, feel pity and sorrow rendition. Look at your own life.... only YOU can change it. If my story can give just one person in the world the strength to carry on, stop them from doing something stupid, help them to face life and re-build.....then my life on this planet has not been as worthless as it has felt since the day I was born!

Only YOU...can change your destiny, improve upon the life you have!

Only YOU... can change your mindset, ditch the self pity and wallowing in 'why me?'

Only YOU... have 3 score years plus ten on this earth.....please don't waste a minute!

Only YOU... can make YOUR'S a fabulous life!

I sincerely wish each and every one of you just that!!

Maria

CONTENTS

Chapters

PLEASE NOTE......

Having listened to all feedback from Volume I, may I please advise this book is published in Crown Format and I want to maintain the continuity of its style of publication.
Its size, which is generally used for Autobiography publishing can be awkward to hold which means some people will fold the book back on itself for comfort in order to ease the 'holding' position when reading.
If you fold this book in half to hold it in one hand....the pages are likely to peel away from the spine and fall out!
This is not a book manufacturing problem....but caused by incorrect handling of the book structure.

To preserve your book in its published condition....do not fold the book back on itself to hold in one hand.

Also....

Actual names of persons mentioned within these covers have been abbreviated or changed in order to protect their identity.

Finally...

This Book contains graphic language portraying the emotions experienced and as per factual events. No offence is intended.

Thank you and enjoy!

Chapter 1

- Escape To The Country -

I wonder what the hell it looks like? Is all I could think in the aftermath of my impetuous actions in buying a house completely unseen, over the phone and paying the asking price to boot!

Well it could not be any worse than some of the places we had already viewed.
It said it was rural in the newspaper advert and I was truly sick and tired of missing out on each property we fancied in the Spring of 1988 gazumping wars, act in haste repent at leisure so the saying goes, well we're just going to have to wait and see I mentally concluded. However in the following hour or so after the call, I was just itching to get out and view the property, the 10 O'clock viewing as arranged the next morning was way too far off for my natural patience levels.
Dillwyn was away on site inspections for the afternoon so I approached the Deputy Manager with my need to leave work early that afternoon for personal reasons. We were hardly under pressure or rushed off our feet in the office and so he agreed on the basis I made up the lost time, done deal Mr and I was out into the car park before he could blink.

As I climbed into my blue Toyota Corolla Hatchback, I raised the sun roof and donned the obligatory sun shades preparing on this gorgeous of days in more ways than just the weather, to view the property that was to be mine and Byron's future home, even if it was only to see it from the exterior. Making my way out of the City hustle and bustle of traffic I eventually found myself on quieter back roads leading to the Welsh Mid Glamorgan Valleys.

13

The Estate Agent had given me very basic locality directions so I had a fair idea of the area I was heading for, as to the exact location of the Cottage, heaven only knows! I found the Village of Llantrisant quite easily and made my way up the steep hill into the heart of the village.

Llantrisant resides within the Borough of what was known as Mid Glamorgan, later re-named as Rhondda Cynon Taff and lay on the Rivers Ely and Afon Clun. Mostly it is still referred to as Llantrisant Mid Glamorgan as generations of locals disliked the new title, especially as it was shortened to Llantrisant, R.C.T.

The Town's name translates as The Parish of The Three Saints in question St.Illtyd, St.Gwynno and St.Dafodwg. A hilltop settlement at an altitude of 565 feet above sea level Llantrisant bears a very rich and ancient history which is truly fascinating.

I made my way into the centre of the village known as The Bull Ring stopping to ask a few people if they knew of the property for sale called Rackett Cottage, but I drew a blank stare from most. Eventually I found the local Post Office and struck gold.

"Oh yes, the Rackett's are out on the back road behind the Mint" replied the Post Master when I enquired. "How do I get there from here?" I asked not locking in for one minute that the man was speaking of THE Royal Mint, the world's leading export Mint making coinage for over 60 Countries each year. Opened in 1968 by H.M.Queen Elizabeth II and employing over 900 staff, the Mint produces an average five Billion coins per annum.

After some brief directions I found myself driving down over Llantrisant Common which is a vast area of 'free' land controlled by the Freemen of Llantrisant where cattle, sheep and horses may graze without rent or obligation.

Looking to my right across the Common I could see rolling hills and mountain terrain and I guessed it was this area I was being directed to in order to find the Cottage. Indeed, I drove up through winding, often narrow country lanes absolutely loving the remoteness of the area I was in. Although the Cottage is only three miles from the Common itself, I felt as if I were driving forever into the middle of nowhere, but even nowhere is somewhere I agreed with myself.

Up one lane and then turning off on to another even narrower adopted road surface into a lane that seemed to be leading back on myself from the direction I had just driven, I found myself truly lost and wondering if I had already gone wrong with the directions. There was no such thing as satellite navigation or indeed smart phones with GPRS back then.

During the Easter weekend hunt that Byron and I had undertaken previously to find a home, we had become accustomed to asking locals for directions and in fact this action in itself had sometimes proven to backfire on us as said locals hadn't realised the property we were seeking was even up for sale. Before we could drive back to the Estate Agents the locals had made favourable enquiries thus thwarting our attempts to purchase. As such Byron had instructed me to 'say nothing to anybody' when trying to view a property we liked.

I drove along this idyllic country lane with only the sun beating down through my open sun roof and the sound of the birds to distract me. I noted the distinct lack of any neighbouring properties, there was no suburban lifestyle to be had here and certainly no 'popping' to the shop or even a neighbour for a cup of sugar if needed.

I drove on slowly past a ramshackle but occupied, dilapidated farmhouse hoping to goodness THAT was not what I'd come to view, forward past what looked like a large Manor House and a small hilltop bungalow that had been built totally out of character with its surroundings?

Down through some winding 'S' bends with a babbling stream running alongside the narrow lane then past a pair of semi detached cottages one of which looked well maintained, the other was in poor and shabby disrepair but there were no names to indicate their identity. I continued up a very steep hill to the top of the adjacent mountain and started by this time to consider I was way off course and had misunderstood entirely where I should be going. I pulled over into a field gateway just as a large tractor rounded the bend heading toward me. Quick as a flash, I left the vehicle to flag down the tractor driver, mindful of my strict instructions from Byron I prepared my question carefully. He pulled in almost reluctantly, much has been the attitude of the locals around here ever since to show any act of helpfulness or neighbourly goodwill. "Excuse me, I started, I'm looking for Rackett Cottage. I was told to go past the new housing development and the cottage would be just after?" I lied. The farmer looked down at me aloft his Massey Fergusson seemingly to take an age to connect his brain to his mouth. "No new 'ousing site round 'ere" he replied stern faced and resolutely. I wasn't to be beaten on this reconnoitre so promptly continued "yes, the Agent said go past the Development and then I would see the Cottage." He just stared at me blankly. With absolutely no disrespect intended to Hill Billy's wherever they may reside in this world, I did indeed start to hear violins playing and wondered if I should beat a retreat. Finally he spoke..."That's The Rackett's down there, and there's NO development round 'ere, I'd know if there was I live 'ere!" BINGO!!

I turned to look over my shoulder back down the long winding lane to the two small semi detached cottages that I had just driven past nestled at the bottom of the hill. I thanked him and he drove off, rumbling his way down the mountain with only the roar of his tractor engine to be heard for miles.

I stood for a moment in the wide open countryside, breathing in the fresh, clean, country air before stepping into the field gateway to stare down from my vantage point up the mountain at the two cottages known as The Racketts' snuggled way below me. To all sides of these two dwellings were vast and endless to the eye open countryside with sheep and stock, horses and odd dwellings scattered across maybe a 3-5 mile radius. I gasped in a breath as I recall thinking "Oh my God it wouldn't be our luck to buy this place!"

I drove slowly back down the mountain and parked outside the two dwellings with no indication of which was which but common sense was telling me the one for sale would most certainly be the run down and sad one at the price stated. No matter I thought, we're young, we have our lives ahead and we can 'do it up!'

As I sat with the car windows open staring at the frontage of the property I took in the babbling stream alongside me, the bird sound of what I thought was a Curlew and the bleating of the sheep. The distant whir of agricultural machinery could be heard if you really listened above the breeze through the hedges and trees.

In a split second I fell in love with the Cottage, it's location was everything I wanted in a rural property, the surrounding fields and woodland were magical and I felt an instant connection with the building itself. I cannot tell you what sort of connection because it made no sense to me at the time, but I felt a strong and uncontrollable urge to be the one to bring this tired, sorry and unkempt building back to life. To give it an identity to be proud of once again, to let it feel some love and warmth from within it's four stone walls heart. There was nobody at home, no sign of life and the afternoon was starting to wane, I realised there was no point in hanging around as I would be back here again tomorrow at 10am and so I drove back the way I had come toward the Village.

Byron had been in London working that day not expected home until very late at Whitla Court and so I made my way home to feed the 'boys' who were by now learning to scale the picture window curtains and could be clearly seen 'dangling' as I pulled up in front of the flat, I wondered how many more new snags and pulled threads I was going to find this time. Mobile communication was in its infancy and at the time Byron's company had equipped his car with a mobile phone that resembled a house brick on the end of a big square box attached to his lower dashboard area.

The Cottage was on my mind covering it like a cobweb of what if's and could we questions? I desperately wanted to get back there to be close to this building almost like a feeling of protection for it....the emotions I was feeling were bizarre and inexplicable but they were what I felt and I could not deny them.

I decided to call Byron from home and break the news of what I had done but the call took on an entirely different slant as my 'simply had to' emotions took over my soul for the second time that day.

"Hi Babe, I spoke brightly and up beat, where you at right now?"

"Hiya Gorgeous, I'm just coming past Reading, be about an hour'ish before I get home, don't worry about a meal for me, you go ahead I can grab something when I get in!" he sounded tired which I gave no thought to.

"Ring me back when you get to the Severn Bridge" I asked. The Severn Bridge being the Toll Bridge into Wales from England. "So I can leave and meet you at Junction 34 of the M4, I have something to show you" I declared in a voice that belied the excitement and happiness I was feeling.

"What do you mean something to show me? he answered, Junction 34 is way past home, what's happening?" His voice sounded concerned but curious.

"I'm taking you to see the Cottage I've bought us!" I declared triumphantly. There was a very long pause on the line

"Yeah, yeah, came his hesitant response, what d'ya mean you've bought us?" His tone was taking on a much more serious tone.

"No honestly, I've bought us a country cottage, you're going to love it!" I was ecstatic to give him my news.

"What's it like and where?" he spat back.

"Near Llantrisant, it's quite run down and they want £45K for it but it could be made gorgeous. You can follow me and I'll show you" I replied.

"Oh for gods sake M (his pet name for me) what have you done? OK, I'll see you at 34!" and he hung up, but I was totally unperturbed by his lack of enthusiasm, I knew it would change soon as he saw the place.

And so we met at Junction 34 by which time it was getting on for 9.30pm and light was fading. I proudly forged the route ahead from the Motorway up through the Village and out into the country lanes that were by now in pitch blackness, no street lighting, no light pollution, in fact you couldn't see your hand in front of your face!

As I approached the cottage in my full beam headlights I indicated from my vehicle for him to pull in behind me. We climbed out from our cars to stand in a pitch black country lane. "There it is, what d'ya think?" I pointed to the dim shadow of both buildings just ahead of us.

"What, where I can't see anything?" Byron was straining to look ahead clearly irritable that he was here to look at something he couldn't even see!

He was right, this was a daft time of night to be trying to view a country residence in the middle of nowhere!

There were a few lights on between both properties but we decided to call it a day and return the following morning as arranged. Back at Whitla Court the conversation soon came around to how on earth I had managed in eight short hours to make a firm offer on a house I hadn't even viewed without at least consulting him and had dragged him out to look at in the pitch black of night to no avail! Get used to it my son was all I could think, I'm a do'er not a thinker!

As always Byron was out of bed at 5am the following morning, pottering around the flat as I slumbered in my pit. A cup of coffee at around 6.45am rendered me at least awake if not alert! The Boys were as ever rolling around the flat locked together in 'prairie ball battle' with Maxwell gaining size and strength over Chester. They bounded up on the bed, purring like two generators volleying for cuddles as they nudged their heads under my arms with me trying to avoid spilling my coffee.

I had organised a rapid day off by calling into the office night shift, nothing was going to stop me viewing my new home at 10am. Byron was just glad to have a day off as far as I could tell. We left the flat just after 9.15am for the drive to the Cottage where we were meeting the Estate Agent Representative.

In the daylight drive through the lanes, Byron began to express his amazement at the locality and rural situ, I of course felt my feathers fluffed at having discovered the place via the newspaper that fateful lunch hour.

We pulled up opposite the cottage and were first to arrive. I was prepared for the vision as I had already witnessed but Byron was a little taken aback at the sad state of repair of the Cottage. "It'll be Ok Hun, I assured him, we can take our time to do it up, no rush!" He nodded in agreement as we knocked the door.

James Bretherton opened the front door as if he were welcoming royalty! A larger than life figure similar in looks to a cross between Big Foot and Shrek appeared in the 'Vestibule' as described as the entrance to the Cottage. Said 'Vestibule' was/is indeed a purpose built square meter of space walled off as an entrance hall from the front door to the main living room of the cottage, let's be realistic here!

His booming voice and peculiar accent led us to believe he was a 'cosmopolitan' sort of chap who was clearly not lacking in self confidence. "Come in, come in" he beckoned, we entered to the immediate odour of sticky sweetness as I recall it. Byron maintains this was the smell of Cannabis...I wouldn't know having never done drugs in my life, but was somewhat curious that Byron knew the smell of it?

We stood politely introducing ourselves awaiting the arrival of the Agent to show us around with the Vendor. As I stood waiting I absorbed the atmosphere of this old building, it was shabby with concrete floors on show, bare stone walls, little in the way of furniture and nothing hanging on the walls.

There were no curtains hanging in the main windows, the dining room looked like something from a gothic, sacrificial scene with flickering red candle wall mounted lamps and a long, bare wooden table with concrete floor beneath. The kitchen was nothing more than a separated room housing a camping table top stove for cooking, no fitted units and a free standing sink unit with a tap on a pipe bracketed to the wall. Upstairs faired no better with a bare minimum fitted bathroom, no shower and a toilet that had flushing issues.

20

The Bedrooms were eccentric to say the least with the front bedroom reeking of something unidentifiable....but again I am unfamiliar with drugs or their smells. Shortly after we had been given the quick 'once around' the Agent arrived. A young buck in a sporty motor, hardly dressed to impress professionally he bounced into the Cottage declaring his late arrival as nothing more than he'd had a late start as a result of sleeping in! Sorry but for me I'd rather be lied to, tell me that Spider Man invaded your bedroom unexpectedly, that a Volcano erupted in your garden without warning, you ran out of god damned fuel on the way....but don't be telling me you failed to get your lazy god damned ass out of bed on time to meet a prospective buyer of a property your company was advertising for sale, who had made an appointment for a viewing time of which you were well aware!!

He was young, he was inexperienced and he was incompetent...on entering the Cottage he immediately engaged with the Vendor before introducing himself to us as to who he was and where from. We were his clients that day, at the very least I would have expected him to extend his hand in a shake of introduction before ploughing into his 'parrot' fashion repartee.

As we had already been shown the interior it was agreed we would all proceed to the gardens of the property. A slight problem here as the back door of the cottage was overgrown with brambles so we ventured out through the front door and walked around the side of the domain. It was indeed a jungle but the owner was intent on showing us his 'water feature pond' to impress upon us his attempts at harnessing the wilderness that was the rear garden.

Oh heavens to Betsy...the water feature was a death trap of a collaboration between sheet plastic sunk into a small area of garden weighted down by stones and an electrical indoor cable strung out through the kitchen window sporting a 60 Watt light bulb on the end. Plugged into the mains in the kitchen it held pride of place an inch or so above the pond suspended off a nearby branch to illuminate the stagnant green water which seemed to have what looked like a condom floating around on top!

21

Byron was horrified and steered me away spluttering his disbelief at the health and safety aspects. We continued around the garden which has the most peculiar layout of boundaries and fences. 'Our' garden, as I had already decided it was to be, seemed to run down beneath the neighbouring property so their own kitchen window overlooked our garden. It was/is substantial in size with a further area tapering off to a point at the side of the Cottage, to describe the basic shape would be to picture a 'Right' pointing arrow if that makes sense with a few odd cut out and added nooks and crannies. It was to all appearances neglected and overgrown with bramble vines smothering the back of the property to the point you couldn't even see the kitchen door. The side elevation of land banked right up to the cottage gable end wall and breached any possible damp proof course by at least three feet, if indeed one existed at all! Rotting Georgian pane windows spelled out much expense to waterproof the property and an equally dodgy looking flat roof to the rear of the Cottage was giving Byron a nervous twitch. The aspect of the Cottage was/is south facing to the rear making for a lovely sunny garden by day, a great plant and vegetable environment. The front was/ is North facing making for quite a dark aspect to the Lounge but there had to be some compromises to be accepted for the sheer rural ambience of the place, its peace and tranquillity, its offering of a completely blank canvass to make our own mark upon as a home.

We all ventured back inside for another 'guided' if you could call it that, tour by the Agent around the interior. He pointed out the beauty of the full house height stone wall to the one side of the lounge, the open plan mahogany staircase, the Inglenook fireplace bereft of any burner but it did have another of those 'dodgy' illuminated lights that had been rigged up around the place. It sported a red bulb giving the stone fireplace a similar sacrificial look to the dining room. The upstairs bedroom doors were quite a selling point for me as they were/are 'ledged and braced' with fairy tale castle type studding giving an almost medieval impression. Similarly somebody had taken the time to ledge and brace panel some of the walls....it's a quaint and unique little property!

In his broad Cardiff accent the Agent piped up "Cor, this is nice innit! My dogs would love it 'ere, wouldn't mind buying this myself!" Hey presto! In one totally unprofessional sentence the Agent had just flung us into a bidding war with the Vendor. Byron was furious as was I.

We expressed our interest to proceed and agreed we would return to the Agents Offices in Cardiff to discuss the property further. As we left hand in hand Byron muttered out of the side of his mouth "we haven't got a cats chance in hell of getting this now thanks to that bloody stupid Agent!" I simply replied "Stand back and watch Baby!" James Bretherton looked cock a hoop as we drove off.
It took just twenty minutes or so to get back to Cardiff City Centre, we entered the Agents Office hopeful and excited but with our emotions guarded as to potential disappointment ....and we were wise to do so!
" Ahhh come in Mr Parnell, hello again Maria, did you like what you saw?" Her questions were plausible but she seemed anxious?

We responded that we were seriously interested to which she dropped her bombshell. "Uhmm not sure how to explain this but Mr Bretherton called us ten minutes ago, he has increased the price of the Cottage to £47,500K. With that she did what most good sales people do and shut up....he who speaks first loses!!!
We were not surprised but very annoyed as it had been the Agent who was supposed to be 'selling' not 'buying' that had caused us this hike in price. Byron was annoyed explaining that the representative Agent had acted unprofessionally causing unnecessary price haggling.....I however was unperturbed because I held an ace up my sleeve. We agreed to pay the new asking price but I personally couldn't wait to get out of the offices and tell Byron that we would NOT be paying any extra at least not on paper!

Details were exchanged and contact numbers swapped and we left the Agents Office as the hopeful new Owners of Rackett Cottage subject to contract! We drove to a nearby favourite lunch time haunt for a coffee and de-brief, Chapter Arts Theatre in Canton, Cardiff.

"I could swing for that little prick!"

Byron was buzzing at just having been stung for a further £2.5K, especially when he had never wanted to spend more than £30K on a home in the first place. I smiled, busting at the seams to relieve his frustrations.

"We won't be increasing the mortgage Hun" I stated staring him in the eye with a wry smile on my face.

"What do you mean?"

"I know something that 'MR' James rip off doesn't know we know." I casually replied. In true style Byron's patience gave out totally.

"What the fuck you talking about, what.... what?"

You see on carousing the Cottage for the second time I had chance to eyeball some paperwork left casually strewn on the upstairs table in the front bedroom...it clearly stated REPOSESSION ORDER issued.

"MR James Bretherton is in no position to haggle my love, the Cottage is up for repossession and the order has been issued, he's very much on borrowed time." I explained.

After some spluttering and disbelief Byron was agog at my ace card player status. Initially I am sad to say we laughed at our own possible good fortune but then we both looked at each other voicing each other's thoughts...."Poor bastard, can't imagine the stress he's under, survival of the fittest and all that but lord how must he feel?" Our sympathies were wasted on this man as you will read further on.

We were now in a position of strength as regards the purchase so Byron contacted James advising his actions had been anticipated but were unacceptable, if he wanted the sale, reminding him we were in no chain, then he would have to accept the additional £2.5K in cash by an agreed date after completion of contracts. Not surprisingly James agreed and almost bit Byron off at the wrist.

The call came through to Rentokil some four days later that our offer had been accepted.....Rackett Cottage was ours to all intent and purpose. We were absolutely elated, excited and emotionally flying.

The wheels of house purchase rolled into motion and as we already had our mortgage jacked up ready to go it just meant a written month's notice to our Landlord who was actually a lovely guy. He wished us well and was sorry to see us go as we'd been 'no trouble at all' as tenants. Our bond was returned as was rightfully ours unlike the last crook of a landlord. We were positively floating through the days like any couple about to move into a first new home together, we talked, planned, hatched, decided, chose colours and argued about how much to spend on furniture and when.

Roughly two weeks after signing for contract James Bretherton called me at work one afternoon.

"Hi, I have to go away on business, might be away during the hand over so I'll need the final payment by tomorrow night."

I explained this was totally unexpected and not what we'd agreed but I'd speak to Byron as soon as possible to see what we could arrange.

We left it that we would call him later that day. Again Byron was exasperated with the guy and we of course knew what his tactics were but we needed to play the game carefully. As it was we could only gather one thousand pounds together in such a short window of time anyway so we called him and advised accordingly. Once again this offer was readily accepted and we agreed for him to meet us at our flat the following evening to collect the cash.

The following day all was in place but it was around 3 O'clock when I got the call from Byron to say he was delayed on a job and wouldn't be able to get back to Whitla Court in time for meeting James, suddenly I was nervous as this guy was clearly a wild card character.

None the less I made my way home only to find James already parked outside the flat, we exchanged pleasantries before he asked outright for his money.

"It's not exactly in my handbag James! I advised, it's upstairs so you better come up."
He followed me to the flat and as ever the boys tumbled down the stairs to meet
me..."Ughh, cats, I hate cats, I'm allergic to them!" I heard James spit out behind me
whilst simultaneously thinking to myself tough shit pal.

He stood waiting whilst I retrieved the £1000 from my bedroom and I counted it out in
front of him. "When can I have the rest? he asked firmly, I want it by Monday." I stared
him in the eye and I could see the level of desperation in his look.
I stated truthfully we couldn't raise that amount in such a short time so we would have
to meet later in the week.
Suddenly he started staring around the flat, "Nice place you got here, I could take
jewellery or some other stuff on retainer." I was aghast..."I've just agreed we'll have the
rest by mid week, take it or leave it James!" I replied rather aggressively hiding the fact
that my knees were knocking louder than a Woodpecker. He backed off thankfully and
made his exit agreeing we would meet the following Wednesday at a local Pub close
to the Cottage. This guy was an out and out waster, what happened to his needing to
go away imminently on business huh?
Byron arrived home to find me 'shaken but not stirred' and we discussed what would
happen next, the kitties were oblivious to it all continuing to spit and fart their way
around the flat no matter what time of day or night...life was a ball and they were
dancing their little hearts out!

We agreed we would meet James at a local Public House known as The Black Prince
in Llantrisant just three miles down the lane from the Cottage. As always Byron and I
were on time and entered this vast building that was/is modern in structure pretending
to be old. My initial memory is of actually 'sticking' to the carpets as I walked in such
was the amount of filth and spillage on the floor. The Pub was and remains neither the
type of establishment or place I would ever want to frequent or be in at any one time!
James arrived some fifteen minutes later sitting himself down at the table with a
determined look on his face.

"Right then, he said, £1500 left to pay I hope you don't want a receipt" and laughed. Byron squared up in his chair, "Can't do it James sorry, you sprung your demands for payment on us too quick after the agreement, you will have to wait until the original date as agreed." James face took on a 'Black Prince' look.

"I want my money Byron." He spoke low and threatening.

"Sure you do James, I appreciate that but scaring my girlfriend in her own home the other night was a bad move mate! Wanting our personal possessions, what the fuck was that all about then heh?"

James and Byron were now eyeball to eyeball across the table.

"Well it's £1500 now or the sale is off!" James didn't flinch in his stance.

Byron was cool and calculated "Well it's off then James, just hope you find another buyer before the repossession order date!"

James was bog eyed at this statement "How the fuck do you know about the repossession?" he spat out.

"Doesn't matter, fact is we do, now are you going to wait for the £1500 or shall we knock it on the head right now?" Byron was taking no prisoners and I sat there watching this battle of wills unfold getting tearful because I so wanted this Cottage.

My man was fighting my corner for my future nest and as much as I felt sorry for James in a strange way, he was his own worst enemy and so full of bullshit and crap that I just couldn't pity him any longer.

"Fair enough, sale goes through but I want my cash immediately after completion OK?" James was rattled. We agreed he could call us after completion and we would arrange settlement.

Letters rumbled back and forth, telephone calls ensued and finally in week four we completed contracts and a date to collect keys was arranged for almost two weeks afterwards.....it was exactly six weeks from first viewing that we moved in and my "stand back and watch me" promise to myself and Byron as we walked out the Cottage door that morning had been honoured.

We took possession of our home on 26th May 1988...it was a Thursday!

I am a Thursday's born child, 'tis said they have far to go and I was certainly on a life's adventure!

Chapter 2

- New Beginnings....lousy start -

All systems go!

Byron had arranged to borrow the box back van from his employers Shine's to transport what pitiful amount of belongings and furniture we owned between us. I had organised a few days off work to move and unpack. We rose that Thursday morning amidst a sea of cardboard boxes and absolutely unable to contain our excitement at moving to our new home in the countryside.

The plan was that I would take the boys and a few vitals such as kettle and sandwiches ahead and Byron and one of the lads from Shines would load up and meet me there later in the day.
I arrived at the Cottage on that sunny, warm morning and on placing my key in the door I felt a surge of love for this pathetic of buildings....I walked in to the empty, damp interior and it simply felt like 'home.' My feelings were inexplicable to me then and now, I had bonded with this house since the day I pulled up outside. It had no previous taints from my sad life, no memories other than those I was about to make, it contained no threats, no pain, it was simply mine to make a home in for me and my man and our future life together. The familiar sickly smell of whatever invaded my nostrils so I immediately threw open all the windows to air the place, the kitchen window promptly fell off it's hinge at this sudden assault on its purpose in life, probably having never been opened in how many years.

I took Maxwell and Chester from the car in their carry boxes and placed them in the upstairs bedroom with water, food and familiar smelling beds and our clothing to settle down whilst we moved in. I don't uphold with all the nonsense of buttering a cats feet to make sure it doesn't stray...what the hell is that all about?

A few hours in the bedroom peacefully with regular checks and when safe later this evening they could come out to join us in their new home....outside introduction would come later when they had settled was my preferred method. I swear to god I hadn't been in the property an hour when I heard an almighty pounding on the front door?

Initially I thought it was Byron arriving and wondered what the panic was, but as I approached the front door through the Lounge I could see a blue car parked outside our front wall. I opened the door to a man short in stature but built like a bulldozer wearing an expression I can only describe as frightening.

"Where's my fucking car?" he demanded and with that he reached forward grasping my arm to pull me outside. I resisted and naturally struggled backwards..."What the hell, who are you? I screamed at him.

"I've been back and forth here for weeks Darlin,' your fuckin' husband as stolen my car, where is he and where's the car?" I was utterly fearful and in shock.

"Look, hang on, I don't know what the hell you are on about!" I tried to explain. "I've just moved in this house today, we've bought it, I don't understand?"

The man stepped back still with his fists clenched at his sides, he had clearly arrived prepared and psyched up for a fight. "Your husband...my hire care, where is it, what's he playing at, I'm gonna kill the twat?" the man continued to push his body forward in a confrontational manner. Whilst his language was abusive and threatening and I was shaking, I suddenly began to put two and two together...he thought I was James Bretherton's wife god forbid!

"Are you talking about James Bretherton?" I demanded.

"Who?" his spit hit my face.

"The guy we just bought this place off, James Bretherton." I pressed on.

I could see by his face he was actually starting to listen to me and realising I didn't have a freakin' clue what he was talking about.

"John Evans! Your husband for fucks sake, you rented my hire car, where is it?"

I was utterly confused. "Look I don't know any John Evans and I'm certainly not married! We, me and my boyfriend just bought this place and are moving in today, I don't know about any car or what you are talking about?" I replied.

His face was a picture of confusion as was mine. He suddenly apologised for his threatening behaviour explaining that John Evans had rented his hire car, a red Ford Sierra some months back but the payments had stopped and he'd been unable to gain any contact from John by telephone or at the Cottage, as far as he was concerned his car had been stolen and he had run out of patience, he was going to the Police next. Ironically I remembered seeing a red Sierra parked opposite the cottage on the day we came to view....I said nothing. I further explained about James Bretherton and it seemed he fitted the identity of John who had rented the car.....the man left apologising for his actions and headed for the local Police Station in Tonyrefail.

As I shut the front door, still shaking from the confrontation I remember thinking this incident won't be the last, something is seriously wrong as regards MR James Bretherton....as always my gut instinct served me well.

Byron arrived and I spilled out the mornings events, he was surprisingly NOT surprised. "The guy's got 'previous' telling you now" he commented before asking if I was OK and where the Boys were.

Our pleasure at moving in was not to be thwarted by a madman seeking return of his car and we plunged into unloading and setting out our sticks of furniture. By six O'clock it was obvious to me we owned less by way of furnishings than a vagrant plus we were sleeping on the floor as we didn't own a bed.

Byron's Mother Glenys came to our rescue with two tiny wooden kids bunk beds, not sure if these were at her house for Byron's nieces to sleep over or whatever but they were to become ours and Byron duly strapped them together to form a makeshift double bed. Our first night at the Cottage was eerily silent, in fact the silence was actually deafening if that makes sense. We woke to hear birds chirping and sheep bleating and the sun shining down on our new life. Maxwell and Chester were already up and exploring the interior of the cottage with most interest being paid to the open plan staircase where they could push each other through the open back of the step and plop to the floor below before racing back up the stairs to do it all over again!

As with all new homes we came down to new smells and a whole new world to explore. Previous cupboard doors as yet unopened were peeked into, the workings and character of the heating boiler were a whole new adventure, the kitchen door to the rear garden was discovered to be nailed shut. Much work was going to need to be done. We had organised a long weekend to move in and so far it had been an awesome few days.

Sunday morning arrived and we were up with the worms, there's something about the countryside to rev your engines early. Byron was at the rear of the Cottage inspecting the boundary fences and I went to the front garden to see what could be done with reclaiming the entrance to the house through the weeds and broken paving.

As I pottered about next door's front door opened and a man appeared. Wearing typical farm labourer's clothing and sucking deeply on a pipe he appeared to be in his early 50's with a weathered, grained look of a farmer...he was of course our new neighbour. I immediately approached the fence extending my hand by way of introduction and greeting. "Hi there, I'm Maria, we're your new neighbours."

My hand remained outstretched as he totally ignored it! He just stared at me holding his pipe in his mouth?

Somewhat uncomfortable I again announced "Umm we've just moved in, but then you know that, nice to meet you." This man, who twenty five years on we refer to as Lurch, has never shown from that day to this any means of hospitality or basic social politeness....he simply stared me up and down before removing his pipe sufficiently long enough to say "Aye" then he returned indoors leaving me speechless.

I mentioned the encounter to Byron who passed comment that perhaps the guy was shy but in my opinion it had just been plain rude.

During our first ten days in our new home we learned a lot about James Bretherton. He had abandoned personal documents in the loft that spelled out quite a 'chameleon' of a character. Seems he had a penchant for setting up non existent business that he established under false identity and then used these names as Aliases.'

As 'newbie's' in the area we stuck out like a sore thumb with our daily back and forth to 'rat race' work in our office garb and cars, this is very much agricultural territory, heels and skirts or briefcase and suit was somewhat looked down upon...we weren't accepted as part of the community then or even now.

I frequented the local Post Office one afternoon only to be given chapter and verse as to how 'John Davies' from Rackett's Cottage had run up a tab at her Post Office cum Store and did I know how to get hold of him so she could be paid?

We ran into similar stories in local shops and pubs, oh and the local Take Away/Fast Food Curry House! MR James Bretherton, aka John Evans aka John Davies had left quite a wake behind him. It was getting on for the agreed date that we were to pay him his final money, by now he had taken to using a 'friend' of his to act as go between so that we could not identify where he was living or staying. Daily piles of mail for him, his two Aliases and now several more new names arrived and at one point we had a 2 x 2 feet cardboard box filled to the brim. I took it upon myself to open some of this mail as I felt we needed to know what OUR home address was still being used for? In the UK your credit history is based on your address and status not your name, as such if he was still jacking up debt against our address we were never going to be able to acquire a credit profile without significant written correspondence as proof of our identities.

Letter after Invoice after Reminder after Final Demand poured out of the first fifty or so envelopes. One invoice in the sum of £356.00 was only days old where he had stayed in a Hotel in London asking for the invoice to be forwarded to his head Office address....our Cottage! Skipping forward a little, at the time we finally got JB out of our hair and lives we held a box full of debt knocking on the door of half a million pounds.

At this point we felt it was per to advertise a Notice in our front window declaring to anyone calling in our absence that James Bretherton and all of his aliases DID NOT live here any longer. We advised the local Police what we were doing and why and felt a little safer when we left for work each day.

A tap on the door one evening presented a short, stocky Farmer with one eye on our doorstep. "I'm Dia!" he declared in a tone that indicated we should know already who 'his Lordship' was? "The Farm up the lane" with which he held his hand out to shake Byron's....hmmm that's better I thought.
We invited him in, little did we know it was asking the wolf to cross the threshold way back then. He strutted around our new home and even opened the fridge door commenting "there's bugger all in it?" We discovered he was the local wealthy land owner/farmer who employed Lurch next door as his Farm Manager, he offered us assistance with anything we needed at any time with a' just ask' tap of the side of his nose and a wink! Hmmm this is one to be wary of I thought to myself. None the less he was pleasant enough if not a little on the cock sure side of arrogant.

The following week, on the Tuesday as I vividly recall, I left Rentokil utterly hacked off with Dillwyn and his whacky system of dealing with the immediate but ignoring the backed up jobs which ultimately he returned to my desk. This action made it look as if I had not dealt with the job in the first place in my capacity as Branch Secretary, which was not true!
I was being used as a scape goat but not in a nasty or cruel way, it was just Dillwyn he was a loveable old sod of a character with a disorganised way of running the Office, how the hell he'd managed to stay in the job so long left me curious?
I pulled up outside the cottage so grateful to be back home in peace and tranquillity and looking forward to some food and then an evening of scraping artex wall coating off the dining room walls. Byron's job this very evening was to dismantle and dispose of the horrid gothic sacrificial lights. There was nothing untoward obvious as I parked up and made my way to the rear of the property as we'd taken to using the kitchen

door as the regular entrance, in fact the front doorway to our home remains to this day vastly unused.

As I navigated the badly worn steps trying to keep my balance I suddenly saw the kitchen door was open....in fact it was much more than open, it had been smashed in and virtually hung from it's hinges. Oh my god we've been burgled stamped across my brain as I dropped my bag and coat rushing forward. It was around 6pm in the evening and still daylight, I scanned the interior and listened for noise or movement but the Cottage was empty....in more ways than one. "Chester, Maxi!" I screamed, where were my boys, oh dear god where were they?

Our TV had been taken, the fridge, the cooker, washing machine, sofa and chairs even the large rug on the floor which was all we could afford whilst we saved for fitted carpets. I clambered up the stairs gulping for breath as tears coursed down my face. Oddly none of my jewellery left on the dresser had been taken, but the bedside cupboard had its contents thrown on the floor and was gone? What the hell was going on? As I rushed for the telephone to call the Police a police car pulled up outside followed by a large white van and then Byron who was by now wondering why these two vehicles and occupants were stopping at our house?

I ran down the driveway shouting "come quick, we've been burgled, how did you know?" The Police Officer put his hand up to silence me explaining there had been a dreadful mix up, Byron leapt from his car shouting at me "what's going on?" and then from behind the hedge I heard mewing, scared to death the boys had fled the cottage and hidden in the field. I scooped them up in my arms whilst Byron dealt with the policeman and two other guys.

Prior to moving to the cottage, good old JB had resided in Somerset, England where he had similarly accrued debts and in particular non payment of his domestic housing rates to Somerset Council.

They had tracked him down to Llantrisant and as he had ignored all their correspondence they held the legal right to ....now let me get the wording correct here... gain lawful entry to his current residence by means of any access that could be used without undue force, to seize goods and chattels to the value of the debt.

Our rear entrance was by no means solid and as such they saw it as a weak entrance point. And so they had taken all our belongings to clear his debt to them leaving us with no written or other explanation other than an apparently 'burgled' home when we returned. Absolutely insane practice and inconsideration as far as I am concerned. Apparently on leaving the property the driver had looked back to see our Notice in the window so they drove to the local Cop Shop to discover they had just stolen all our belongings not JB's. The Officer returned with them to ensure there was no unacceptable behaviour or fractiousness as our goods were returned. The Somerset Bailiffs were exceedingly apologetic for their actions and for the shock and trauma it had caused me on returning home. On hind sight perhaps we should have taken the matter further but I was just so relieved that it had been a grave error, our goods were returned and my babies were safe. A few days later an envelope came in the mail containing an official letter of apology and a gift by way of recompense for our distress, a fully paid for weekend at the Holiday Inn Hotel in Cardiff City to include Penthouse Suit, champagne and canapés on arrival, a Restaurant candle lit table for two and full use of the Health & Spa facilities for the entire weekend, all we had to do was turn up and sign for the bill at the end which would be forwarded to the Somerset Council. Needless to say Byron and I enjoyed a fantastic weekend shortly after whilst his parents babysat the boys!

We had been in the cottage less than two months at this time and the week had arrived for JB's final payment.

As ever his go between called requesting payment to whom Byron advised "tell James on yer bike, no further payment is being made!" After all we had signed nothing to the effect, it had all been verbal which is not always as effectively binding as people are led to believe.

The telephone rang almost immediately that Byron hung up.

"It's James, what d'ya mean you're not paying?" he demanded.

"Exactly that James, oh sorry, or is it John, or Ian or Robert?" Byron replied.

A moment passed before I heard with my ear pressed hard up against the receiver alongside Byron's, "I want my fucking money and I'm coming up there to get it, you're gonna regret this!"

"Be our guest, Byron answered, there'll be quite a few of us waiting to see you again, the Post office lady, Curry house owner, pub landlords oh and Somerset Council Bailiffs, think the Police want a word as well, plus I have a box full of outstanding invoices from all over the world to give you...shall we say 7pm tomorrow?"

The line went dead and we never heard from or saw James again.

Chapter 3

- Bye Bye bugs...hello plugs -

The Cottage was taking every penny we could muster to renovate and as most refurbishment jobs generally go, we'd start one repair only to unveil another three jobs that needed doing as a result! It was almost constant three paces forward and ten back, we had bought a veritable 'money pit,' a house that had been neglected of maintenance for many a year.

Byron's job was going from strength to strength with his promotions up through the ranks to Sales Management but with it grew his annual sales targets involving long hours on the road and frequent stops away from home on site projects.

I battled on discovering my innate self taught talents and skills for house renovations of just about any description. I tackled cementing, artex'ing, wallpapering, painting, wood distressing, gardening, tree felling and just about anything else that was within my power to lift, screw down, nail, paint or hang, that we couldn't afford to pay a professional to do.

By now we were into late Summer of 1988 and it had been a long and eventful year to date. I knew in my heart I couldn't stay at Rentokil as I was dreading getting up of a morning, and dragging my proverbial satchel to school as the saying goes, I was sick to death of opening blood soaked mail with squashed innards of god knows what every morning and Dillwyn was driving me insane. I made a promise to myself that I would change my life and so I announced to Byron I was leaving my job. This might sound a rather thoughtless, disrespectful thing to do when in a relationship but you see I have always looked out for and taken care of myself, I have never failed to put bread on my table and money in the bank.

I had no doubts whatsoever that I would continue to earn whilst I sought further full time employment by simply returning to Employment Agencies and signing up as a

'Temp.' There was always contract work to be had and it would give me the breathing space I needed.

Byron was of course exasperated, we had just taken on a mortgage, utility bills and a renovation project and booked our first holiday together in Tenerife...was I compos mentis or what for pity's sake?

We had borrowed an Apartment in Tenerife owned by a client of Byron's, for a two week break. Since Barcelona, this was my first real holiday abroad and I was looking forward to feeling the sun on my bones and a chance to spend some leisure time with my man.

Passports and other necessities attended to we finally organised for one of Byron's work colleagues to have a 'country' holiday in our home free of charge as long as he would look after Max and Chester. Tim was a fabulous guy and there was never any doubt that he would carry out his duties with aplomb!

We boarded the flight and took off for our first real holiday together, I was more excited than a kid at Disney Land and it felt nothing like the flight I took to Barcelona. Why? Because I was sharing it with someone right alongside me that I knew would stop the wheels falling off my luggage and spare me the panic of having to find my way around the Airport.

We arrived at the Apartment situated in Playa del Las Americas and there was certainly nothing to dislike about this privately owned dwelling with views across the azure blue pool below, the private gardens and a balcony to sit out on to take it all in. For the first time in my life I felt my ship had docked, I had a life of my own with someone who loved me and cared about me.

The next ten days were fun to say the least, we swam and sunbathed, or rather he swam I dog paddled, we walked the strip and ventured down to the lovely area of Los Christianos, we took excursions and trips like Tourists do on holiday.

Then came the day when Byron tried to hang glide me off the side of Mount Teide without a parachute! We hired a Mini Moke the local transport vehicles for tourists and headed out for a drive. Byron had been given a venue to visit much recommended by his friend who owned the apartment whose instructions were to follow the main route by vehicle, do NOT follow the mountain track!

So we set off in glorious sunshine in shorts and tee shirts in our dinky blue mini moke, half way into the directions the surfaced road ran out! It quite literally stopped dead, thereafter was an option to proceed along the grit and gravel or veer to the left along what looked like a well used single width lane. Don't even think twice about which route Byron took as we headed off on the lane with me hoping we wouldn't meet any oncoming traffic. Oncoming be damned was the least of my worries as the temperature dipped the further along we travelled, I was freezing. Then the wind got up and I found myself sitting on the right hand side of this 'baby buggy' nearest the sheer drop down off the mountain, indeed there were cloud formations BELOW me!!!! My panic button was well and truly activated, I don't do heights, I cannot fly unaided by motorised jet engines and I certainly ain't got bloody wings! As Byron motored on in defiant Indiana Jones style I was clinging on to anything within reach in my 'doorless' chariot chanting prayers to my Saviour!

The real problem was the roof of this vehicle which was a canvas canopy, it suddenly took on a life of its own billowing up fuelled by the wind that actually lifted the wheels off the ground as we drove along!
 I started screaming, Byron told me to shut up and stay calm but for the first time started to look a touch concerned at the predicament we were in! Around the next bend on this freakin' 'ledge' of a so called road we encountered a full scale avalanche of rocks and debris from above totally blocking our way forward. The Moke continued to bounce around as the wind used its canopy as a hot air balloon and all I could see was the sheer drop down the mountainside.

The usual arguments began between man and girlfriend as to how I told him so and he was too stupid to listen, so how the hell do we turn around? Well, hard as this is to imagine I clambered out whilst Byron executed the most precarious of ten point turns on what was effectively a mountain ledge until we were facing back the way we had came. I was never so relieved to see the first tarmac of true highway!

The holiday continued but not as smoothly as one would envisage. With just four days to go to the end of our holiday we received a telephone message via the security people who looked after the complex. Byron's friends ex-wife was travelling out to use her rights to her ex-matrimonial apartment as agreed in the divorce proceedings. Oh great, just great! The 'Friend' had arranged alternative accommodation for us in a neighbouring friends apartment immediately above the most popular nightlife club on the island! We obliged and rapidly packed up and shipped out to said new accommodation just a short distance from where we were.

The final three nights in Tenerife were torturous as we were kept awake by Boom Blasters and music that literally reverberated around the walls of the building we were trying to sleep in until 2am of a morning. Tenerife was indeed a holiday to remember but never to be re-visited.

Returning home was somewhat of an anti climax as we re-entered orbit into grey Wales and its rain fall and work that I didn't want to undertake any longer. I promptly drafted my resignation to Dillwyn and Rentokil and prepared for another change in life. It was late Autumn 1988, a time when most people think about 'digging in' to survive the oncoming Christmas expense. Me? No, nothing so responsible entered my head, this was just another situation to deal with.

I handed my resignation to Dillwyn on a Friday morning, he looked at me long and hard as he held the envelope in his hand..."What's this?" he queried.

"I think you know Hun." I answered honestly.

"Maria, if this is what I think it's impulsive...that's your nature!"

I did not take kindly to being told my actions were impulsive. "Dillwyn I cannot deal with this job any longer, or in fact deal with you, I spoke candidly, I am up to my back teeth with trying to cope with your eccentric way of managing the work load, I'm sick to death of getting blamed for things that are truly not my fault!" I looked him square in the eye as I expressed my dissatisfaction. To my honest surprise he nodded and said "Sit down. You're a very special lady Maria, you have a character to be admired. I'm sorry I've let you down in this job but I'm too old to change." His words stay with me to this day...Dillwyn was trapped in an archaic way of conducting his job role.

I neither condemn him or condone him for this, I simply couldn't survive in such an environment any longer.

A leaving party was promptly convened which saw all the Office and Sales staff, with the exception of Moaning Mona, enjoying a local restaurant meal in order to bid me farewell and good luck! It was a lovely event and I actually felt sorry to be leaving, the Sales guys were effusive with their praise and appreciation of how I had managed their paperwork leaving Dillwyn to make his own statement. This he did in style and attracted many comments and raised eyebrows... as the meal finished and I was presented with cards and a few gifts, Dillwyn rolled out the flaming Zambukas to raise a toast to me....he then handed me a single red rose across the table looking me square in the eye saying " We'll all miss you Maria, you are a very, very special lady!" A buzz of comments went around the table but Dillwyn was oblivious as to the statement he had just made and engaged my stare eyeball to eyeball, we exchanged a silent knowing acknowledgement, nothing more. And so my Rentokil days were at an end....life was about to change again dramatically.

It was around this time that I became officially engaged to be married to Byron. We had discussed getting married somewhere in the future and of course the obvious first step was to get engaged. On hindsight this was perhaps all a little immature for us to be indulging in at our ages but the romance was on a high. We had shopped for a ring and I had chosen a double set, twisted knot diamond ring mounted on shoulders.

It had needed some alteration as I have quite large fingers for a woman and the day had arrived for collection from the Jewellers work shop. Byron was aware of this when he asked me at breakfast time if I wanted to meet for lunch at one of our regular haunts. His plan had been to collect the ring and present it to me over lunch.

I was completing my last few days at Rentokil and was de-mob happy to get from there, Dillwyn had given me a particularly stressful morning and moaning Mona had caused a fractious confrontation over my booking out one of the Vans on a job Dillwyn had not authorised but the Dep.Manager had? I left at 1pm to meet Byron and I was wound up and stressed out. No sooner had we sat to eat than Byron commented on my mood, I snapped back and we had words. I remember just walking out telling him I'd see him at home. Back at work I reflected on my bad mood and concluded that I had taken my frustrations out on Byron and owed him an apology. I drove home ready to make my peace and anticipated the fireworks I would encounter as Byron is no pussycat in the temper department!

His car was already parked up on the rough area of ground at the side of our cottage which is now our driveway. I could see life within the house via lights and Max sitting in the front bay window swatting no doubt an imaginary fly on the curtains. Kicking my shoes off and dropping my handbag in the 'Vestibule' I opened the Lounge door to the most comical of sights.

Byron was on one knee in front of the fireplace......in full Dinner Suit attire from the waist up, below this....all he wore were his boxer shorts and one sock?? He held a ring box in his hand containing my engagement ring.

I stopped dead in my tracks trying to contain my astonishment and spluttered "what ARE you doing??" He laughed with me as he explained that he had the ring in his pocket at the coffee shop lunch time but as I'd been in such a bitch of a mood he had decided to delay giving it to me. He had rushed home early to dress up and present it to me in grand gesture followed by champagne. However on getting changed in the bedroom he heard me pull up and he was only half dressed so had rushed down 'as he was!' We laughed and laughed as he placed the ring on my finger and we became officially engaged to be married and his semi naked proposal was highly original.

Initially, I registered with all the local City Recruitment Agencies and within a matter of days a position became available in an Estate Agents Office in a City outskirt Town called Rhiwbina *(pronounced Ru By Na.)* I duly turned up for duty on the Monday morning, it was just another job to go to far as I was concerned whilst I hunted around for something more permanent. The Offices were sparsely furnished with two Agents whom I rarely saw as they rushed in and out, but they left mounds of Dictaphone tapes to be copy typed, something I had not had experience of before.

It was peaceful without my daily work load crawling around my table, or bits of body parts dropping out of opened envelopes. I was very much left to my own devices, something I like as the loner in life had forged me into. The Dictaphone machine was a mystery to me? It was early afternoon on the first day before I was asked by one of the Agents if I had completed the first of his Tapes? "Just getting to them" I brightly assured him in a manner disguising my anxiousness as to how the hell this piece of kit worked? Thus perhaps one of the least embarrassing moments of my life occurred, there have been greater ones!! I promptly picked up the headset and mounted it on my head as you would wear a headband....I looked like a sodding Telly Tubby animated cartoon character with antenna attached. His face was a hysterical picture of shock and disbelief at what the hell the secretarial agency had sent him. I sat there giving it my best Miss Money Penny efficient appearance as he slowly approached diplomatically declaring that he felt I would be more comfortable were I to wear the earphones with the apparatus hanging below my chin. Red faces all round but I simply blustered my way through in ever self survival style.

A few more 'temp' assignments ensued which meant home life/finances continued pretty much as normal before an interview loomed up for a PA to the Managing Director of FRAM Europe in the huge factory development opposite the Royal Mint and just three miles down the lane from where I live.

FRAM Europe UK (Continental trade name SOGEFI) manufactured car components and filters for worldwide distribution. The factory itself was a sprawling development with the Offices off to one side in a separate block.

Rafael Martinez was the Managing Director who I arrived to meet for my interview along with the Personnel Director, Wyndham Lewis and Operations Director, Alf Johnson at 6pm sharp one November evening.

I was shown to his plush albeit very outdated office on the first floor where everyone seemed to be waiting for my arrival, I felt quite vulnerable entering the room with these three older, professional, senior management men staring at me.

Up tipped the defiant chin and the survival instinct kicked in..... "good evening Gentleman!" I spoke clearly and confidently.

Wyndham was the first to speak in his broad Welsh accent "Come in Maria, take a seat." Whilst I was aware of Alf's perusal of me I was acutely aware from the corner of my eye of Rafael's riveting appraisal of me. I was to replace his beloved retired secretary her name escapes me all these years on, but I seem to have the name Mair in my head?

The real memory of that evening was that upon entering the room my senses were bombarded with the smell of someone's aftershave and that someone turned out to be Rafael himself. Oh my goodness me, it was pure unadulterated testosterone and I breathed in its sexuality!

Rafael himself was a fabulous guy in his early fifties maybe in 1988, average height and stature of a man who looked after himself, Spanish and well educated, spoke beautiful and eloquent English and was a pure gentleman to the bone, married with a family that spent their time at home in Spain whilst Rafael lived a Batchelor's job life in the UK.

He was a deeply committed man to both his job and family, he was gentle and kind but was nobody's fool. Unlike Dillwyn he was totally in control of his Directorship level position and he managed his workforce of a few hundred with pride and discipline.

FRAM held two business premises in South Wales, the sister company being situated in the rural Town of Abergavenny some 25 plus miles from Llantrisant so he spread himself weekly between the two locations running the empire.

The interview was intimidating to say the least but I held my ground declaring my answers to very searching questions honestly and openly. I had already drawn my conclusion of Wyndham whom I was wary and distrustful of. Alf seemed a pleasant enough guy but again I had this impression of a 'wolf in sheep's clothing.'

Rafael was the least active in the interview as was to be expected given that his Human Resources and Operations Directors were there to carry out the interview. Mid answer to a very blunt question from Wyndham as to my obvious age and potential childbearing abilities which could affect my future employment, Rafael spoke up. Nowadays I don't think such a question would be deemed legal in employment law but here I was sat in front of three full blooded red males being asked directly if I had any plans to become pregnant, Woah!!

"Castilian or Basque?" His question was simple and direct, and completely incomprehensible to me, I had no idea what he was asking me?

Up came the shoulders and out tipped the chin as I replied in defiant not to be put down attitude, the only Spanish words I knew "Lo siento me habla muy poco Espanole por el momento!"

Both Wyndham and Alf looked jaw struck in surprise that I should speak Spanish, little did they know. Rafael however simply stared back at me for what seemed like hours but was in fact seconds before winking the most provocative but understanding wink I have ever been the recipient of up until then. He smiled wryly and nodded his approval of my answer but proceeded no further.

He knew full well that I hadn't understood the original question but respected me enough not to humiliate me in accepting my simple statement of "I am sorry but I speak very little Spanish at the moment."

Pleasantries were exchanged and I left feeling as if I'd bollocks'ed up the whole interview. Within 10 minutes of leaving FRAM I arrived home just up the lane wondering if I had stood any chance whatsoever of gaining this job on £11,500 per annum working 8.30am to 4pm Monday to Friday as a PA for Pete's sake to a Managing Director of an International Organisation....here I was, unskilled, unqualified and flying by the seat of my pants to survive life as always, what the hell was I thinking of even applying!

Less than 72 hours elapsed before I received the call telling me the 'Offer' letter was in the mail. I was cock a hoop as was Byron. Not only on my doorstep saving time and travel costs but almost double financially what I had been working for previously. The Cottage would have extra disposable income at its beck and call and so life was about to change dramatically once again.

Chapter 4

- When Personnel...becomes way too personal! -

I was 28 years old, gutsy, feisty and able to take care of myself given all that life had
flung at me so far. I respected those who treated me with respect and civility, then as
now I don't give what I don't get simple as!

I was nervous as I rolled into the car park that first morning in my battered old blue
Toyota Corolla, I was welcomed, inducted and plonked in my office outside Rafael's
but more than that I didn't have a clue what came next? Alf was in the office directly
behind mine through paper thin walls and was present more times than Rafael.

Alf was by then in his mid 60's I am guessing and was as ever pleasant, somewhat
akin to a long lost grandfather....but something didn't sit right with me about him.

In all the time I spent employed at FRAM I was never once given a tour of the Factory
floor, I arrived and left there some 16 months later having never viewed the interior
workings of the production lines or having met the workforce, sad really because I
know they were a great bunch of local people. Mind you, I heard tales daily of the
women who swooned in Rafael's wake as he patrolled his 'Lines' leaving his lingering
Agua Brava aftershave aroma that simply knocked us all dead in our tracks!

The Cottage was by now well and truly underway as a labour of love in regeneration.
We spent every waking and spare hour out of work tackling its needs, it was like
bringing a house back from the dead. Originally known as Rackett Cottage we had
decided to change the name because of the trouble encountered with the previous
owner and we sought inspiration from our surroundings. Curlew Cottage, Hazelnut
Cottage, Brook Cottage nothing sat right in our hearts until the day we realised the tree
in the garden was a Cherry....voila, Cherry Tree Cottage was about to be named and
claimed.

It wasn't done officially and is still listed as No.1 Racketts Cottage in the annals of
wherever. Rackett being the name of the local wooded area to the side of our home.

I couldn't live with the original cottage name given that James Bretherton had been a complete Racketeer and that we needed to disassociate our address with the black credit rating it had acquired under his name. We were the talk of the area for a while, name changing of a local property being every other local residents cause for concern of course....I don't think, push off and mind your own!!

We spent many weekends and long evenings working on the grounds of the property and within until we could see some form of change, some mark of our own on what was to become our 'forever home.'

My next memory comes from early 1989 when we noticed an advertisement in the newspaper 'Swansea school being demolished, stone and wooden beams offered for sale.' Swansea is a magnificent City West of where we live by 50 miles or so and is rich in culture and history. I wasted no time in calling the number to lay claim to the wooden roof trusses and internal beams that could be used to restore our old cottage to its former glory. Previous occupants attempts at modernisation had seen the guts of the cottage ripped out and I wanted to restore its previous old world charm.

Saturday arrived and Byron had yet again borrowed the Shine Food Machinery company box back van, we set off for Swansea roughly an hours run. We located the school being demolished quite easily and set about negotiating with the Site Foreman for costs on quite a number of 4 x 2 inch old wooden rafters.

Duly paid for we loaded up between ourselves around 30 wooden beams of various lengths, my top arms were starting to take on the appearance of a world class muscle woman from all this DIY. Time to depart saw Byron needing to reverse this three ton van out into a busy Saturday highway packed with traffic.

As ever Mrs Me In Control whizzed out into the middle of a two lane highway like a well trained Traffic Cop hand signalling for all traffic both ways to stop so we could emerge into the flow.

Swansea City New Theatre was situated directly opposite the demolition site with it's enormous plate glass window frontage, lord knows how many feet high and wide but knocking on the door of I guess 50 feet!! I stood proud and confident holding up a single lane of traffic either way whilst waving Byron out in reverse from the demolition site.... neither of us gave a seconds thought to the fact that at least six feet of wooden beams extended beyond the rear tailgate of the van....ooops!

As I stood there hand signalling Byron to come back, back, back, car horns took off like sirens in a crescendo.

Scorpio patience never far away, I signalled to drivers either side to have some god damned patience and wait....little did I realise their alerts were for us to STOP DEAD! I don't know why but I suddenly looked up and backwards only to realise our extension of beams from beyond the rear of the van was within six inches of shattering the front plate glass windows of Swansea's New Theatre....I screamed STOP louder than I knew I had a voice capable of! Byron jammed on the anchors and a crisis was averted.....doing up an old Cottage was not going to be plain sailing I could tell.

Back at the Cottage we unloaded the heavy oak beams and set about installing them. The next few weekends saw my transformation into Miss Whip Lash as Byron erected these beautiful, old lengths of wood that had seen much of their own history in situ along the ceilings of our home. I would follow behind with a length of chain literally 'whipping' the wood to further distress its appearance thus creating the battered look associated with old country cottage beams. Our joint DIY antics are legendry over the years to come.

A large RSJ metal lintel spanned the centre of the Lounge as a main supporting beam which was ugly but obviously necessary. So Byron set about 'cladding' this with the oak lengths. I recall it was an early evening after work as he once again set about a few hours DIY, we were in fact living in a building site by this time, when he suddenly sat down writing a letter on a blank sheet of paper. Curious, I approached asking what he was up to? I am making a 'Time Capsule' he stated matter of fact. Of course you are Darling, as one does!!!! He proceeded to write a description of me and him, who we were, our names, our ages, the name we had given the cottage, the identity of our two cats and when we had taken up occupancy. He then wished the future 'Finder' of this time piece as much happiness as he hoped we were about to enjoy in our future at Cherry Tree Cottage. Byron then encased the letter inside the main beam and sealed it up, it remains there to this day and I realised just what a sensitive and romantic man I was about to marry. This is by no means a singular act of his 'sensitive' side as and when he deigns to demonstrate it.

That night I realised that I did not truly own Cherry Tree Cottage, we are but its present time guardians for how ever many decades until the next new guardians come along.

Built Circa 1875 this small dwelling has seen many inhabitants in its time and I tried to unearth a little of its past. As far as I have ever managed to find out the Cottage is named after the local wood which is Racketts Wood. Local maps and literature seem to indicate its existence from around 1850 to 1875 as a local stock Drovers watering hole. Through the decades it passed to a family with the man of the household being a Carpenter by day and a Tailor by night....this piece of history proved very interesting to me in the following years as you will read later on.

Families ensued thereafter one of which turned the upstairs of the Cottage which was at the time a simple one room up, one room down configuration, into an Aviary come chicken house, the mind boggles. In very recent months of real time 2013, I have discovered that at some point in the mid 1940's early 1950's a family lived here who were the lowliest of low, the poorest of poor as such the term 'dirt poor' refers. This meant they lived in the Cottage which would have had simple dirt floors with nothing more than the windows and a roof to call home. There were no facilities or utilities; domestic sewage would have been into a bedside bucket and carried across the fields to be disposed of, drinking and sanitary water would have been drawn by hand from the local streams, they survived on what they could grow or farm. This family, according to a knowledgeable village local of several generations standing, produced 12 children, 11 of which died during their infant and junior years due to illness and disease and are again, allegedly buried around the fields of this dwelling as no formal funeral would have taken place. This account of my home's history will also bear meaning to me in later years as you will read further on.

We merrily continued with our self renovation DIY and many laughs and tears followed. Such as the day we decided to reclaim the rear kitchen door and release the back of the building from strangulation of blackberry vines. We started on our hands and knees at the door threshold and literally hacked our way out and to each side, we discovered crazy paved pathways that had clearly been overgrown and lost from sight for many a year. Follow me said my intrepid leader and you won't get caught by the thorns, I rarely do as I am told by Byron but on this occasion I did! He hacked his way forth flinging debris back over his shoulders only to lasso me around the neck with a six feet vine that he was still tugging away merrily at the other end. The thorns dug in deep and I tried to grapple with the vine screaming for him to stop moving. He jumped up staring at me in disbelief saying "for god's sake woman what have you done now!" "You nearly strangled me you stupid B*****!"
To which he replied "Well what were you doing standing right behind me, it wasn't my fault!" No it never is Mr P and if I had a £1 for every time I have heard you bleat that since I'd be a millionaire'ess....in fact I am thinking of having your headstone engraved with "I died, it wasn't my fault!" or better still your other old chestnut.... "I was only trying to help...!"
Follow me he said and I did but ever since I have stuck to the safest method of 'follow me, I'm right behind you!'

Then of course there was the incident of the excavation of the side wall of the Cottage, the ground banked right up to the wall breaching, if any existed, damp proof course. We hired a mini excavator on tank tracks and started digging out a pathway to clear and make a side access path from front to rear of the building. Byron broke his shovel and pick axe handle after gaining several feet clearance, we still had around twenty five feet to go so he told me to stay put whilst he went to the Merchants to buy replacements, he would be gone half an hour. Not content with sitting around I wanted to get on, I climbed aboard this dinky toy of a machine and tried to work out what gear lever did what? I found out how to make the bucket go up and down and how to move forward and backwards so how difficult could it be? I would carry on and surprise him I thought. Not entirely clear how far back from the wall Byron was planning to dig I started gouging the bucket into the ground removing clods and lumps of earth and mud, the hole got deeper and deeper and now seemed out of shape with the original width of the pathway Byron had pegged out. Oh dear, too late to fill it back in as here came the Foreman. His face was a picture of disbelief and horror.... "Get off there NOW!" he bellowed at me, I felt like a scolded child and leapt down from the excavator. "What the hell are you doing woman, I said leave things alone whilst I was gone....Awww no M what's that?" He stared down into the six feet deep hole I had made which was now at least two feet deeper than the original path level he'd started making.

Sheepishly I tried to explain that I thought I would carry on to keep the project moving and save him some work...."yeah but we're making a pathway not digging a bloody grave!" We both looked down the hole and started laughing..."Ok, let's keep the hole and we'll turn into the log store, but don't go digging any more holes right!" he declared, maybe I will, maybe I won't I thought as I've never been one NOT to have a go!

We laboured on into the Summer and Autumn of 1989 working around the clock coming home from work to carry on with refurbishments. Everything we touched unveiled at least three other repair jobs before we could carry on, the cottage was zapping us of cash so we decided to re-mortgage to raise much needed funds for new windows and other essentials such as a fitted kitchen and a real cooker. We effectively doubled the mortgage we had but it was necessary if we were to achieve a habitable home.

The garden was pretty much still a wilderness and we spent every weekend in any decent weather and some indecent weather reclaiming it. Whoever had lived here in decades gone by they had laid out a very pretty little cottage garden with low stone walls, nooks and crannies such as an old stone coal house and an elevated stone wall area to the rear of the garden which we immediately recognised would make a superb elevated patio sitting area for long summer evenings, it was elevated by some six or more feet affording a great viewing area of the surrounding fields and mountains. The day came whereby we set about clearing the slab steps up to it and unearthing the overgrown patio area itself.

"I'll go first and pull away all the old loose stones and pass them to you to stack there..." Byron pointed to an area where he would be able to access these stones easily whilst rebuilding. Like a fool I nodded and donned my heavy duty gardening gloves. The first few stones were large so he turned to hand these down to me but as the going got easier higher up the steps he started tossing the smaller stones back for me to catch. We were going great guns in a fluid motion when I stood up to catch my next stone only to have a mating trio of SNAILS tossed back at me over his shoulder...they hit me in the cheek smashing the shell of one and it drooled down my face plopping to the ground. Screaming like a banshee and furiously scrubbing away at my face with the hem of my jumper, Byron turned to see what all the fuss was about. Gasping and feeling sick I shouted at him "for god's sake man they were snails, oh my god, oh my god, arrrghhhhh"! I was dancing around like I'd been prodded up the bottom with a hot iron. He simply laughed before stating "get on with you, they won't hurt you, I thought it was a stone."
"I'm going to swing for you if you do that again" I snarled before stomping off to the kitchen to bleach my face!!

Other such delightful escapades of our legendary self renovation antics will follow, we now happily refer to ourselves as the 'Laurel & Hardy' of DIY.

I'd been at FRAM some eight months or more by now and although the status of being Rafael's PA carried with it some perks, such as a Secretaries paid for trip to Zurich by the travel company I regularly used for all his flights abroad, I was becoming bored and agitated. I was in fact the highest paid 'coffee maker' I've ever known because that is all I seemed to do. Board meetings were frequent and regular so one of my main duties was to ensure the Boardroom was laid out correctly, fresh coffee on tap and Directors lunches organised. As for any actual secretarial work there was little for me to do because Rafael generated little in the way of paperwork, he had his senior management to undertake all that was needed via their own departments. I would sit for hours during the day watching the traffic drive past my large picture windows, I would visit the Accounts department where I had made several down to earth friends and we would have a laugh and a chat. But there were a few individuals who didn't like me for whatever their sad reason, I was the Managing Directors PA and thus seen as a cut above my station, I dressed glamorously as my figure allowed me to then. I tried to always look smart and efficient but my character has always been that of an over friendly puppy. The two didn't mix in the opinion of some of the workforce, I should have acted aloof and distant like some of the other senior secretaries did.

I began to notice cryptic comments made in my presence and quite frankly, some trouble making going on behind my back filtering back to senior managers?

I ignored it for a while assuming it was just classic office bitching and jealousy, but it continued to spread, even to the Abergavenny Offices.

Rafael as I said was a lovely guy, a gentleman and very professional in his work. We would have a chat often over a coffee in his office and share a little family information about each other, he seemed genuinely interested and appeared to enjoy my company. He was away often during the month travelling abroad or to Abergavenny leaving me to occupy my days with virtually nothing to do. Alf would dap in and out but mostly spent his time on the factory floor....I began to resent the time I was wasting when I could be home DIY'ing. What I really wanted was work to occupy me, I am a grafter not a sit about do nothing, twiddle my thumbs and paint my nails type of Gal.

The offices were tired and old fashioned so I set about rearranging the filing cabinets to make more space, I cleaned out the desks and then emptied out all the cupboards disposing of anything that appeared to be junk or not needed. This kept me going for a few weeks but I soon found myself back to watching the clock handles crawl around the face. I wasn't a 'lunch' person in those days, a simple piece of fruit and a yogurt were what kept me going from Breakfast till Dinner and helped me keep in shape, thus I never attended the company canteen. This was seen as me being anti social by some of the staff and was yet another nail in my coffin as I finally discovered.

The discord really started I guess during May of 1990.

I had treated myself to a silk chiffon blouse that had a square cut neckline in the prettiest shade of mottled caramel pattern on a cream background which I teamed up with my signature knee length black skirt, stockings and 3 inch heel court shoe. Jewellery was minimal but always stylish and solid gold, my make up was day fresh and light but always perfectly applied.
I felt that I looked good and would be a liar if I said that at the age of 29 I didn't enjoy the appreciative glances from the men. Particularly those who visited from SOGEFI, Italy. Bruno and Jesus (*pronounced HehZeus*) were the most regular and both, particularly Bruno, were strong Latino handsome with magnificent bodies. As full red blooded males they made no effort to disguise their lust and would appraise my appearance muttering in Italian to Rafael in suggestive tones of voice. I knew they were saying sexual things about me but it was irrelevant as the only man in my life was Byron, end of!

The Company Chief Accountant was a man called Keith Drew, a tall guy who liked to think of himself as the company 'Richard Gere,' married with a young child but having an affair with a young 18 year old from the offices which he thought nobody knew about. He was indeed stringing this poor girl along promising to leave his wife and give her the earth and heaven forbid she believed him. I became party to this information because she lived in the row of cottages about half a mile from our cottage and we often met and spoke whilst walking the lanes. As she became friendlier, she would come to my office for a coffee and a cry on my shoulder, she saw me as a big sister figure and I felt angry at the way Keith Drew was treating her.

I had cause to go to his office one morning with documents from Rafael and he sat back at his desk beckoning me forward whilst he signed them. I bent forward to sort each that needed filing, I was neither indecently dressed or showing any cleavage in my chiffon blouse.....but Keith saw fit to report my dress code to Wyndham Lewis in Human Resources stating I had bent over his desk like a 'hooker' showing off my breasts and as far as he was concerned I was disgracefully dressed for my role as the MD's PA!

My ass was hauled to Wyndham's office where I was told to button up my blouse and dress in a more respectful manner. Respectful to whom? My blouse was buttoned to three inches below my throat and not capable of showing any breast, what's more Keith bloody Drew shouldn't have even been looking! I was extremely annoyed given that I was in a job role where no uniform had to be worn therefore they did not have the right to dictate what I chose to wear providing I was dressed respectably and I considered I was, so what the hell was going on? Later that day I found out from the young lady that she had told Keith that I knew of their affair....plop went the penny! Big headed Drew was proactively trying to demonstrate the power of his position and the type of grief he could cause me if I blew his cover. I felt the old 'Paul Roberts/Plessey' annoyance and the need to let Drew know I was no pushover!

A couple of weeks passed before the next incident which involved my car, the old blue Toyota. I was being summoned back and forth to the Abergavenny offices and the long return trip was pushing my engine to blowing a gasket. Byron and I decided to use the weekend to look around the sale rooms for a change of vehicle. His being a company car meant he had a brand spanking new model every two years but I wasn't going to be able to afford anything 'newer' than a couple of years younger Model of anything. Again, the internet and other such easier means of locating a new car was not available at the time so after breakfast we set off on our shopping trip.

It didn't take me long to find a stunning Bronze colour, 3 Litre Toyota Supra Turbo with pop up frogs for headlights, low profiles and the obligatory sun roof but this one was electric wey hey, in fact everything was electric and ultra modern compared to my 'old Betsy!!' A tad on the heavy side of having run the clock, the mileage I was assured was nothing to worry about as being a 3 litre it could probably go twice round the clock before scrapping. I fell in love with this huge car and the deal was struck. Tucking myself in behind the wheel after kissing old Betsy goodbye, I felt a million dollars and with such 'ooomph' under my bonnet. I loved that car who's registration plate was SEP 173Y so I named him 'Seppy.' The engine was throaty and powerful being a turbo model, so when I cruised into work on the following Monday morning to the agog stares from the Security Gate Officers and a few of the office staff I felt proud as punch. I parked a few bays down in the car park from the Directors cars which were BMW's and top of the range Fords.

It was around 11am when I got the call from Human Resources and Wyndham in his usual superior, up his own ass voice. Wondering what could be the reason I ambled over to his office.

"Ahh sit down Maria" he gestured to a nearby seat. "I see you have a new car?"

Initially I thought he was asking out of interest about the motor but no...!

"We're a little perturbed Maria that you should be driving such a prestigious vehicle and it's even bigger engine size than Rafael's, what are you playing at?"

My mouth dropped open like a falling brick.

I stammered to get control of my words and gripped the arms of the chair I was sat in.

"What....what am I playing at? What the hell do you mean what am I playing at? My face was a picture of total disbelief at what I was hearing.

Wyndham continued "I don't think you should be driving a better car than the Managing Director of this Company, its a bit of an insult really don't you think? Almost as if you are trying to be somebody you are not."

I exploded, sorry but job and salary or not who the hell did he think he was.

Staring Wyndham eye to eye I unleashed my Scorpio temper undiluted.

"For a start, you pay me a salary to do a job here, that does not entitle you to tell me how to spend MY salary! Rafael drives a 5 Series BMW which in itself is a 'prestigious' motor." Wyndham tried to butt in on this outburst but I was having none of it. "I am expected to travel back and forth Abergavenny but my old car couldn't cope with the mileage, I upgraded so I could keep up with the demands of my job and you have the audacity to ask me what I think I am 'playing at,' how dare you be so bloody offensive?" Wyndham was...well Wyndham! Impervious to anything he didn't like or want to hear, he disregarded my outburst as if it had never happened.

"I see, well in that case would you please park your vehicle further down the car park away from the main Directors bays from now on, that's all Maria, please shut the door on your way out."

I really wanted to drag him across his desk and wipe the supercilious look off his face but I walked out and left his door open.

Rafael was quiet and distant when I got back to the office, I knew he knew what had just taken place, what I couldn't figure out was why such a lovely man would allow such an insane reprimand to take place?

On the drive home I decided not to tell Byron about this latest upset at work because he would start panicking about our income and go on at me about how I've had more jobs than a barmaid pulls pints! So what, I thought, you have to kiss a lot of frogs to find a prince....I was still looking for my prince of a job.

Inevitably I started to call in sick on a regular basis because I simply didn't want to go to this place of work any more. I loved being home pottering around the cottage and cooking, nest making I suppose, but this couldn't go on so I returned to work as normal.

I avoided the trouble makers as I identified those to be at all costs, I despised Keith Drew and I was careful about every single thing I did at work lest I should be once again chastised for absolutely no good reason.

Arriving at work one morning I noted Rafael's car was absent from the car park when I had been anticipating him to be in, I thought no more of it and made my way to my office. We had interconnecting doors between the offices but for some reason from his to mine and my outer corridor door had been locked which was most strange. I dug out my spare office keys from my bag and opened up hanging up my coat and switching on lights as was my normal routine.

Turning to me desk I saw a note from Rafael, it said " Maria, I am in Abergavenny for the day, try to stay out of trouble or call me first." The last word was heavily underlined. At first I laughed at the comment but then started to ponder its meaning.

The morning wore on before Alf Johnson came in asking if he could have a word in his office. By now I had come to dread these requests and followed him through to his office wondering what the hell was wrong now.

"Sit down Maria" he gestured to a seat. Here we go again I thought.

"I notice you don't ever go to the canteen for your lunch, why is that do you think?"

By now I was sick to my gut of these archaic dinosaurs of management running FRAM with their pathetic attitudes.

"Why do you want to know?" I counteracted.

Alf took on a tight lipped look, "Well we don't really approve of eating at your desk, that's why we have a staff canteen" he replied.

Before I could respond he continued "The office always smells of oranges and I note there are orange juice drips on the carpet all around your desk area which will need cleaning." He stared at me in a most confrontational manner.

I explained that the 'drips' as he called them were actually from a Coca Cola bottle that had exploded on opening for one of the board meetings and that I had tried to clean it to the best of my abilities and that I didn't want to go to the canteen for my lunch because **a)** I didn't partake of lunch other than some fruit or a yogurt and **b)** I disliked the stench of nicotine in my hair and clothes let alone when I was trying to consume food. In those days smoking bans did not apply in the workplace.

He accepted my explanation but instructed that I was to no longer eat at my desk. For the sake of peace and quiet I simply agreed and walked out. This place was becoming too much for me to tolerate, what the hell was wrong with these people?

Later that afternoon I had cause to go to the big store cupboard in the corner of my office, opening the door I was faced with a single stem red rose in a dainty glass vase with a hand written note alongside from Rafael.....it was written in Spanish? It took me aback somewhat, you are probably reading this thinking the same thing as I did then but I had no way of translating his note, I tucked it in my drawer and awaited his return. The following morning he arrived and I knew he was in the building long before he alighted the stairs because I could smell his sensual, masculine aftershave aroma wafting up the corridor.

A little after 10am I popped into his office on the pretence of handing over messages but the first on the top of the pile was his note. I said nothing but sat down slowly and quietly opposite him, we were like two poker players calmly eyeball to eyeball waiting for the first to break the tension and silence, he won! "The rose was beautiful, thank you" I opened up the conversation. Rafael gave nothing away and simply nodded. "Would you like to tell me what this says?" I pushed the note closer to him. Rafael picked up the note and stared at it for what seemed like minutes but could have only been seconds, he then screwed it up and popped it in his trouser pocket...."No. My messages please..."

I sat for a further few seconds but he refused to look up and busied himself reading his messages...I had been dismissed. Returning to my office I concluded that the note was of romantic content for which he now regretted his actions. Hmmm very interesting, what on earth is going to happen next I thought to myself, I often wonder what was written in that note, I never ever got to find out?

I did not have to wait long as the next incident was right around the corner. Byron and I had stripped out all the Louvre Panel cupboard doors in the cottage, we had about a dozen or so in good condition and too good to dump. I promptly popped a notice on our staff board at work offering them for sale. There were plenty of couples on the factory floor doing up their own homes who may be able to make good use of them. In my inimitable style my card read with some humour, " Qty 12 Louvre doors for sale, good condition, no door handles £40 or make me an offer, you may just catch me in a good mood!" It hadn't been on the canteen board 24 hours when I got the call from Wyndham to attend his office.

"Ahhh sit down Maria" he gestured to a chair I HAD already sat down in.

"You placed a for sale card on the canteen notice board I understand" I simply nodded in agreement feeling that I was being victimised. Was this a conspiracy to get me to hand my notice in so they didn't have to sack me? Was Rafael so pissed off with my lack of shorthand and typing skills? No it couldn't be for that reason because he rarely generated anything for me to type. I must have looked disinterested and away with the fairies because I heard Wyndham say "Excuse me young lady I am speaking to you."

"About what exactly Wyndham, what have I done now?" I queried.

He looked at me in a frustrated manner, "I would have thought we are paying you enough of a salary not to have the need to sell off your junk, it's totally inappropriate for a Managing Directors PA to act this way, and what were you thinking of putting 'make me an offer I might be in a good mood' ridiculous behaviour for your status in this company Maria!"

My heart was beating in my ears with blind fury. My Scorpio temper was in full flood and I knew I just couldn't hold my mouth any longer.

"Have you never sold anything in your life Wyndham? I asked, and those doors are not junk thank you very much, you people don't live in the real world. What is it with this place, you all act like a bunch of dinosaurs and as for status...how fucking pompous can you be!" I stood up so abruptly my chair fell over...for the first time Wyndham appeared flustered.

"Now sit back down, you are the most senior secretary in this company, we won't have you acting in this manner...." I gave him no chance to continue. "Act in what manner, like a normal human being you mean, you've tried to dictate how I can dress, what car I can drive, how I can eat and now you want to control my actions... you're unreal, the lot of you, sack me I don't give a shit!" with which I stormed out of his office leaving the door open.

As I marched purposefully back across the car park to my office block intent on having this out with Rafael once and for all, who should be coming out through the main foyer was Keith Drew. He took one look at me as I aimed to pass him on the steps and said with the type of smirk on his face anyone would want to remove with a sand blaster "..something wrong.....AGAIN Maria?"

I stopped dead in my tracks and turned slowly to look at his smug, arrogant face before saying "stick to playing with the little girls, now fuck off you worthless piece of shit!" His mouth dropped open in total shock, with which I proudly turned on my heel and strode off. I guessed I was counting my days at FRAM after that but I truly didn't care.

Having expected the heavens to drop on me the next day, no mention was made of the incident with either Wyndham or Drew but I was at an all time low in the job, I loathed going to work simple as.

Byron and I had discussed and set a date for our wedding, it was to be 15th December 1990 which gave me around five months to get organised.

I put my secretarial skills to good use and set about planning our wedding like a military operation.

The actual proposal of marriage was in true Parnell style unique to say the least. Byron's Grandmother Gladys, on his mother's side had passed away. She lived in Porth a small town only 3-4 miles from where we live but the house had never changed in all the years she lived there. Set in a long street of typical Welsh Terraced Miners houses, with the front door opening direct onto the pavement, she lived in damp conditions with no heating other than a coal fire, an outside lavatory at the end of the garden and gas lamp lights on the wall. In 1990 this was inconceivable to most of us but that's how she lived, refusing any government aid or assistance, stashing any pension or money she came by in a shoe box under her bed.

Her death had led to some family conflict between siblings as to who would be left what and in fairness to Byron's mother Glenys, she washed her hands of this nonsense, her only desire being that her mother was despatched to her Maker in peace and with dignity.

Items and belongings went missing from the house and each Sibling blamed the other subsequent to her death. I recall much anguish and frustration but ultimately Byron and I were called on to empty the last contents of the house. It was a dark evening so I am guessing around October time... we arrived to find a skip (dump container) parked on the road outside the house and we promptly set about doing as were instructed by Byron's parents....to clear out the last of the items to empty the house and slam the door shut!

It was around 7pm pouring with rain, traffic was whizzing past us as Byron gave me a 'bunk up' into the dump skip. "You get in there and I'll pass up the stuff to you OK!"

We continued for half an hour or so with Byron ferrying bags and boxes of paraphernalia from the house and up to me in the skip to evenly distribute.

At this point I noticed something shiny and twinkling in the back end of the dump skip. A brass bedstead had been deposited by earlier relatives helping clear the house and I was keen to see if it could be salvaged as a family antique for our own matrimonial bed.

"Look Byron...is that what I think it is?" I questioned as he approached with the next armful. He duly clambered up and started rooting around amongst his Grandmother Gladys's no longer needed belongings.

"It's a bedstead" he declared...."I know that, can it be salvaged.....we would have a family heirloom, your Grandmother's bed!" I replied.

We tugged and unearthed, pulled, huffed and puffed and eventually brought the bed head and it's frame to the surface of the dump skip....the rain lashed down, we were soaked to the skin, the traffic roared past within feet and suddenly Byron stood up amongst the debris and cast off's of his Nan's life. He looked at me in a strange way..."What's the matter, you OK?" I queried. With the rain dripping from his nose, ears and chin he simply said "Will you marry me?" I remember scrabbling across the skip to fall into his arms laughing and spluttering "Yes!"

I remain convinced to this day that mine may have been the most 'grubby' of proposals being that we were stood in a rubbish bin at the time...but hey, who the hell cares!! Within a matter of weeks the date had been set for December 15th 1990, and the plans began for the wedding I had always wanted.

Work at FRAM carried on in its inimitable soul destroying fashion, but I had invited Rafael and his wife Amy to the wedding and he promised they would come.

During these latter few months of my time at FRAM between the July and November of 1990, I had resigned myself to the fact I would be leaving the company by foul means or fair and during this time I decided to enrol at a College of Higher Education in Newport, some 35 mile down the motorway for a Fashion Design and Dressmaking Course that would culminate in a National City & Guilds Qualification. I felt it would satisfy my creative needs to make things and also help me as I had decided to make my own wedding dress from scratch.

We simply couldn't afford the costs of a gown and a wedding but I hoped to achieve as near damn it as I could. There was never any intention to be hypocritical and 'marry in white!' I was after all a Divorcee and knocking on the door of 30 years of age.....the 'foo foo flounces' of a wedding gown were not what I wanted but I DID want a wedding dress and so decided to design something that was 'quirky' unusual, it resembled a Spanish Flamenco dress in shape but without the flounces. However I digress....

Chapter 5

- Worst(en) ....things can happen! -

I sat in my office one afternoon contemplating how many strung together paper clips it would take to measure a mile of my utter boredom...when the phone rang, "Call for you Maria, personal" I heard the switchboard lady say.

It was Byron's youngest daughter on the line, she would have been around 16+ years old then but was always less mature than her age. She was sobbing her heart out and gasping for a lung full of breath.

"*(Name protected)* what's happened, tell me, are you alright?" I demanded. She continued to try to speak in short, traumatised gulps. At this point she was standing in a telephone kiosk around the corner from her mother's home and had no idea what to do next.

With some 'motherly' coercing I got her to tell me what had happened, bearing in mind these kids had been 'poisoned' against me by their mother this child didn't know who was her friend or her enemy and this is what had happened:-

Byron's ex wife was an alcoholic, not registered or treated as such, but an alcoholic none the less. Her temper was vile and her 'use' of their children to get at their father knew no bounds. As a majority of ex wives tend to do, she was intent on her hatred of me, of Byron and any means she could achieve to hurt Byron or cause me grief.

This poor girl had stepped off the school bus as she always did around 4.30pm, the short walk from the bus to her home was able to be observed from the front window of her home where her mother sat and watched on this particular day. The ex wife's plan was to possibly shock her child into a mental breakdown, I can see no other reason for her idiotic, selfish and hateful actions. TO WHAT END I asked myself, what the hell did she hope to achieve against Byron or I in carrying out her following horrendous actions?

As Byron's youngest daughter stepped from the bus, her mother watched from the house window then leapt into action, rushing upstairs to place a homemade noose around her neck before descending just enough stair treads so that she wouldn't actually hang herself, which is what she wanted her daughter to see and think as soon as the girl put the key in the lock!

To this day and despite all family dissent that has since transpired, I will never be able to comprehend what that poor girl felt as she opened her door to view her mother hanging from the stairwell. It appears she raced up the stairs managing, of course, to disentangle her mother from the rope with the ex wife acting the part to the hilt.
In shock and upset the daughter engaged in an argument with her mother who then threw a full cider bottle at her daughter striking her in the back of the head and knocking her to the ground. At this point, like a terrified creature, the daughter fled the house heading straight for the telephone kiosk to call her Dad, he was unobtainable out of his office, so she called me at my office sobbing her heart out in pure fear. I kept her on the line whilst I managed to contact Byron's parents on another phone, they immediately left to collect her from the kiosk and take her to their home. As I was not allowed to leave work, I tracked Byron down and detoured him to his parents home where he concealed his anger whilst comforting his youngest daughter.

Byron's eldest daughter had by this time moved in with her boyfriend and so his youngest daughter came to live with us at the Cottage whilst we all tried to sort out what the hell was going on with her mother!

September Enrolment night arrived and I headed off to the College feeling excited to be doing something new and looking forward to learning how to create beautiful clothing.
The College was buzzing with activity when I arrived, people milling around everywhere, picking out their class rooms and courses from the main arrival board. I felt a real connection back to my sad school days and wondered how I would have felt

back then to have sat any exams whatsoever, to have attained any qualifications, I actually felt so robbed of that side of my life and to this day still dream sometimes that I am back at school and I'm trying to tell everyone I shouldn't be there now because I am 53 years old (laughing.)

I rolled up at Room 4D for the City and Guilds Master Fashion Design and Dressmaking Course.
There were around twenty of us that started out on the Course that evening but only 6 of us completed the exams 2 years later!
"Comm in, comm in, find yourselves a seat, nice to see so many of you." I heard the Tutor's cheerful greeting as we filed into the room.
As we all settled, coats off and facing the front of the class, she introduced herself.
"Goot Evfening, my name iz Hannah Worsten, I am your Course Tutor for za duration of dis Course, I am pleeced to meet you!" She spoke good English in her broken German accent. My entire body froze as a spear of past history seared through my brain!
Oh my good god!! How many Hannah Worsten's can there be living within such a close proximity to Newport/Chepstow? My ex husband Andrew's ex girlfriend Penny's......MOTHER?? No way.....no, no, no, no way...cannot possibly be was howling through my head.

YES way!!

Hannah worked her way through the Register, and doled out our paperwork and we started the evening's tuition. Seems she had not made the same connection to my name Maria Price as I had to her's. The coincidence of her name and being German was just too great for it NOT to be the same woman. I decided to make casual enquiries to confirm but felt sure if it was her...and if she did make the connection to me, then my chances of passing this Course were a big fat zero before I'd even started.

68

Later that evening as she walked around the class chatting to us I had chance to have a brief word.

Hannah approached my chair "Hello Maria, gosh you've travelled a bit for za Course, most of zer Students are locals."

"Hi, yes I live in Llantrisant but it's not too bad, about 70 miles round trip" I replied.

"Are you local Hannah?" I fished dreading the answer...

"About za same as you, I live in Chepstow, iz not too far on zee Motorway."

I smiled and in a split millisecond decided to proceed further rather than waste anymore time on a Course I didn't have a hope in hell of being judged and accredited on fairly.

"Chepstow you say...Hmmm, what part? You wouldn't happen to live in Severn Avenue, Tutshill by any chance? I queried feeling I'd gained the upper hand.

Hannah was totally taken aback ...."...do I know you? Yes, that's right...how do you know where I live?" her face was a picture of innocent surprise.

"You are friends with Jean Price, yes? Andrew Price...Penny your daughter..." I pushed home information she was utterly shocked to hear.

Suddenly I could see a decade earlier flooding into Hannah's mind and her face turned to steel.

"Maria.....Maria Price.....you married Andrew, yes?"

"That's right, yes I did." I answered eyeball to eyeball as she looked me up and down from head to toe.

"How is Penny?" I asked in a casual manner.

Hannah was utterly thrown.... "Uhhh, yes thank you she iz goot! Married now, living in Svitzerland, I have a grandson....I uhh...I ....well I must get on."

She rushed back to her desk and the remainder of the evening was spent with her casting surreptitious glances over to my desk.

I drove home not really knowing where all this was going to lead and reiterated the events to Byron. He was as surprised as me but we agreed I would return the following week and see how things went. If Hannah was going to make life retaliatory difficult then there was no point in me continuing....but let's see shall we.

I returned to FRAM feeling like absolutely everything was against me in life to shake off my past and make a new life with the man I loved.

Plans for the wedding were well underway as I arranged everything from a Vintage Rolls Royce, to flowers, cake, wedding favours, gifts for the Bridesmaids who were to be Byron's two Nieces around 8 and 10 years old at the time, my Chief Bridesmaid who was to be Byron's secretary as we had struck up a friendship and I located a Church that would actually agree to marry us as Divorcees, plus a reception venue. Most of my planning and booking was undertaken at work as I had no other time to do it and nothing to actually do as a job at FRAM.

It was a Monday morning when I got hauled into Wyndham's office and reprimanded for my personal use of the office extension phone .....I offered to pay the bill but it was just another nail in my coffin, whatever!!

In true style of my character....it was all or nothing and so I set about designing and making not only my own wedding gown but two bridesmaids dresses, a chief bridesmaid gown and Byron's waistcoat and bow tie all fabric/colour coordinated and for good measure I decided to make the table wedding favours as well! I had 14 weeks left! It was manic to say the least, 23 Yards of cream Duchess Satin for my gown, 56 Yards of Antique lace edging and overlay, 867 seed pearls and sequins all hand sewn and that was JUST my gown!! I was like the Tailor's Mouse...worked around the clock....

It was early one Sunday morning when Byron's daughter knocked on our bedroom door saying she could hear 'crying' at the front of the cottage. I immediately leapt out of bed fearing next door's young teenage daughter was perhaps in some trouble?

In my dressing gown I rushed downstairs to open our front door but could see nothing until I heard a pitiful whisper to "help me." As I stepped out the door and looked to my neighbours frontage of the house.....I was devastated and in shock to see indeed, a young teenage girl but it was not my next door neighbours daughter.

She sat huddled up trying to conceal herself, totally naked, and bleeding from head to toe with cuts, wounds and brambles embedded in her flesh! I screamed instinctively "Oh my god, Noooo!" as I rushed between the garden fences at the split same moment my neighbour opened her front door and both her husband appeared as did Byron at our door.... my common sense kicked in. This girl had either been raped or had suffered a murder attempt...I yelled at both our male neighbour and Byron to "get indoors, out the way, NOW!" My fear was that in this poor girls terror she would freak at the first male she saw screaming 'he did it!'

I yelled at Peggy my neighbour who was standing in utter shock..."get a blanket, anything, please!" I couldn't let go of the girl as she had by now almost passed out in my arms.

Peggy returned with a blanket and we bundled her into Peggy's home where she sat in total silence, shaking uncontrollably. I asked her if I could look at her wounds and at first she blanked me, but then as I stroked her arm and spoke reassuringly that she was safe now she peeled back the blanket to the wound that was obviously hurting her the most. Her shin bone had snapped at the ankle and come straight through her instep, it protruded by some inch or more....I gagged and forced the vomit back down my throat. I took her arms in mine and could see she had various rope tie burns around the wrists that had dug in deep, rips and tears to her skin still with the bramble bushes embedded within....her other foot was cut badly and her face was swollen and red....the inside top of her thighs was reddish/purple and she was bleeding badly from the vagina....she had human bite marks all over her, I knew right then she had been raped!

No matter how I try I cannot recall her name...it as if in shock I have blanked her from my memory so that she remains just a girl on a doorstep in the middle of nowhere.

Peggy phoned for the Police as I sat with her, she then started to speak to me very quietly and in a very hoarse voice as if she'd been screaming for hours.....and indeed she had! "Please, wash...I..sob...want to...sob...wash!" I looked at Peggy and we exchanged a knowing look....if this girl had any chance of her Rapist being caught they needed to examine her 'as found!' I felt cruel and horrible as she begged to be cleansed of his filth!

We kept her calm and warm and she spoke of it being her 18th birthday party and she'd met a man in the club whilst out with her friends, he invited her to another party he knew was taking place out of town telling her she could enjoy Champagne and food, unlike the down town club she was in.....stupidly she agreed to go with him and left the club alone with him. He drove her to the disused farm a quarter mile up on the mountain, in front of our cottage in the middle of nowhere, by now she had panicked and started to resist him but he locked the car doors electronically, she scrabbled to climb through his sunroof whilst he bit at her legs and then climbed out to drag her through the sunroof and across the farm yard. He then tied her to the 'lambing post' in the barn before repeatedly raping her over several hours during the early morning hours. The 'lambing post' is equally as repulsive as far as I have been led to understand, being the post that any lambs born who are deemed to be no good have their heads smashed against to kill them outright within minutes of birth.

After several exhaustive hours she managed to escape and fled straight down the mountain to the only two houses in her view. She stopped for nothing, no gate or fence or hedge ploughing straight through anything in her way in terror.....thus her injuries were severe and lifetime scarring.

Only somebody who lived locally at sometime in their life could have known that the storage farm yard he drove her to was disused. He knew he would not be seen or his vehicle detected.....it turned out after investigation that he was a local man, known as a very strange character all his life and unbelievably at the time he raped this poor woman, he was out on bail for a nightclub stabbing!

Peggy's house was suddenly deluged by Police and cars blocked the lanes with blaring sirens. Byron and his daughter remained in the Cottage, and Peggy's husband stayed out of sight as I explained what could happen to them if this girl freaked out, many a wrong accusation can be made in pain and panic and let's face it men were her most detested of creatures right at that moment.

My total disbelief culminated when a Police Woman and her male colleague walked in to stand before this wreck of a girl....they stayed silent, they just stared at her for what seemed an age to the girl's total discomfort and then the PCW said "What's your name?" There was no compassion, no sympathy, no consideration of her feelings....nothing!! I was aghast and tried to speak out but the PCW told me to be quiet....for a few moments they grilled her before leading her away to the waiting ambulance.

The CID Detectives invaded my home for a day or so and we were questioned as was Peggy next door. I recall the Rapists name being referred to as John and just imminent to the Court Hearing he pleaded guilty to his heinous crime. We were told we were no longer needed as witnesses and I believe he was sentenced to many years in prison where I hope he remains to this day, rotting!!

Not long after this Byron's daughter moved out and almost immediately then left Wales to live with her sister in London.

FRAM was just somewhere I HAD to go by day unfortunately and the time was coming close for me to leave. I left there one lunch hour to go to the local Stationers to collect some sample books for wedding stationery. I popped into the local Tesco supermarket en route to pick up some evening meal supplies and it was here that I saw a huge parked up Porta Cabin/Trailer bearing the sign 'Breast Cancer Test Wales.' As I walked back to my car from doing my shopping I mentally noted the number off the side of the trailer....I didn't realise at that time you have to be 50 years plus to have a breast cancer test, I just thought it would be a good idea to have a check up to be on the safe side.

I collected the sample books and returned to FRAM. The afternoon was stretching out ahead and as ever with nothing to do so I decided to call the number and make an appointment to have a check up, responsible health care and all that.

And this is what actually took place; please note I cannot actually remember the guy's name so am hypothesising.

"Hello, Sales, Rob speaking how can I help?"

Me; "Hello, I'd like to make an appointment please."

Rob; Hi, yeah sure, who do you want to see?"

I thought this a bit of a strange question.....?

Me; "Well whoever I need to see...?"

Rob; delayed reply as he pondered this answer..." Uhh well what is it you want, maybe I can direct you to the right Department?"

IS this guy a Muppet? I am now twitching with impatience.

Me: "Right Department? I want to make an appointment for a test, please."

Rob; by now utterly confused. "A test, what do you mean, a test...?"

Me; "Oh for goodness sake...I am trying to make an appointment to get my breasts checked, can I speak to the Nurse or a Doctor please?"

Rob; Heavy clearing of throat and wicked laughing ensued...."Ahh I see, now I am with you..." More chuckling and laughing..."Darling I'll check your breasts ANY DAY...but this is the number to call to actually HIRE the porta cabin unit!!"

Me; Shrivelled with embarrassment, places phone back on hook and headed for a glass of water. Ooops!!

The wedding stationery faired no better.

There was a young guy working at FRAM in Gate Security, I cannot even recall his name but he was on a mission to be recognised and if that meant a date with the MD's PA...he was going for it! I first became aware of his attentions when cream cakes were delivered to my office from him to me, then a small bunch of flowers and he always took the chance to delay the entrance barrier when I arrived at the factory of a morning so he could have a quick word telling me how glamorous I looked or that he liked my hair! I was probably his senior by 5 years or so and disinterested but wanted to be kind to his feelings so just politely tolerated his endeavours to gain my interest. I knew the day would come that I would have to put him straight.

I had been asking around the offices if anyone knew of a calligrapher or someone with decent handwriting as mine can be a scrawl. I wanted someone to write up the fifty invites to our wedding and didn't trust my own handwriting.

Guess who applied for the job? Mr Security man assured me he had undertaken a calligraphers course on a local night school course and would be delighted to ...'quote' me for the work. I took him at his word and duly passed the guest list and freshly printed invites to him...3-4 weeks passed and I was getting twitchy as the wedding was approaching fast. He assured me he was on the last leg of the list and I could collect them that Thursday.

"Can't you bring them into work?" I asked.

Him; "No best if you collect from my home in case anything should happen to them, it's safer."

I was in no mood to question this as I was juggling several million balls with the wedding already. He gave me his address and like a fool I went to collect.

He opened his door in a Village a few miles from where I live with his shirt unbuttoned to the waist bearing a milk white, hairless chest that would have looked good on a boy of around 9 years old! Trousers and casual slip on shoes completed his 'seduction' ensemble along with a bohemian beaded thong around his neck.

"Come in, don't mind the dog he's a bit randy at the moment....bit like me!"

I stopped dead in my tracks...bearing in mind I'd had no experience whatsoever of dogs at this stage of my life and it was bad enough coping with a horny security guard let alone his dog!

"Are the invites ready, here's the money." I held out the agreed amount and waited...

"Wanna a coffee?"

"No thanks, I'm in a rush, loads to do for the wedding" I replied.

"Aww go on, just a few minutes....I'm an artist you know, wanna see some of my sketches, their upstairs, come on..."

With a resigned sigh and lack of any further patience, up came the Scorpio tail lash...

"My invites, NOW! There's your cash and back off Buddy or I'll cripple you where you stand!"

His face was a picture....he was most certainly not ready for a real woman, probably having only encountered teenagers in his pathetic love life experiences.

My invites were handed over and I left in a flurry of tossed hair and the guzzle of my twin exhaust pipes on the Supra, job done!

Job done....NOT!

On arrival home I started checking through the invites and list and oh my good god....

I joke you not when I tell you there were bits of food stuck to my invites, names spelled incorrectly and even people paired up to the wrong partners...he had completely botched fifty invites at a cost of some £300, there was even something that looked like blood stuck to the inside of one of them!!

I threw them all in the bin having learned a valuable life lesson. I immediately re-ordered with the Stationer but time was critical and we were now just weeks from the wedding, chances are the people we were inviting would already have made plans as the 15th December is so close to Christmas!!

Work at FRAM was becoming more and more fractious if this could be believed.

Rafael had engaged a PA at Abergavenny thus he had a PA in either establishment.

I just hoped she had more to do than I did! Her name escapes me but this is normal with me when something or somebody is of absolutely no consequence to me...I simply wipe them from my radar. Although I do have the name June in my head?

She began to meddle with Rafael's mail, withholding letters and documents I needed to pass to him in time for meetings and deadlines at Llantrisant causing me to look a fool, she was trying to gain the upper hand in the war of the perfect PA! I already knew I wasn't one so what's your problem lady? I tackled her about it one morning by phone but soon realised I was playing straight into her hands. "Well if you can't do your job Maria, that's not my problem" was her flippant comment, I was enraged.

I rattled off my resignation naming and shaming all who had pissed me off in my months at FRAM...and why! I entered Wyndham's office that morning without invite much to his annoyance and slammed my resignation on his desk...."Here you go, you malicious little weasel...I finally quit, I'm gone, I'm out of your prehistoric hair...go running to Rafael all you want, there's my month's notice!"

For good measure I kicked his 'visitors chair' out of my way and left the office pausing only to push the door back open behind me, my temper knows no bounds when it explodes! And life was about to change dramatically once again!!

Regrettably, during my month's notice and around the month of October, I became ill. I had suffered most of my life with serious monthly menstrual pain causing me to lose consciousness on times, and had on occasions been seen at the local Accident & Emergency Hospital fearing appendicitis or worse. But this was the worst ever, I had collapsed at home one morning after Byron left for work. We were due a delivery of central heating oil and the delivery driver found me on the Dining Room floor spark out. He called an ambulance and I was off to hospital once again.

The Doctors' concluded that I needed to see a Specialist which could take a few months, however I held private medical Insurance as part of my salary package at FRAM so I was booked to see a Private Specialist almost immediately.

He had no doubts whatsoever that I suffered from Endometriosis and scarring of the womb with possible polyp growths and admitted me to BUPA the Private Health Care Hospital in Cardiff within days.

I was slightly worried at this stage because the wedding was only weeks away and so much still to do plus I had never spent any actual time in hospital and this condition sounded serious to me, Byron was naturally concerned but kept his calm composure.

The morning for me to be admitted arrived, we were shown to a very smart private room with my own TV, fresh flowers and a tray of coffee on arrival.

The Nurses were very attentive and helpful, finally they left with instructions for me to undress and don the clothing on the bed ready for me to be prepped for theatre where I was to undertake a full D&C operation.

Byron sat reading the hospital forms whilst I duly dressed in the clothing provided, the gown was a bit on the small side of a napkin size leaving not much to the imagination and as for the hat, I wasn't sure it was going to keep my long hair in which kept sliding out through the holes for your ears?? I placed the hat on and pulled the hole over each ear tucking as much hair back in as kept slipping out.

Theatre staff arrived with a trolley and I was gently and respectfully loaded aboard now starting to feel very nervous indeed, it didn't help that they seemed to be enjoying a damned good joke between themselves whilst they wheeled me off to theatre, a bit of reassurance for the patient might have been nice.

Some time later I found myself back in my room feeling absolutely horrendously ill and wearing my HAT, but it wasn't on my head. It was where 'they' should have been to start with as panties around my ass (laughing.) Another minor embarrassment in life as I realised I had put the theatre knickers on as a hat hence the joke en route between the nurses!

A few days saw me swiftly back on my feet and back at FRAM where I duly completed all the medical forms and sent off my Hospital bill which totalled some £2875 for settlement by my private medical insurers. I was due to leave FRAM for good by the middle of November which was just two weeks away so I set about packing up my belongings and generally preparing to leave the Company.

College was going OK and I was enjoying learning the fascinating art of drafting and cutting patterns for clothes which I had designed and sketched, albeit all my own wedding attire. Hannah was very cool with me, I was NOT one of her favourites in class and we politely skirted around each other for the two years I undertook the Course, however and professionally, she did not deny me any tuition I needed and for that I respected her despite it was obvious that she clearly and passionately detested me! Her main area for 'punishment' with me was Grade time, my marks were only ever given the basic pass levels because although she couldn't 'fail' me as my work was satisfactory or good, she sure as hell wasn't going to give me my true worth and at one point I became very annoyed about this on one particular mock exam.

The remit was to design, cut and make a suede jacket, I did so putting all of my heart into making a garment I didn't want to as it was robbing me of valuable time on my wedding wear manufacture, I achieved the Jacket in record time. The pass mark was set as 65/100...Hannah awarded me 64! I was furious and headed for her office.

"Hi Hannah, can I have a word about the marks awarded for my jacket please?" I asked politely.

"Not now Maria, I am busy" she replied without even looking up from her chick magazine!

"Is that so, I retorted, well you're not too busy to pin your ears back lady far as I can see! I know you dislike me and have no intention of doing me any favours on this Course but if you are going to 'fail' me on an assignment, damn well do it by more than one mark which was bloody petty, at least try and disguise your revenge!"

Hannah said nothing as I stomped off back to the class room.

The following week, myself and two others were asked to re-sit our mock as the marks we had been awarded 'didn't make sense' given the quality of our Course Portfolio's to date....I could smell red herrings every where and was exasperated that I was now just three weeks from my wedding with still much to do and now I had to make another god damned jacket arghhhh!!

Just as the predecessor who occupied our Cottage many decades ago...I worked through the night as a Couture Seamstress/Tailor, often missing out on going to bed at all. I was exhausted, but the jacket was designed, sketched, cut and made up in less than 12 days....and awarded 86/100.... result!

The morning arrived....my last day at FRAM, I was in a carefree, happy go lucky mood, nothing was going to spoil this day as I felt like a bird released from behind the bars of its cage. There was no leaving party, only one or two cards from the very few friends I'd made there and certainly no demonstration that anybody cared I was going...so what? I cared not as this miserable chapter of my life was rapidly disappearing as the clock counted down to 4pm.

I popped the kettle on at just past 3pm to enjoy a final cup of coffee. Whilst it boiled I decided to go check the mail box in Reception for any end of day deliveries so that I could at least leave my desk clear of any outstanding admin for Rafael who was due back any minute. A corporate magazine, a few internal memo's and a letter addressed to me were in the box which I opened as I strolled back along the corridor to my office. The opening paragraph that I read hit me in the head like somebody smashing me with a brick!

"Dear Mrs Price
Thank you for receipt of your completed Claim Form in relation to your recent Hospital treatment. We regret to advise this Claim has been declined for the following reasons......."

I sank into my chair reading and re-reading the letter in disbelief. My medical insurers were refusing to settle my private treatment bill of £2875 on the basis that my condition was a 'pre-existing' ailment. This was to become my very first encounter with Insurance companies and their 'loop hole' devious protocol.

Here I was three weeks away from paying out our only savings to get married, jobless and now facing a massive bill, I was devastated.

My heart was in my mouth only guessing at a fraction of what I was going to hear from Byron and the panic that would grip him! I decided that I would appeal and fight the decision but for the moment, the wedding had to take precedence.

Rafael breezed into the office minutes before 4pm and called me through to have a word. We generally de-briefed about the day, some chit chat about the wedding with him confirming his attendance and then.....

He looked me in the eye very directly and almost searching for his next words, I fell silent wondering what was coming? For the first time I truly looked at Rafael, he was indeed a very handsome man, tanned, healthy apart from his chain smoking, with a worldly wisdom about him, there is no doubt I appreciate the maturity of the older man.

"Mareeea, my name rolled off his tongue in his strong Spanish accent, I don't know what to say?" His eyebrows were knitted together in an almost pained expression. "I couldn't get involved you understand? My position...."

I listened although not sure I understood what I was hearing?

"You should have come to me that day....was too late, you handed in your notice to Wyndham, I couldn't over rule that or it would have been obvious."

By now my head was shaking from side to side in a quizzical manner...what on earth was he on about?

He gazed across the desk at me with a look on his face that I had never seen, it was pitying of me, angry with himself, sad and hurt all in one expression best I could read? Suddenly and slowly, 1 + 1 = 2 started adding up in my brain as a multitude of events started to falling into place.

I sat a little more upright in the plush leather, deep padded chair and stared back at him eye to eye. His expression was deeply sad, his eyes moist....his voice carried the hoarseness that only being upset can convey.

"Rafael....have I missed something here?" I questioned.

He slowly nodded his head in confirmation but said nothing.

"The rose, the note....am I right?" I further queried.

He nodded still in silence. As the realisation hit me that Rafael had feelings for me I suddenly understood why he had allowed me to be persecuted at FRAM, why he had allowed the insane reprimands to take place, he couldn't step in and defend me because his feelings for me would have been obvious. His position as the head of the company compromised.... oh my god!

I fought to find words in my head that would ease this poor man's clear discomfort and embarrassment right this second... "Oh Rafael, I'm so sorry. I love Byron, if he wasn't in my life I wouldn't have missed a thing, I promise you!" I heard myself say.

As his face took on a weak smile, a single tear ran down his left cheek which he rapidly wiped away as he stood up to come around my side of the desk. It was time to say goodbye so I reached out my hand to shake his but he ignored it, placing his strong arms around me with his aftershave invading my senses he hugged me tighter than a bug in a rug...I got the feeling Rafael was lonely, he needed some human contact, he held on to me not seeming to want to let go. As we stood apart, both a bit wiser in life's lessons, I leaned forward to peck him on both cheeks in final farewell. Rafael placed his hands on my cheeks and I realised he was going to kiss me. I knew that I should have stepped back but I could feel his pain from whatever it was he was feeling. I was rooted to the spot as he kissed me full on the lips in the type of deep and sensual kiss that only a man of experience can deliver. I do not deny the urge to respond was difficult....the Latinos have a masterful way with women, I wanted to but I didn't in loyalty and love of my own man Byron. Finally he released my lips and his grip around my shoulders....he looked, once again, embarrassed but at the same time relieved? Why? Perhaps because he had finally demonstrated what he felt, got it off his chest, who knows? He then handed me £50 worth of Gift Vouchers toward my wedding gift list and we bid our final farewell to each other...I doubted I would ever see him again let alone at our wedding.

FRAM was over....and life was about to change dramatically once again!

Chapter 6

- I Do ...and I did -

Saturday, 15th December 1990 arrived as a beautifully sunny, crisp, frosty, freezing cold morning, the wedding service was booked for 11am.

The previous evening had seen me packing Byron off to his parents for the night armed with all his wedding attire, instructions to his Mum about various things, a box of wedding favours for him to deliver to our Reception Venue and a phone call to be made to our florist confirming all was going to plan for the chapel and table decorations, my bouquet etc. My Chief Bridesmaid, Jacquie was due to arrive at the Cottage for 6pm so we could have a girl's preparation night and a meal and a few drinks..... except she didn't!

I showered, plucked, preened, waxed, primped, painted and paced around the Cottage until 7.30pm when I finally realised she wasn't coming. My penultimate wedding night was spent on my own with my two cats, eating a microwave meal in bed watching TV! No telephone call and no answer from hers? I was utterly confused at what was happening... I couldn't understand how she could be so inconsiderate as to leave me in the lurch like this? I worried myself sick that she'd had an accident, was in some way not able to contact me for whatever reason....my pre wedding night was a disaster!

The following morning saw me up at the crack of dawn, cats fed and proceedings swinging into action. Byron's dear and much loved Dad, Les arrived and was the most loving and attentive Father of the Bride I could have ever hoped for. Then Byron's Sister Barbara, lord help me....the Dominatrix! Difficult woman to befriend, control freak and a veritable pain in the arse! She and I have never got along and NEVER will! Finally Jacquie showed her sheepish face....
"What happened?" I instantly demanded.

"Oh I knew you'd be OK, you know what you're like, I couldn't get the horses in and by the time I did, I didn't feel like driving all the way up here" she stated matter of fact.
I was deeply angry.
"Lost the use of your fingers as well did you...a phone call would have been nice!"
"Oh sorry, I thought you would have been busy and partying..." she trailed off at the look on my face.
We commenced getting dressed and the general hype of a wedding morning started to kick in around Cherry Tree Cottage...sounds daft but I could feel the Cottage absorbing the happiness. The Vintage Rolls arrived and the Bridesmaids were duly dispatched leaving me and Les, my dear Father In Law alone to talk.
He held my hands as I paced the lounge with the cats about my feet, he told me I was a perfect Daughter In Law, he told me his Son was a 'good boy' and that he'd 'been a bit hard on him' in his life. I smiled knowing that Les was emotional right at this minute...he was a truly lovely man, RIP Lesley Parnell.

As we awaited the Rolls to return, skidding its way up and down our country lanes in the heavy frost, I was nervous as hell and agitated. I popped into the kitchen and for whatever reason decided to water the plants on the window cill.
As I poured water into the first pot the damn thing splashed back sending a spray of muddy droplets toward my gown.....quick as a flash I felt Les's hand on my shoulder yanking me backwards.... "What you doing, bloody hell that was close!" he shouted as the droplets fell to the floor. Suddenly he took on a real parental, stern and angry face... "Now go in there and sit down, NOW before something else happens!" I burst out laughing at his little face crumpled...he put his arms around my shoulder saying "Com'on now girl...I'm supposed to be looking after you!" I like to think Les and I always had a very special relationship...he was wicked and a rebel...but then so is his Son!
The Photographer arrived and with all home shots taken, then departed, leaving me and Les to head for the Chapel.
Chauffer to Les, "Uhh Mr Parnell, we have a problem..."

Les, "What d'ya mean a problem Butt?" (Welsh for Mate)

Chauffer, "The car is playing up, I can't get it started, I think it's the cold weather.."

Me out of window, "What's wrong Dad?"

Les, "Nothing, go inside, it's too cold for you out here!"

Les to Chauffer, "Lift the Bonnet..."

I could see the pair of them tinkering around under the hood and the sudden thought hit me that my wedding transport was broken down....oh for goodness sake....come on life, cut me some slack will ya!

Les and the Chauffer continued for some twenty minutes until they got sounds of life from the engine...I was utterly relieved as I was now LATE for my wedding my 5 minutes.

Les locked up the Cottage and we clambered aboard this beautiful old vintage motor. Just half a mile up the road as we approached the first climb out from our lanes the car spluttered to a dead stop! Les had his calm head on...."Now I'm telling you girl, stay there!" He climbed out and once again the 'tinkering' began. Then they rolled the car backwards and tackled the hill again and did this a further three times before it was agreed the car wasn't going to climb up this hill unless pushed!

I have never seen two men more ashen faced as they spoke to me through the window.

Les, "We're going to have to roll it back to the flat stretch of lane so we can do a jump start on it, you're going to have to get out and walk up the lane to where we can pick you up once it's started..."

Me, "Dad, you're joking me...look at the state of the lane, my dress and shoes...oh no!"

Les, "Stop moaning, c'mon get out, quick now, we're late!"

Hell's bells tell me something I ain't panicking over already why don't you!

I scooped up as much of my 23 Yards of silk as I could and disembarked into the lane. As they rolled the Rolls backwards I headed forwards up the lane carrying my skirts in my arms... the first to pass me was a local 4 x 4 who nearly drove off the road in disbelief of his eyes! Then the local Postie went past in his van with a similar reaction...eventually, and picking my way through the mud and horse droppings in the lane in my satin cream wedding shoes, I reached the junction at the top of the lane and patiently waited, shivering in less than 20 microns of silk lace to my upper body and in -3 Degrees Centigrade with white frost glistening on the ground. I stood alone, in a country lane, in full wedding gown, freezing my ass off as my Rolls chugged up the hill with Les and somebody they had flagged down pushing as hard as they could behind, thank you my wonderful Dad, a sight I will never forget! Finally we are underway but by now I am 40 minutes late for my wedding....

Arriving at the Chapel was magical in my memory. There were guests everywhere, the local residents in houses were out in their gardens to watch the Bride arrive...I felt really special for once in my life. With the usual arrival shots taken we entered the Chapel for my walk up the Aisle on my very proud Father In Law's arm.
Jacquie was behind herding the two little bridesmaids. I was totally flustered with the morning's events and thus my mind was blank of all the rehearsals we had attended.
"Which foot first to lead off Dad..?" I asked.
"Oh for god's sake just walk!" I heard from Jacquie behind....
Hmmm, what is going on here I thought to myself.
I entered the Chapel aisle in a bubble of happiness with my wonderful and beautiful Father in Law proud as punch on my arm...he was to be my little bit of 'arm candy' forever after. Byron looked utterly relieved and on the brink of panic...I tried to mouth "I'm sorry" to him but of course he was never going to know why until I explained about the car. I remember a buzz of admiration of my gown going around the Chapel and then facing the Vicar and the Ceremony began, all I could think of was how HORRIFIED I was at the Chapel flower decorations....what the hell had gone wrong? Large, fat candles quite literally had a bit of red ribbon tied to them and some very tacky green holly embellished paper decoration wrapped around the bases. Where the hell were the flowers I had ordered?

We had chosen The Holly and The Ivy as a Hymn but they had printed all six verses....try singing them...trust me it's hard going, it went on, and on, and on, and on (laughing.) I do believe the Congregation were totally relieved to escape the Chapel at the end.

Not one of my photographs shows my Chief Bridesmaid Jacquie, smiling? She moaned about the cold weather, her dress, and questioned how long she would need to stay at the wedding?? I was too pre-occupied to pay her rudeness due attention.

We eventually arrived at the beautiful Miskin Manor Country House, some two miles from the Chapel for our wedding reception. Again the photos were taken and I was delighted to actually see Rafael and his wife Amy in the guest line up...bless him, he had honoured his promise. As we caught eyeball to eyeball he winked his provocative wink and nodded his head in approval of whatever, me, the day, the ceremony who knows?

The Welsh Harpist struck her first cords and we took our seats....I felt like I was floating through this day of magic.

The Speeches were just the best....nothing silly, all very mature, kind and highly humorous. Byron's Brother In Law, Edward was Best Man and absolutely made for the job...he entertained the wedding guests like he was made for the stage. At some point the wine and champagne overtook his vertical abilities as he dumped a large glass of red in my lap... my gown sporting a nice pink stain was the least of my worries as I noticed Jacquie's latest squeeze's chair was vacant, the meal uneaten?

I managed to catch a moment to approach her and ask where her Boyfriend was?

"Where's Geoff?" I asked directly.

"Oh he couldn't make it, something came up at the yard."

I registered this reply with the inconsideration and contempt it deserved..

"Thanks a bunch Jacq, we've just shelled out £50 per head for a meal your boyfriend is too busy to eat having been invited weeks ago!" I was furious.

"And whilst I'm at it...what is your problem Lady? You agreed to be my Chief Bridesmaid and all you've done so far is let me down, you fucked up my photo's with your miserable face and now we're left paying for a meal your boyfriend can't be bothered to attend to eat! C'mon tell me what's this little game all about because I am fucking stumped?"

Jacqueline had the good sense to look worried or I swear I would have decked her where she stood.

"Ohh it's you, isn't it! You got it all sorted haven't you, the lovely country cottage, the only decent guy I've met in years...you're bloody PA job.... you make me sick!"

I just stood there...OH ...MY...GOD!!! Am I stupid or what, how the hell did I miss the green eyed monster in my midst, let alone invite her to be my 'right hand woman' at my wedding? Two women of roughly the same age just 6 months apart, add Byron, plus a Secretary opposed to PA....plop, plop as the pennies fell into place...well what d'ya know!! Another lesson in life learned the hard way.

Jacqueline showed up at the evening party venue for barely an hour just to show her face and disappeared....never to be seen or spoken to again. It left me pondering the question of why I couldn't seem to make any true friends?

Our Wedding Evening Party was held at a nearby venue known as Fairwater Leisure Centre...a sports centre that was affordable and convenient for all guests to travel to. The evening was a lovely affair and everybody seemed to enjoy themselves....none more than my new Brother In Law Ed. He was well tanked up on the day's hype, the success of his speech and booze. A drunk always speaks the truth they say....

Ed was propping up the bar in the leisure centre as I walked past, he caught hold of my arm as I passed.

" You happy love?" he asked.

"Yeah, course I am...you having a good time Bro?" I smiled back at him.

"Yeah, I am...god I could lick you all over from your....!"

WHOA UP MY BROTHER IN LAW!!!!

Booze talking, nothing more than..... "Yeah, yeah, whatever Hun, can you get me a glass of champagne please, I've lost the last one!" With that he staggered off.

I hit the dance floor with my husband.... I hoped the moment would never end.
Suddenly tap, tap on the shoulder as Brian Trask wanted to dance with the Bride...
Byron as ever the gentleman stood down.
"Hiya Babe"
Brian was a remarkable ginger haired cross breed replica between an Irish
Leprechaun and a Jack Russell....an Installation Engineer in Byron's company, around
45 years old, divorced with a son he idolised.

"Hi Brian...you've just broken up my wedding waltz with my husband Hun!"
Brian, "Oh bugger him....I know where you are going on Honeymoon, iss gonna be
great, yur gonna love it in Ireland!"
Byron caught hold of Brian at the scruff of the neck and gently guided him to one side
saying "Thanks Bri....you just ruined my wedding surprise!"
I was agog at this point because I knew we couldn't afford a honeymoon, it had never
been in the budget....Ireland....oh my gosh!
"No worries Mate, I'll make sure it all goes OK!" were Brian's last words as he
staggered off across the dance floor.
We looked at each other, "what did he mean?" I asked...Byron shrugged his shoulders
and said..."who knows, daft old sod, but he's bloody spoiled my surprise
Gorgeous...I'm taking you to Ireland for a three day honeymoon, it's all we can afford."
I wrapped my arms around Byron's neck and we danced our way off the floor.
The night dwindled to an end as guests left, Byron and I stayed to clean up the room
and leave it in a decent state for the Centre staff, we finally hit the Cottage at
3am....only for me to learn the Ferry left at 6am, so my wedding night was somewhat
of a hurried affair amidst the rose petals that had been secretly strewn in our marital
bed....!

Just six days later on the 21st December 1990, the TV News headlines were that
Geraldine Palk was brutally raped and repeatedly stabbed to death in the grounds of
the Fairwater Leisure Centre, Cardiff where we had just held our wedding evening

party. Just 26 years old, a Secretary living in Fairwater, she had been out at her office Christmas party...she made her way home by taxi walking the last few yards to her home when her murderer struck, he dragged her into the quiet grounds of the Leisure Centre leaving her to die alone in the watery ditch at the perimeter of the grounds. Her mother Cynthia, a retired Nurse never recovered from her grief. Walking past her daughters last known point of life, Cynthia was struck by a car and killed outright less than a year later. Barely a year after that, Les her husband died.... an entire family was brutalised, tortured and wiped out in the blink of any eye! RIP Geraldine, Cynthia and Les...may your remaining family glean some peace in life. Whenever I think of my wedding day...my thoughts turn to you all, God Bless!

Ireland was an experience to be remembered but NOT for the Country and its culture albeit this is spectacular in itself....but because Brian bloody Trask accompanied us on our Honeymoon!

With our cats catered for, we swiftly packed bags for our Honeymoon and departed for the Ferry point some two hours away...by now I was running on pure adrenaline and I'm guessing so was Byron, probably even more shattered at his necessary 'quickie' wedding night antics!
We arrived at Fishguard Port in West Wales and boarded the Ferry. Within minutes...here comes Brian Trask, we were speechless but intrigued. "It's all planned my beautiful couple, I got you a meeting with the Capitan on Deck and a wedding breakfast....and I'm personally escorting you to the Hotel in Wexford, I got it all sorted, just follow me!"
Byron and I were too damned tired to argue the toss and how the hell was Brian so bright and breezy when we were exhausted and in alcohol recovery mode??

As promised we were summoned to the Deck of the Ferry where the Captain welcomed and congratulated us on our marriage, he allowed me to steer the ship for a short distance and toasted us with a glass of champagne....Byron was proud as a lion and I was numb with all the lavish attention and formalities...I felt real for the first time in my life!

Locating our motor on the lower decks, we all disembarked on Irish Soil ....
Here he came, our Caped Crusader in his little battered white Ford Escort van. Brian was short in stature around 5 feet 2 inches and of slight build with wiry ginger hair, balding on top. His permanent grin belied the tough matrimonial times he had endured and the wicked twinkle in his green eyes gave him the appearance of a psyched up gnome!
"Right, follow me, we're going straight to the White Horse Pub/B&B, I got it all in hand boss" he said to Byron through the open car window. I swear to god if he'd had a tail it would have been wagging like a metronome on crack!
It seemed to take forever as we followed him through Town after Village after Hamlet until we pulled into a very quaint old Irish Establishment and made our way into Reception to book in. The plan was for at least a few hours sleep through the morning to come before we could even begin to enjoy our Honeymoon....my only concern was that Brian....CHECKED in too? I was beginning to worry that my Honeymoon was going to turn into a Ménage de Troi!

As we entered the Hotel Room there were flowers absolutely everywhere...I was teary eyed. Seems Brian had organised a welcome from The Shine Food Machinery Company to do Byron proud. We headed straight for the bed for nothing more than pure rest! As I pulled back the cover there were condoms and rose petals, champagne corks and god knows what covering the mattress ...took us 15 minutes more to clean up before we collapsed into the deepest sleep in each others arms that we have ever enjoyed.

Wexford is indeed a truly beautiful place on God's earth. We slept most of that first day, venturing down to the Hotel Lounge early evening only to find Brian propping up the Bar. You couldn't not like this guy, indeed I loved him and often babysat his son, even took his son for a trip to the Museum in Cardiff.... but as a Gooseberry on my Honeymoon, he was pushing his luck!

As we entered the Bar a roar of clapping and congratulations took off with complete strangers patting Byron on the back and shaking his hand, shaking my hand and wishing us all the very best in our married life. Brian was dancing around the Bar whipping up the crowd like a well honed Publicity Agent! Drinks were flowing across the Bar, we didn't need to put our hand in our pocket all evening and for this I never had the chance to say a deep and sincere thank you to the Residents of Wexford who were in the Pub that day, my friends of the moment, you were awesome and god bless you!

Eventually Brian explained in great detail why he was irritated that he had to leave us to our own devices and return to the UK leaving us the last two days of our Honeymoon alone. I found myself saying "Awww really Bri, you sure Hun? Ok well no matter and we cannot thank you enough for all that you have organised" and I actually felt myself meaning it in a funny sort of way! Byron on the other hand shook his hand firmly and hugged him tight before saying... "no worries Mate, now fuck off and leave me with my woman will ya!" We all laughed as Brian sashayed off down the highway heading for Newport, South Wales, UK via the earliest ferry.

The following two days were amazing, we toured Dublin and stood before the statue of Charles Stewart Parnell...just maybe somewhere back in the annals of history could he be in our family tree? We experienced the amazing ambience of the Irish Pubs, real Guinness and toured the Stuart Crystal Factory watching real crystal glass being blown by hand.
Charles Stewart Parnell... Born in County Wicklow 27th June 1846 - Died October 6th 1891 *(Google researched.)* An Irish Landlord who became a Founder/Leader of the Irish Parliamentary.

I found the City of Dublin and indeed Ireland a fascinating Country...I just wished we could have spent more than three short days there....my wish was to be granted many, many, many years later.

On our final morning we came down to breakfast as the 'late arrivals,' we were on Honeymoon after all! As I descended the stairs into the restaurant I could see the room was empty and most all of the breakfast tables already cleared.

"Arhhh good morning to you Mrs Parnell" I heard the waiter's bright and cheery greeting.

"Morning, sorry we're late, is it still ok for breakfast?" I queried.

"Yerrrrs, top of the morning to ya, bet the Mr has been keeping you busy, not a problem!"

My eyebrows seemed to join my hairline at this comment!

I continued and indicating to just the four remaining tables laid out for breakfast..."Uhh where would you like us to sit?"

His response was pure Irish logic... "Arhhh any where you like my lovely lady, anywhere you like......as long as it's HERE!" he pointed to a table nearest the kitchen swing doors. Fair enough I thought, smiling to myself....the Irish blarney amusing me and Byron alike.

Ireland remains a firm favourite Country in my heart for many reasons, not just my Honeymoon but for it's deep and rich culture, the natural and unselfish hospitality of it's population and it's sheer unadulterated environmental beauty.... Ireland...Auntie M LUBS you...oh yes she does!! *(Terminology; 'Auntie M', a title as yet to be created and publicised via Face Book in years to come.)*

Chapter 7

- A Daughter is a Daughter...all her life!"

We arrived home from Honeymoon on a high. Life for once was all that we could have hoped for and our future stretched out before us like an exciting web of 'what leads to what?'

The Boys were right as rain and like we'd never been away, Tim had done his job admirably and enjoyed a well earned mini holiday. The Cottage looked more cosy than ever as we re-girded our loins to plough into further refurbishments this close to Christmas. As the new Mrs Parnell, I felt like I had shaken off all the past shrouds of taint and bad luck...my life was starting, right here, right now, I was 30 years old, it had been a long time in the making but at last I had arrived ...in my own life, with a man who adored me and a family of cats, a lovely country home and a career...well Ok that was still work in progress!!

Arriving back from Honeymoon and as mentioned, I had been horrified with the Church Floral decorations and wrote to the Florist to complain asking what had gone wrong and why my original order had not been adhered to, before I was prepared to settle the invoice? Within days I received a County Summons suing me for non payment of my order. Again, I telephoned and wrote but the owner of the shop was indignant and refused to discuss my original order with me. We were instructed to attend the local County Court Office where Byron and myself along with the Florist and her husband sat before a judge who quite frankly was appalled that she hadn't been professional enough to at the very least discuss my complaint for goods and services rendered before taking such drastic actions as to sue me! The florist was rude and hostile whilst in court resulting in the Judge awarding Byron and myself a 50% discount in our wedding floral costs. This wasn't the issue...a few flowers didn't spoil our wedding but when you consider I'd ordered Autumn/Winter decorations for a Christmas wedding and I got Spring/Summer colours and flowers and paper tape to tie off the church like a murder scene....surely I had a right to complain? Yet another 'whatever' chalked up in my life.

Christmas came and went, as did New Year 1990, we enjoyed the simple pleasures of the festive season, our home and our pets.

January 3rd 1991; The phone was ringing as I came downstairs from the bathroom. Standard response on picking up the hand set was "Hello?"
" Maria? It's Fran...you'll have to come straight away, Mum's Dead, you HAVE to come, Oh god...she's dead!" Was what I heard.
I didn't speak, I hung up in total and utter, drop to the floor on my knees shock!
With my hand still on the phone I realised I didn't even know where my Mother lived...so I carefully selected 'last number redial.'
My Sister, Frances was a mess...her sobbing was heartbreaking to listen to but I almost felt detached, like an outsider, when had they ever included me in their life as mother and daughter...daughters?
"Fran, it's me...I don't know where Mum lives...where do I go?"
She gave me the address and I hung up once again. Byron had been in the Lounge watching TV but was by now alerted to something going on....I wandered past him without speaking to go upstairs and dress. On returning downstairs, I made my way out into the dark of night toward my vehicle and without shoes on... "Maria... what the hell is going on?" I heard him say as if he was somewhere down a tunnel with an echo.... "Where are you going, you've got no shoes on?" he continued.
I felt eerily suspended in life... from the euphoric highs of marrying the man I adored to this 'slap in the face' wake up call out of the blue, about the mother who couldn't care less if I breathed or died, but news of her demise had hit me like a sledge hammer!
" It's my Mum..." I said in the most pathetic of tones of voice.... "She's dead!"
Byron just stared at me for what seemed like a lifetime before he came to me wrapping his arms about me muttering..."Ssshhh, Ok, Ok, it's going to be OK, I'll come with you."

We drove to Newport to the address I had been given...my sister and Ray, her husband were already there as was my Mother's live in partner that she had moved 'on to, Derek'....all news to me I'm afraid. The atmosphere was rank with grief and confusion and total chaos.

As I walked in my Sister started babbling about god knows what, her voice on the verge of hysteria. I looked around the sad, one bedroom'ed, Council flat that had become my mother's final resting place....it sickened me! Her newest Partner Derek was appraised immediately on sight as being the worthless, useless, piece of shit he transpired to be...I am RARELY wrong in my judgement of the human race!

The Undertakers arrived within minutes of me and Byron, I was eaten apart with the inability of being able to say a real 'goodbye' to the woman who never cared a hoot about me...she was my Mother for gods sake!! I felt like she was the only post left standing in my life field...and now it had finally been kicked down...I was truly alone for the first time ever, a Sister who was less than useless didn't count!

Byron drove me home that night in total silence...he didn't know what to say....and I didn't know how to speak, to express the depth of the grief I was feeling.

My Mother's funeral was mostly organised by me with some input from my Sister Frances who was too reticent to do too much due to cost implication. I could understand this given their meagre existence on benefit payments due to Ray's serious ailments.

I moved forward in numb, jerky, PA organisational methods... the cremation date was set I wrote a tribute to my Mother to be published in the local Newspaper Obituaries.

I couldn't understand why I felt so emotionally broken at the death of a woman who couldn't care less whether I lived or died?

Her funeral day was yet another momentous experience for me as we arrived at the Funeral Home...Doris Joan Hext, latter Bishop, latter Trute was dressed out in her coffin and looked a fraction of the woman I remembered thanks no doubt to formaldehyde. I approached her coffin in a somewhat autopilot manner, I kissed her cold, lifeless forehead and looked down on the face that I had somehow forgotten to remember in my life. In that one split second of contact of my lips to her forehead...I forgave her everything, I don't know why, I cannot explain and I don't intend to try! My Mother was dead...end of!

The congregation was a mixed and motley crew of people my Mother had befriended over the years. My Sister and Ray were highly emotional as the service took place, Byron squeezed my hand tight...but as for me...nothing, nada, nowt! No tears, no outward emotion, nothing! I felt dead from the neck up!
I sang the hymns, I enacted what should be done...but as for feelings? Numb!
A lady approached me...maybe the term lady is too complimentary... "so you're her other daughter huh...you cruel cow, you haven't even shed a tear" and with that she lashed out as if to slap my face. I caught hold of her hand before anyone else could see what was going down.... all I could think to say was "get lost you stupid bitch!"

We arrived at the Crematorium in Cwmbran, Monmouthshire and the service concluded the demise of my Mother's life. It was a small and informal affair, I recall the congregation standing as her coffin rolled through the final curtains of her life...I tried to imagine how I would feel were I her in that box right now? I continued to stand staring after the conveyer belt long after the coffin had disappeared from sight... no tears, no emotions, no nothing...I felt truly abandoned and alone at 30 years old...crazy I know, but to me, although she never wanted me, she was like a post in a field out there somewhere...and finally the post had been kicked down...I was truly the last in my line!

- Chapter 8 -

- 'Fashioning' a new career! -

We scattered Mum's ashes on The Winter Rose Bed at the Crematorium in Cwmbran.......I have never returned to it because to me she 'died' elsewhere in my life a long time before that!

The Cottage was taking some sort of shape and as we headed into the start of 1991 there was a lot to be sorted out...not least a job for me for a start. I once again hit the Employment Agency rounds and managed to acquire some Temporary Office work covering staff sick leave and pregnancy leave. As long as a wage hit the bank each month I wasn't bothered what I did for it within reason and Byron was content as long as we could jointly meet the bills.

Spring approached and as ever the gardens at the Cottage were work in progress. There has been a large Cypress Tree growing in the most awkward area of the driveway and we had agreed at some point it had to go....maybe my chosen date wasn't quite appropriate?

Byron was away long haul in the UK that day, I arrived home from my 'temp' job earlier than expected and set about our obligatory three hours of DIY per weekday evening. Looking at the tree as I reversed into the drive I decided this was to be my task for the evening. Byron was due home around 7pm so I had just enough time to chop it down and cook dinner.

I parked SEPY in the usual place but as I switched off the engine, one of his headlamp 'eyes' popped up of its own accord making my car look like a drunken frog! Damn it, I thought, hope Byron can fix it because I'm not driving around with a one eyed car! After a quick change into my 'labourers clothes' I set about ransacking Byron's tool shed for equipment. Hatchet...too small. We didn't own a chainsaw (thank GOD!) hammer and chisel....maybe not? Ahhh ...a huge Axe.

I did feel sorry for this living entity as I approached it doing my best impression of the 'Axe Murderer' but it simply had to go. I licked my thumb and placed it in the air as Byron had showed me how to in order to check wind direction.... I couldn't feel anything? Bloody great check that is, I thought to myself! Well it can't matter that much so I'll just start chopping. SEPY languished 'sleepy eyed' around eight feet away from the tree.

The first wield of the axe saw a large splinter of trunk fly past my left cheek...goggles and a helmet were not part of my Risk Assessment and Method Statement back then...in fact I don't think either existed then!! Several heaving axe swipes at this trunk later saw me gasping for breath and sweat running down my face. Not to be beaten and needing to see the joy on my Husband's face when he pulled up and realised I'd saved him yet another weekend job...I continued to hack away merrily.

As the sun started to dip in the sky, the tree started to lean precariously.....IN THE WRONG direction. I suddenly realised it was going to topple across the driveway and in doing so was most certainly going to smash down right across SEPY's bonnet! The trouble was that I now had an immediate decision to make...wedge myself between the tree and car to minimise impact damage or let it fall and smash my car up!!!!
I dropped the axe and leapt between the tree and car. The Cyprus was only 10 -12 feet tall but you really cannot appreciate the weight behind such a growth until you have to hold it up. As I grappled my way through branches and twigs, I heard a car pull up at the gateway. At this stage I was laying across the nearside bonnet of my car with a fir tree on top of me.
I heard Byron long before I saw him...not difficult I assure you with a mouth like his!
"Jesus Christ I can't leave you alone for five minutes, what the fuck are doing woman? If you've damaged that car I'm not paying for it!"
Slightly battered and bruised I hear myself muttering "Hi Hun, do you think you can get this off me, is my car OK?

Suddenly in one heave the tree flew off me like the wind had blown it away. "Leave things alone will you, you don't know what you're doing. For god's sake M, what if I hadn't got home tonight?"
Good point mate....I'd have been sleeping under a 'Fir' blanket on the bonnet of my car!!

I lamely tried to explain I had wanted to save him some time and effort whilst he pulled twigs and debris out of my hair and stood me upright albeit I was shaky, and on retrieving his beloved axe he declared .. " and you better not have blunted this I'm warning you!"

A few weeks passed and life continued in ParnellLaLaLand (*Term to be explained in years/chapters to come*) as any normal married couple in a new home. We had started acquiring some pieces of furniture and growing vegetables in the garden and to be honest, felt utterly like we were living the good life!

It was Monday morning as I dressed for my latest 'Temp' job position in some office somewhere in Cardiff City. I kissed Byron and drove off up the lane....as I dropped down the hill and rounded the bend, there he was! Stretched out across the lane like he was sleeping but with his tongue lolling out and his eyes wide in panic, his entrails seeping from his anus. I slammed on the brakes screaming "Chester, Noooooooooooo!" I rushed from the car as another vehicle was heading toward me. Throwing myself on the floor to scoop him up, praying he was still alive and treatable, I was blocking the road...TOUGH! Byron had by now left the Cottage and had pulled up short behind me as I rocked my dead baby in my arms. The guy in the other car looked utterly intolerant as Byron scraped me off my knees to one side of the country lane, moved both mine and his vehicle and eventually the guy passed with less than a gesture of anything! I carried Chester home and we buried him under the Goat Willow Tree in the garden...he had been hit by a car on the country lane which less than a dozen vehicles a day use, why oh why couldn't he have stuck to the fields and mountains on his daily roaming? I went to work, albeit late, but was chastised for being so emotional...my temporary Boss told me "pull yourself together, it's JUST a cat!"

I recall looking at the man with utter contempt and hatred....Chester was never 'just a cat.' He was the sickly little babe I couldn't leave behind, he was my baby boy and someone I loved with all my heart and soul. I began to develop my true understanding of those who genuinely love and care for animals...and those who don't. The one's who don't have never figured seriously in my life ever since, end of!

Animals deal with death far better than we humans. Maxwell neither looked for or pined for his sibling and by now was growing into a beast of a cat. Max was a positively huge Tabby and enjoying the rural surroundings he lived and foraged in. I of course tried to compensate for my grief by lavishing even more love and attention on Max, he tolerated this but was at the very least indifferent.

College was coming to an end for me, my Course Final Exams were looming up. For some reason I was nervous, not my normal style but I guess I wanted this achievement badly. I had, after all, never acquired any form of academic qualification in my life. I needed basic recognition that I was 'good for something!' The very thought of passing this exam, at over 30 years of age, actually signified to me that I really DID have some intelligence, knowledge, ability. You know those type of things you achieve at 16 years of age when leaving school...the very things I had been robbed the chance of! Guess my chance was coming late in life....

The Exam day loomed up and my Course Portfolio was 'as ready' as I could make it, out of my hands from here on.

On the morning of the exam I felt physically ill, but determined to give it my best shot. I knew damned well I was never going to get a Distinction at 90+ marks, I hoped for at least a Credit at 76+ marks....BUT had probably resigned myself due to the Hannah/Jean/Andrew/Penny and Me Pentangle to a basic Pass. Whatever was going to be ...was going to be. On this day in history/in my life I learned to accept that what was going to be....was NOT necessarily what I should accept in life! From here on in this life story, I forged my own destiny, accepted NOTHING was cast in stone, I believe this is called self belief!

I graduated from Adult Education College with a Credit at 85/100 and thus my Fashion Career began.

Chapter 9

- *Living the dream...* -

From this point of my life is where I started to move into the 'Bitches' era of the title of this book, I have met many thousands of people in my lifetime, some I wish had never, ever crossed my path!

With my grand City & Guild Accreditation Certificate I had obtained a skill in my life, something I truly knew how to do, a craft, an ability and I pondered as to how I could put it to good use. After all I had initially only undertaken the course to create my own wedding attire. The Temp jobs were coming and going, life was reasonably normal but I hated every second of sitting in offices somewhere around the Capital City bashing away at a keyboard with absolutely no interest in the job I was doing. The Fashion Course had awakened something within me and I realised that my true interests and love lay with 'making and doing' thus I was loving refurbishing our home, making my own wedding clothes, cooking, gardening....I am never happier than when I am creating something.

It was Summer 1991 when Byron and I decided to take a holiday abroad and with much enthusiasm we chose Barbados as the destination and I set about organising the trip of a lifetime. I couldn't believe that I was actually getting to see some of the World. First Spain then Tenerife, Zurich and now the Caribbean. Two glorious weeks of sunshine, sea and spectacular touring.

With everything sorted and Maxwell catered for at a nearby Cattery, we left for the airport and the time of our lives landing in Barbados some eight hours later after a brief stop off en route. We made our way by Taxi to the Town of Oistins in the Parish of Christ Church.

The small Island of Barbados (*in the lesser Antilles*) is truly exquisite, or at least it was then, I know not if it has lost any of its charm in the decades that followed. Just 21 miles long by 14 miles wide it is sectioned into 11 Parishes with Bridgetown being the Capital and largest City in the Parish of St Michael.

We were Self Catering in Oistins with our Chalet situated right on the beach in the Bay of Oistins. Stepping out of our door straight on to the beach with the Caribbean sea lapping at our feet was absolutely incredible. The Chalet was humble, habitable, clean and totally functional but could hardly be called 5 Star as some of the St James Parish Hotels would have been. It didn't matter to us, we were entranced with the culture and the Island. As always the first couple of days saw us acclimatising to the heat, finding our bearings and generally sussing out the amenities. We enjoyed the beach by day until late afternoon when we would venture out to walk between the Parishes savouring the diverse array of bars, restaurants, shops and venues on offer.

The Brits on holiday can be as comical as any TV sketch and I'm afraid we added to this reputation on our second evening whilst out walking in the Town of St Lawrence. Deciding where to eat, I spied a gorgeous little restaurant nuzzled back off the road with landscaped and palm tree gardens, gentle music on the evening breeze and a seafood menu to die for posted outside in it's posh illuminated glass case.

"Oh let's do this one" I urged as Byron studied the menu prices rapidly trying to convert everything back to £GBP.

We approached the restaurant door which was locked...this seemed very peculiar as there were people eating inside? An intercom buzzer alerted us to the door being electronically unlocked and we entered into what I can only describe as being an Oasis of Opulence. Magnificent wall to wall glass fish tanks with some of the largest, odd looking and vividly coloured aquatic species residing within, some I am guessing were on borrowed time until the menu called for them! Crystal chandeliers glistened from the ceilings and mirrored alcoves with huge displays of fresh cut flowers adorned the hexagonal shaped dining area which was then sectioned off into snugs and nooks on two elevations with couples intimately dining in their own little bit of privacy.

Palm trees swayed gently as the air conditioning breeze ruffled their fronds and a rather stern looking Barbadian lady dressed from head to toe in Yves St Laurent designer wear, and they weren't 'knock offs,' stood before me staring at Byron and I as if we had just 'crawled' let alone stepped through her door!

"May I help you" she enquired with her mouth seemingly fixed in a superficial smile that belied the rest of her face as her beautiful violet blue eyes and nostrils narrowed in distaste of something?

"May we have a table for two please" I asked politely with which she seemed to freeze up. Many seconds passed as she cast her eyes over Byron and I as if examining us for suitability to actually breath oxygen!! I suddenly got the message...it was US she was in distaste of.....was I wearing the wrong colour flip flops or something!!!!

It may have been Byron's Hawaiian style tee shirt and his ACTUAL RAF PT shorts which he resolutely refused to be parted from, thread bare even then, they managed to survive a further 16 years before he grieved for their ripe demise, but he was wearing leather Loafers for goodness sake? As for me, I wore a pretty little tee shirt top over a rather expensive pair of Designer shorts, Chanel fragrance and my brand new flip flops, so your problem is lady?? As we glanced around it was clear we were in THE most expensive dining establishment on the Island as I could also see cut crystal glasses and solid silver cutlery on the tables... "I will just check Madam if we have any availability" she spoke in that tone of voice that told me we were leaving via the nearest back door entrance! Feeling somewhat humiliated Byron came to my rescue over my shoulder.... "As you can see we're on holiday, he spoke to her in a friendly voice, perhaps we could reserve a table for another night against this?" He handed her his American Express card.....well slap my wrists and call me cynical as her smile melted into pure liquid and her eyes alighted on me with the same look your bank manager gives when you deposit a lottery win. "No, no Sir, just let me check I am sure we have a table, walk with me" she ushered us thankfully not to the centre of the restaurant floor but....to the most hidden and secluded of all tables where we sat like 'day of the Triffids' amongst the overgrowth of trees and plants hidden from view of any other Diner, I swear to god had the place closed up that night nobody would have even known we were there. However her attendance to our table was second to none as each time she popped back to enquire if 'all was OK' I could see Byron's Amex card mirror imaged in her eyes!!

The meal was as you would expect....award winning and two hours later she breathed a sigh of relief as we departed leaving her millionaire client Diners' to gossip about the riff raff that had just tainted their watering hole.

Laughing to ourselves about the obvious faux par we had caused the night before we resolved to find a more local and friendly eatery, we did so in locating Rosie's Lobster Hut a short distance further on from M' Lady's establishment.

Rosie's was your basic Barbados shack serving honest to goodness, daily fresh caught lobster and beers...good food, great people, a laugh and joke and folk who made you feel right at home. We ate, many, many times there throughout the remainder of the holiday....after all, how much lobster can a girl enjoy....drooling even now!

A new couple arrived in the downstairs Chalet some 4 days into the holiday. An elderly couple, he was reminiscent of an ex Major and his wife the meek and mild woman who spoke little. They duly claimed their sun beds on the patio and pretty much kept themselves to themselves....until the morning we decided to give the sightseeing a rest for the day and kick back on the beach outside our door.

I prepared breakfast whilst Byron went down to 'German' some sun beds for us *(no offence intended.)* "I just spoke to the couple downstairs, they seem pleasant enough" he said.

Later we took up our lounging positions and slathered on the Bergasol sun oil.

It couldn't have been half an hour before I heard it....a distinct 'mewing.' I sat up staring around, everybody was comatose on their beds...I lay back down. There it was again, tiny and pitiful...'mewing?'

This time I could see a tiny scrap of a kitten making its way from the hedgerow to me across the patio. Of course, I called to it and encouraged its approach, a dear little thing probably some 12-15 weeks old and mostly white more than tabby, it wrapped itself around the legs of my sun bed and purred away to itself contented with the ear tickles and love it was receiving. Byron sat up wondering who I was talking to and scooped the little mite up for a cuddle, "Hey there little one...hello."

Almost immediately a booming regimental voice bellowed across at Byron.... "PUT THAT PUSSY down...you brought your own!" Byron was speechless, we laughed out loud as the elderly gent chuckled to himself at his own joke before dropping back down to snooze in the sun! What the hell was that about came to mind but it did make us laugh.

The holiday continued in much the same bizarre fashion....but then we were the Parnell's on holiday, what do you expect?

Some six days in we decided to hire another mini moke...I found myself praying there were no mountains on the island! The young lad arrived just after 10am one morning as agreed with a pale blue moke...in fact come to think of it from Tenerife...are they ALL pale blue?

No canopy...my first relief! Byron signed the papers and handed over the cash with which the young, tanned, dred locked and almost naked but for a pair of 'cut off' Bermuda's lad handed him a short length of broom handle. "Ya gonna need juice Bud, just use the stick OK." the young lad declared before sauntering off to his lift back to who knows where.

We looked at the sawn off broom handle noting it's chipped out markers by the Gallon. "How quaint" Byron was laughing like a drain. "Takes me back to my 'rough it' Air force days" he declared. I on the other hand felt like we were about to drive a whole heap of trouble??

We set off for the North of the Island intending to sightsee 'The Soup Bowl' a favourite surfing area near Bathsheba. This locale is quite prehistoric with its outcrops of rock formation in the sea, great crashing waves where I am guessing the Atlantic meets the

Caribbean Ocean, the whole ambience is of barren, rough, climatically powerful existence....the Surfers love it for the height and roll of the waves crashing on land. We walked, breathing in the briskness of the air whilst our bodies 'glowed' with the humidity of the inland temperatures. We shopped in a small town buying trinkets and keepsakes of our holiday, I was deeply attracted to a boxed sea shell, but it was no ordinary shell. This one was called the Crucifix shell and is indeed shaped exactly like the Crucifix. It is fragile and immensely delicate...you may as well be staring at our Lord on the Cross, it is eerie but beautiful. I purchased this and no matter how stupid it sounds felt immediately 'peaceful?'

We made our way back to Oistins along the basic road network when suddenly the 'Moke' spluttered and died, no fuel! We were between Parishes and lets be honest, the nearest town couldn't be far away given the length and breadth of the Island but Byron was being Byron as usual, jumping up and down like a demented frog on hot coals. "Bloody stupid stick, it said 2 gallons....should have taken us there and back with some to spare...!!" Trying to think practically I said "Look, calm down, I'll stay with the car you go and see if you can find somewhere, a town, fuel, it's only 1pm plenty of time before it's dark, I'll be fine I promise."
This seemed the only sensible solution short of abandoning the vehicle and walking 'home' to Oistins or the nearest taxi service, known as ZR's, pronounced ZedR's, not ZeeR's.
We were just about to kiss goodbye wondering if we'd ever see each other again when a vehicle loomed up on the horizon in the distance...the road was very long and straight and it seemed forever before it actually got to us. I planned to hop out and flag it down asking for directions or assistance but no need as the car headed straight for us. He pulled up just in front and made his way to Byron... in a deep Barbadian accent this gent of the highway tipped back his hat and chuckled "Woss up my Maaan, ya da got probleeemmms?" his local drawl was musical. We explained our predicament....
"Uh huh, well ya gives me $10 bucks an' I be back wid da fuel faster dan the sun go down me Maaan" he declared holding out his hand for the cash and chuckling away to

himself with a twinkle in his eye. Byron handed over the money...it seemed insulting to insist Byron went with him, he had after all stopped to help of his own volition, however as we watched him disappear back over the horizon we were already hatching plan B and resigned to having just given away $10.

Oh ye of little faith as an hour later here comes our knight of the roads bearing a gasoline can....still chuckling he poured it into the tank for us and shook Byron's hand before ambling off to who knows where that was his original destination before getting way laid by us. Thank you my lovely man for being kind, helpful and above all honest, bless you!

Three more very vivid memories stay with me from this holiday;

Several days after this event we decided to visit the Capital City, Bridgetown. We duly loaded up the Moke planning a tour of the shopping area before heading for a beach 'afternoon and picnic' somewhere between Holetown and Speightstown further North. Bridgetown was bustling and colourful and everything you can imagine of a Caribbean City. The road network seemed reasonably easy, if not a 'free for all' at some of the junctions but it was the local 'Youth' who in my opinion spoiled their Country's much needed tourism. As we pulled up at traffic lights, two young men in their 20's leapt into the back of our vehicle declaring they could 'show us the sights' for a price! It was scary in that we were in a queue of traffic, unable to pull over, my bag and purse was behind my seat at the feet of these guys and they weren't taking 'no thank you' for an answer. As we declined their assistance they became more intent on staying in the Moke...as the lights changed Byron had the good sense to pull off the road, he turned to the lads thanking them for their assistance explaining we were on our way back to our apartment, we didn't need it. "Yeah, yeah man, a good time yeah? We show you...$20 bucks!"

Byron stood his ground, "thanks Guys another time OK. I'm parking up now, we're off to our Hotel! With that Byron gestured to me to get out of the vehicle and I grabbed my bag...the two guys hopped out muttering some dialect verbal and left us be...we immediately drove off heading out of town.

Feeling a little rattled it was my first encounter with some of the locals and their 'pestering' of holiday makers, I would probably never cope in the likes of some of the Eastern Markets and other Countries where poverty can sometimes cause similar behaviour.

My last recollection of our Barbados holiday still makes me squirm and Byron fall about laughing to this day.

We were nearing the end of the holiday and decided to book up for one of those 'tourist excursions.' A glass bottomed boat would ferry us to a pontoon half a mile out from shore where those who wanted to could snorkel and sunbathe, enjoy a BBQ and generally kick back. Sounded heaven....in my case turned into a watery hell!

The boat trip out was mesmerising as I virtually laid on the floor of the boat marvelling at the colours and fish species I knew I would never in my lifetime see again.
We arrived at this large floating piece of wood in the middle of the Caribbean Ocean large enough to accommodate up to 30 people with the ferry boat anchoring to it.
We all disembarked on to the pontoon and were duly issued with life belts, snorkel and flippers. Within minutes many had left the pontoon and were happily snorkelling around the ocean, some within feet of the landing craft others were venturing much further abroad. Byron ensured I was happy to stay put and sun bathe given that I cannot swim, before diving into the deep waters to snorkel...no life jacket...he enjoyed deep sea diving whilst in the RAF and his deepest free dive without air was 50 feet.

Eventually as I stretched out in the sun I became conscious that only myself and a gentleman of Spanish or Portuguese nationality were left on the craft.

Fifteen minutes or maybe more passed with swimmers popping back and forth the pontoon, Byron checked in twice but was otherwise preoccupied with a sunken vessel he'd seen beneath the waves, before once again it became very quiet with only the lapping waves for noise background as I stood up to get a drink from the make shift Bar.

Senor I'm In Love With Myself had risen from his sun worshipping and was patrolling the pontoon.... "Ola" he spoke to me with a wide toothy grin. "Hello" I replied politely. "Ahhh you English, no?" Seemed a contradiction but I assured him I was. In his broken English he continued... *"Su Nada, Si?"* in a questioning voice. As he was gesturing toward the water I guessed he was asking if I would swim. " No, I no nadar, nada, nader!" I tried to piece together something he would verbally understand. He was tall, maybe 6' 2", bronze, jet black hair, the hairiest chest I have seen since my Father's with a gold chain around his neck sufficient in weight to anchor him to the pontoon! "Si, si, Nadar...ees good!" he persisted.
I responded as politely but firmly as I could...."NO, I no want to nadar OK?"
He laughed ...."ahh I speak da English, you no sweem heh? eees ok yeah, you 'av thees," he tugged at my life jacket. Getting somewhat irritated by this 'Spanish Fly' I continued..."thank you, yes, but I don't want to swim!" He looked genuinely hurt at my rejection of his assistance so I foolishly tried to make amends. Using my hand to gesture slitting my throat and then further in a waving gesture such as a swimming fish plus shaking my head negatively I tried to explain that I actually really couldn't swim. Oh dear lord he read all the wrong signals and eagerly gathered up a snorkel mask jamming it over my head and urging me to use the mouth piece. As I opened my mouth to protest, he pushed the apparatus home assuming I was going along with the plan!!
Before I could spit it out he launched me off the side of the pontoon into depths of ocean I can only continue to have nightmares about.

I hit the calm sea doing a very good impression of an Octopus having an epileptic fit! (No offence intended to sufferers, simply a mental image of my behaviour.)

By now I had the ENTIRE snorkel mouthpiece inside my lips giving me the appearance of a woman with a guinea pig stuffed in each cheek, I didn't know whether to suck or blow. I disappeared beneath the waves ensuring my snorkel pipe filled with sea water.....as I bobbed back up to the surface I could see the idiot who had launched me to my death smiling on board the pontoon gesturing to me to swim! I vowed in my panic stricken brain that were I to survive this drowning...I was going to take him apart limb by limb but not before I had plucked each singular hair from his chest using boiling hot wax!!!!!

I continued to flail around causing myself to rock up and down, under then up as a result of the life jacket, I was gasping for air and my mask was totally steamed up, I couldn't see, breath or gain any life giving stability.
Suddenly from somewhere underneath my crotch a hand propelled me to the surface and simultaneously ripped off the offending plastic suffocation equipment from my face. "Breath....stop panicking, breath, breath...come on, breath!!!" I heard my hero's voice somewhere down a panic stricken tunnel....Byron was in front of me looking as cool as a freakin' holiday maker enjoying snorkelling whilst I was dying!! He kissed me and held me as he trod water, calming me down....a stupid term to me as how the fuck can you tread something firm that isn't there??
"What the hell you doing with all that in there you daft bitch?" having swiped the snorkel mouthpiece from my mouth I felt immediate relief as my cheeks deflated. He removed the entire snorkel from my head, blew out the tube and spat in my mask...I was appalled and disgusted..."I'm not wearing THAT now you've gobbed in it!" I wailed.
"Put it on, now breath and keep your spout above water, come on, it's not difficult" he declared. I did as I was told and started to calm down now that I could cling on to

Byron with my arms wrapped about his neck and my legs entwined around his waist....as long as he was afloat...so WAS I!

"Gerrof me woman, let go, what were you thinking of getting in the water anyway?" Byron asked before I prised my one finger from his neck to point at the bastard idiot on the pontoon who pushed me in!
"Him....he did it, he pushed me and I told him I couldn't swim..." I spluttered.
"OK well you're in now, come on hold my hand and we'll stay close to the boat, you'll enjoy it....it's character building." Two things pierced my brain...how the hell can you swim with one arm whilst holding me up and how the hell is this character building....'learning to die in one easy shove' was NEVER in my need to have qualifications!!
As Byron helped me to float around the pontoon I built up the courage to upturn and face down in the water....OH MY GOD!!!!!!!
I was never prepared for the vacuous space I saw before me, the depth I was bobbing about in or the sheer beauty of the vision before me.
I suddenly forgot about my fears as the life jacket kept me afloat, I soon grasped the mechanics of breathing through the snorkel tube and suddenly this underwater world was my oyster. Byron stayed close by life guarding my every move as I found a new confidence in the water...I couldn't believe the sights I was taking in...a 'purpose sunk' wreck of a ship that was most effective BUT the little fish that kept coming right up to us were amazing. Byron called them 'Sucker fish' for the want of a more specific title but they were crazy crumpets...loving having us around, nibbling at our arms, tickling our legs.

I was living the dream....floating in the Caribbean Ocean, my man on life guard duty within feet and experiencing sights I NEVER thought I would ever see....when suddenly on my right side I felt an enormous dragging sensation as I got sucked under the water once again....we were both submerged when Byron grabbed me and we looked straight in the eye of a Giant Turtle who glided past me before Byron propelled me to the surface gasping for air once again. This beast was awesome in size and dignity...I will never, ever forget this vision in my memory. By this time I was ready to call it a day...Byron shouldered me up the side of the pontoon and I recovered from my ordeals...enjoyable or otherwise. Mr Stupido had by now got the message and left me well alone I guess fearing the wrath of Byron's return....but we ended this excursion none the worse for wear and I for one was glad to hit solid ground!

Our last days on the Island were taken up with souvenir buying and generally kicking back before we returned home to the daily work grind and refurbishment of the Cottage.
"How do you fancy a run up to Needhams Point just our side of Bridgetown?" Byron asked.... let's go!
We drove around for a short while taking in the sights and I stopped to buy some Bananas and vegetables for our evening meal...it was a road side stall with two ladies in attendance. They eyed me up and down as I approached and chose my goods, on asking the payment price the larger of the two women spoke up.."Hey girl, ya got some goooooood stuff there, you gonna be cooking good tonight... $30 bucks!" No please, no thank you, no kiss my ass! I stared at what I had in bewilderment...NO WAY did this amount to $30....$10 more like? I tossed the bag back on their stall as I declared "$30 bucks heh...here you go...ENJOY!" and I walked away leaving them shouting Barbadian abuse behind me.
I explained to Byron what had happened and we agreed that I had almost been a victim or 'tourist rip off.' Best to eat out again that evening and mean while we would enjoy a few more hours on the nearest beach.....

As we pulled the Moke into the makeshift car parking area close to the beach, the heat was intense, the smell of the Caribbean sea intoxicating and we couldn't wait to for a cool off dip in the shallows. I gathered up our bags and some bottled water whilst Byron checked there was nothing of value left on show in the vehicle.

They came from absolutely nowhere, like shadows from behind palm trees....four Barbadian youths were suddenly surrounding the Moke and us. I sensed a feeling of aggression immediately but Byron was way ahead of me and already on guard. He spoke directly to the pack leader and no nonsense briskly... "What d'ya want lads?" he asked giving direct eye contact. The lad in the front grinned a brilliantly white toothy smile against his bare ebony skin... "Ya do left yer winnnkie on Man, yuz get flat barrtry yeah?" with that he let out a maliciously evil laugh whilst flicking his hand in a gesture of insolence, the others joined in. It was obvious we were being targeted by the local hoodlums, I stood stock still watching Byron's every move. He was not about to take this 'bullying' that was for sure.... "My WHAT?" he spat at the lad.... "Yer Winnkeeeie, Man, diss light right here" he prodded the drivers side indicator light with his flip flopped toe, which indeed was still flashing. Byron squared up and returned to the Moke to switch it off...."Dat be $10 bucks Man...for us be showing you!!" Byron laughed a insurgent laugh whilst pushing past the youth who had by now stepped up closer to us and the car. "Yeah right...now fuck off and find something useful to do boys!" Byron gave me one of his 'move it, now' looks and I climbed back into the moke, the lads were by now agitated and demonstrating threatening body language. Byron revved up the engine and we drove straight through the middle of them and out onto to the main roadway heading back to our accommodation.

All in all it was an adventurous and exotic holiday and one I shall never forget!

Chapter 10

- Accounting for my next step...! -

Back at home life was unchanged except I needed a 'proper' job. I started to apply for interviews and soon attained a position as Secretary in a City Accountancy Practice. It was a small company but the Partners were keen to build the business and work was coming in faster than their present Secretary, Lindsay, could cope with. I started there late Summer 1991 and the job lasted some 9 months. I actually enjoyed Owens, Thomas & Co Accountants, they were a young bunch of keen business men and for a while I tried to kid myself the secretarial career route was for me....but it never had been and never would be!

There were moments of angst as one of the Partners, Patrick became more and more frustrated with return of my work for typo's and I think the ultimate for him was the day I copy typed one of his letters to an important client, a Barrister I believe, the letter made no sense to me as I struggled to decipher Patrick's scrawl. I typed up the letter and spoke to Patrick who called in to the office to say he wouldn't be back that day. "I have your letters ready to go" I commented...."Ok well 'pp' them on my behalf and get them in the mail, put the copies on my desk for the morning" Patrick instructed, which is what I did.

The following morning Patrick was like an enraged bull as he approached my desk..."did you send this?" he demanded in a very angry tone waving the Barristers copy letter in my face. I was shocked at his temper display...."are you totally stupid or what...?" he continued by which time I was annoyed and upset. It would appear that Patrick had written a letter of congratulations to his client the Barrister declaring "I am delighted to hear you have taken Silk!" This being a term used in legal quarters to acknowledge when a legal 'Bod' passes their exams etc. Because I could neither read his scrawl or make sense of the sentence I had typed.... "I am delighted to hear you have been taken SICK!" Thereafter my days were numbers at OT&Co as Patrick was the Senior Partner!!

The usual staff party for Christmas came and went and I had started to resent Patrick's constant 'targeting' of me for any least little thing that went wrong at work.

I had also by now started to 'dabble' heavily with my dressmaking skills and around this time a story hit the newspaper headlines of a young girl living in Swansea City, some 50 miles from where I live.

The young lady in question, Suzanne, had paid for a gown and was awaiting her final fitting just days before her wedding. The shop went bust overnight leaving a trail of debts and broken hearted brides to be. I read the story thinking to myself how distressed she must feel when suddenly a light bulb switched on inside me. I could cut patterns and sew...why don't I offer to make her gown for her and help her out of this predicament. She would have to pay for all the materials but I would ask for nothing more than some recognition in the paper for having helped her out and maybe this would bring in a few orders for garments, I could perhaps make some part time money with my design and sewing skills?

I contacted the Newspaper who duly put me in touch with Suzanne. At first she was naturally cautious as to whether I was some sort of sicko crank but it transpired her wedding was still three weeks away...so plenty of time for me to make a replica gown if she could show me images of the original and pay for the materials.

I met with her at her home and still her family were wary of me....at the time I didn't understand why in my innocence of what life deals people, but eventually they believed my intent was honest and up front, all I asked was for some form of recognition in reply to the newspaper original story. Little did I know but for the grace of god go I in years to come....

Fabric ordered and patterns cut, we were underway as I threw myself every spare hour into the production of this beautiful Duchesse Satin Gown. I sought no self glory or costs for the many times I travelled back and forth the 100 mile round trip to Suzanne's for fittings. Her gown became reality within a matter of 10 days with last minute finishing's to be undertaken. Suzanne was elated and emotionally very grateful, I was exhausted.....and my employers were well and truly pissed off with me as all I could talk about in work was helping this young girl, I was perpetually tired from my wee small hours sewing and my secretarial work was suffering accordingly.

I am thrilled to say that the gown was a total success as an identical replica to her originally chosen and lost one. The making of this gown satisfied everything within my creative inner needs and it was obvious to me I needed to do something about it. We were invited as celebrity guests to Suzanne's wedding and I was acknowledged in the speeches as being 'woman of the hour!' I hadn't expected anything more than her delighted and relieved face on completion of my abilities to re-create the wedding gown she had fallen in love with but been robbed of....to be publicly thanked was a total overwhelming honour!

This singular event gave birth to my very first business enterprise.

It was clear to me now that I needed to work for myself. I wasn't cut out to be a Secretary and certainly not a crap one! I couldn't face another thirty plus years in this type of work until I retired. I decided, almost overnight, to launch myself as a Fashion Designer...it was after all what I had trained and qualified to be! As a Sole Trader, 'Labello Angelina' Designer & Couturier (after my middle names) was launched. I began marketing for business.....and my goodness me work started pouring in!

Within a few months I was called for a meeting with one of the Senior Partners, I guessed what was coming and I was asked to make a choice between being their Secretary or running my own business as clearly, the two running tandem could not continue as far as they were concerned. I took a deep breath, thanked them for my time with them and resigned my position on the spot. I felt the door I needed to step through had just been opened for me, this was it, time to put my money where my ambitious mouth was and take that giant step forward. On just one month's pay off salary I set up my sole trader business *Labello Angelina* as Winter descended on 1991 and we slid into Christmas. Byron was naturally worried that I could 'cut the mustard' having no business skills whatsoever, but I set about enrolling on local government business courses and joining 'Network' clubs along with short courses on sales and marketing, before too long I had developed a very recognisable presence around our local area via my business card, stationery, advertising and word of mouth. I left no stone unturned and was enjoying actually being financially self sufficient, I felt that I had made something of myself at long last.

The Cottage was coming along in bumpy steps of improvement given that we now had limited funds to throw at the projects but it resembled a warm family home and we had the rest of lives to sort it out....didn't we?

- Chapter 11 -

- *A Model life....* -

Byron helped me set up our Guest bedroom as a Sewing Workroom and I couldn't wait
to get in there each day to progress with my customers orders. It started small with
more 'alteration' work coming in than 'Bespoke Commissions' but I was determined I
wouldn't get caught in the trap of staying as a 'make good and mend' seamstress. I
used this 'bit work' money to cash flow whilst I sought bigger and grander work.

The first real good luck break was in 1993 when I teamed up with a local Hairdressing
Business in the Town of Talbot Green near my home. A lovely lady by the name of
'Mrs S' ran the business and still does to this day, she was/is a like minded character
and determined to place her business at the top of her trade. Mrs S was go ahead,
gutsy, a real work hard try'er in life and she set her sights high undertaking many
Regional/National competitions in hairdressing demonstrating the skills of her staff
under her personal tuition. 'Professional Hairdressing Partner' contracts' ensued and
her business flourished, it is still highly reputable. Her foresight was if anything a little
before its time in the back hills of Wales as her techniques and prices were considered
zany and expensive...but she never once lost sight of her goal and remains at the top
of her pole in Hairdressing.

Mrs S and I forged a friendship and an understanding of how our two businesses could
embrace each other in providing clients who needed both our services for weddings.
We worked together to 'court' custom that we could cross refer between us. It was to
coin the phrase.... 'a marriage made in heaven!'

She was ahead of me with business contacts at this stage and was able to organise
Fashion Shows for her hairdressing skills with her Models wearing my designs and
garments.

It was clear to me that my 'Cottage Industry' had outgrown it's premises and to be honest, whilst I was at home working, the telephone rang at all hours, some very unacceptable hours and I could never actually shut the door on my job and walk away. I may be in the middle of preparing Dinner of an evening and suddenly remember I had forgotten to sew an 'inner wedding gown train loop' or something as diverse causing me to return to the work room and often burnt offerings for Dinner that were forgotten in the oven!! This lifestyle could not continue...I spent many evenings in front of the TV when Byron came home, and after Dinner, with someone's wedding gown on my lap delicately hand sewing thousands of crystals or pearls onto the Bodice...it was far from relaxation or an out of work life!

I needed a business premises and set about looking for one.

It was late 1993 when I located a Studio to be rented within a building locally known as the *Model House, Llantrisant.* Situated in the heart of the Historic *Llantrisant Village,* just four miles from home, this majestic building is steeped in local history.

Situated in what is called *The Bull Ring, on Swan Street* between the Parish Church to the West and the Castle to the East according to documentation *(Wikipedia 2013)* it was the first Workhouse in the County of Glamorgan opening its doors in May 1784 adapted from a row of Cottages on Swan Street.

The Union Work House was built in 1884 on the Bull Ring where it stands today behind the Town Pump and was named The Model House in the optimistic belief that it's occupants would lead a model life of Christianity, two Pubs a Shop and a Cottage were demolished to make way for the expansion of the Workhouse.

The building was closed as a workhouse in the early 1900's, progressing to become first a Boarding House, then an Inn and later a General Store called County Stores. Known as corn flour and provisions merchants, linen and woollen drapers also selling boots and shoes, I guess you could say a 'one stop' shop! The site was bought out in the '50's by 'Planet Gloves' who manufactured gloves there until the late 1960's after which this majestic three storey building stood empty and neglected for many years before being bought by the local authority to convert into a local Craft & Design Centre. In 1989 the Model House re-opened it's doors as a registered charity funded by the Arts and Crafts Council and enjoys around 35,000 visitors a year if not many more nowadays. It houses a Gallery displaying the art and works of British Crafts People on the ground floor with the above levels of the building given over to rented studios for local artisans. It was within one of these Studios that I relocated my fledgling business and life was about to change dramatically once again!

Chapter 12

- Versace, Armani, Chanel and Laurent -

Eagerly looking forward to having a 'real' business premises I set about packing up my workroom at home and preparing for the fact that I would actually be going OUT to work every morning...but to my OWN business, I was deliriously happy.

I moved into my new premises feeling like a real 'achiever.' For the first time ever I felt a sense of worth about myself and a confidence I didn't know I could feel, I had after all been so used to being put down and reprimanded for my 'lack' of abilities and made to feel worthless all my life! So far I had managed to push myself to attain knowledge and skill and I wasn't about to waste my opportunity.

Amidst this happiness, thinking nothing could spoil anything for me I awoke one morning to find no Maxwell? He had become very much a 'roamer' and was a giant of a cat, I had no fear of him feeding himself off the land but wondered how many days he would be gone this time. I carried on thinking little more of it because he always returned like he'd had a fantastic lads weekend away, eating me out of house and home and then he'd be off again on another adventure. I used to drive past fields of hay bales miles from home to see him perched aloft one sleeping in the sun. He enjoyed the life of Riley, they say a cat will encompass 10 miles from its home base on its wanderings.

Maxwell, my beloved Tabby Terror, rescued from a Cardiff City Animal Shelter and deposited in the bliss of the countryside with the world as his oyster would have been around 6 years old that fateful day that he left home for good, for whatever reason? As the days wore on I realised he had gone, we were heartbroken in our worry of not knowing if he lay injured somewhere, too sick to come home, Byron spent days wandering the fields and mountain looking for him at his usual haunts. We never found him, we resigned ourselves to the fact that maybe he'd got in to a fight he didn't win perhaps with a fox. Was hit by a car on the lane and crawled off to die or perhaps being as large as he was and such a grey tabby...had he been shot by the idiots who take pleasure in hunting around here, mistaken as a large rabbit? In any event our boy was gone and it took us months to come to terms with it.

It's fair to say that wedding attire was my main source of business but I enjoyed this because it gave me chance to vent my creative mind on some of the most flamboyant styles of gowns and attendants wear that you can imagine. The Suits and Day Wear also came in but it was truly the wedding gowns that I could unleash my design talents on and my customers loved being able to come in for private Consultation with their 'Designer' and watch as together we dreamt up their dream of a wedding gown. I worked closely with my clients and I won't say it was all plain sailing because as anyone involved in the 'wedding market' knows it is a highly emotional arena to be a supplier of any service or product within! A Bride is a hormonal and emotional creature, nothing must be a problem....when Suppliers often let me down with deadline delivery of materials, it could on times be the end of the earth and result in a right tirade of abuse to me from the customer and her family. Ultimately, I would work steadily forward sticking to my Plan of Work and all materials would filter in, the gown would appear weeks before the wedding date so no further panic could ensue and inevitably I would be praised and glorified for my endeavours....all previous animosity simply blown to the wind!! I got used to it, it was the way this sector of my business appeared to work, all I could do was remain as professional and organised as I could be but as any business owner knows.....once you introduce a 'third party' in any service there will always be problems beyond your own control no matter how hard you try to avoid it.

My daily life was any woman's dream as I selected, handled, discussed, ordered and worked with fabrics designed and manufactured by the world's leading Fashion Icons. Versace, Chanel and Armani were household names to me....I read and studied extensively, I dined out on fashion documentaries and top flight fashion magazines, I travelled back and forth to London regularly attending Fashion Exhibitions and visiting top class fabric suppliers many of whom saw me as a tadpole in ditch water back in Wales, but I was not to be overlooked. Whenever I undertake something in my life I give it my all and I wanted to be taken seriously in what I did. I did not however want to 'make a name' for myself in the Fashion World because I knew what pressure and stress that would bring, all I desired was to be considered a reputable Fashion Designer/Maker in Wales who could provide quality in both product and value for money.

Inevitably work and orders became to great for me to manage alone and so in 1993 I sought staff who could assist me. You cannot possibly begin to imagine how difficult it is to find anyone who is prepared to become a *'Couture Seamstress.'*
You see there is an enormous difference between someone who can domestically sew, someone who is a 'machinist' and someone who can produce precision manufacture working to ANY cut pattern creating truly 'bespoke' workmanship. As ever I had set my sights sky high, I had sold myself very well, I had orders coming out of my ears with only me to create them. I interviewed and trialled many applicants...and was beginning to lose hope when a lady called Adrienne M came along. An ex-RAF woman bordering on Amazonian stature she dwarfed me and was most certainly not impressed by any of my airs and graces....Armani may as well have been coalman for all she knew about him and his empire!!
I met her at her home deep in the Ogmore Valley in Mid Glamorgan and was deeply disturbed by her 'lifestyle.' I know I shouldn't have been and it's all about live and let live, but Adrienne's home was in my own personal opinion disgusting to live in! There is nothing kinder I can say...

The house was on three storeys and the family appeared to live in the basement and the main living area was a bomb site of an affair. My feet actually stuck to the carpet, there was food dropped and left to rot where it fell, what furniture there was in the room was obliterated from sight by clothes, shoes and general paraphernalia strewn across it. Dirty cups and plates sat where they were left from maybe days ago and as for decor....there was none! Paper dangled from the walls where damp had caused it to peel, mould grew inside the windows and as for the kitchen which led off this room, it was a environmental officers dream of a prosecution case. Food half eaten just sat on dirty plates from days ago, the sink was full of dirty crockery, I've seen cleaner speed bike dirt tracks than the top of the cooker and everything smelled of decay.

Adrienne offered me a coffee which I politely declined asking to proceed with the interview, the real point was that if she could do the job I had no right whatsoever to judge or condemn her or the way she chose to live, I just couldn't get my head around why such an articulate and ex services woman would live in this manner?

We discussed the job and debated pay rates, I viewed samples of her work and eventually it appeared to me that Adrienne could certainly give me the quality of work I was looking for so I offered her the job. She seemed genuinely happy as she walked to the front door with me and we agreed she would start at 9am the following Monday in the Studio. As I walked away toward my car my nagging thought was that she wasn't telling me something and I couldn't afford not to know, it would affect everything in maybe weeks to come....I took a deep breath and turned to speak to her. "By the way I meant to say Congratulations, when's the baby due?" I asked nodding to her grossly enlarged tummy. Adrienne smiled before replying...."I'm not pregnant!" Red faced and with duck and paddle coming to mind I tried to make amends explaining that her billowing black tunic over sloppy jo leggings had given the impression but she held up her hand waving me and my embarrassment away laughing to herself. This one incident was a source of much humour between us in the years to follow.

Adrienne and I became a solid team, we worked well in harness and there's no doubt about it she could make a piece of fabric sing. Her quality and precision of workmanship was to be admired and she was a 'rare' find as together we never found another that could even sew a straight seam let alone create a 'pad stitched lapel' in all the years we worked side by side. Adrienne and I had an affinity for creation, we could stand before a bolt of fabric costing perhaps a mere £800 and without even speaking to each other we would know what the other was about to say, "watch the grain, it's warped," "it'll over run the selvedge on Pattern Pce 7," "Don't forget to cut on the fold for the godet and seam it in at least three inches beneath the button placket!" We were a force to be reckoned with in the sewing room and for a year or two worked alongside each other living and suffering the many highs and lows that being in the fashion trade can bring. As the 'front man' of the operation I was always the one to meet with the clients to design and sell, at some point the client would come to meet Adrienne and this was generally where most problems happened as Adrienne had no people skills, no sales and marketing ability and no tolerance whatsoever of weepy, whining brides or clients if so much as a seed pearl fell off the gown/suit during fittings. She often offended clients with her outright manner and I was left to pick up the pieces. Despite many chats, requests and eventual ultimatums Adrienne refused to change her ways and it was something I just had to learn to manage and disguise. If it was a choice between her frequent bad manners and her workmanship...there was simply no competition!

Mid 1993 my Toyota Supra car died a death, it's boot had rusted so badly I often parked it several doors down from my clients homes so they couldn't see what a 'scrap yard' condition it was in. My business and my required 'dress code' did not justify driving such a wreck of a motor but I couldn't afford to change it and despite the business holding its own, it was by no means languishing in huge profit. Despite wearing top of the range clothing designed and manufactured in my own work room, I drove a car that advertised 'champagne tastes, beer barrel pockets!'

I borrowed Byron's company motor wherever I could given that he enjoyed prestige vehicles supplied by Shine Food Machinery and had by now climbed further up the ladder to Senior Management, but it wasn't always convenient. Thus one Saturday morning we decided to take a drive around the garage forecourts of Cardiff in search of an upgrade that was affordable on maybe a 2-3 year finance loan.

There wasn't much within my price range, or perhaps I should say what my small business could finance and eventually we ended up at a City Centre showroom viewing a black Ford Sierra 1.6ltr Saloon. The curl down at the side of my mouth said it all. The car itself was immaculate as an ex demo model...but it wasn't SEPY! There were no gadgets, no electric toys, no sunroof, no pop up headlights and certainly no 3 litres of turbo power with overdrive under its bonnet. But it was within months old of being a brand new car....I'd never had a brand new car and was assured by Byron and the Salesman I would enjoy being relieved of the continual running costs and repair bills and above all there was no rust! Hmmm but my fashion career called for a little bit of stylish oomph in what I drove, my clients were all well heeled and affluent people, at the very least I needed to be in a sporty motor of some description. It was all of course a front but it was one my clients subscribed to and I felt the Saloon didn't support the 'elite' image I had marketed and portrayed as best I could.

 I'm not a snob or a socialite but I was being forced to become both in order to maintain the 'business image!'

I test drove the vehicle, it was like driving a golf cart in comparison, I was resigned to hating the car but needed a more reliable form of transport. The deal was struck and I part exchanged my beloved SEPY emptying out the contents of my car into the replacement with a heavy heart. I swear to god I was emotional driving away, abandoning my beloved Supra at the garage to be scrapped off no doubt.
We had been home an hour or so when Byron insisted I check out all the bits on the car so that I knew where the 'spare wheel' was and the jack lift etc. We squabbled as we approached the car, he was irritable that I couldn't raise some enthusiasm toward the motor and said I was being childish. He popped the boot from within the car as my mouth fell open in total shock!

The tiniest little black kitten sat in the middle of the boot space looking up at me, squinting in the sudden daylight, and mewed the most pathetic' where's my mummy' cry. He was in pitiful condition, I scooped him into my arms shouting to Byron "Oh my god, look at this!"

Byron was as shocked as I and we couldn't even begin to imagine how the little mite had got in there in the first place but we felt obliged to call the garage to ask. The garage was called Evans & Halshaw Motors, Cardiff, I dialled the number and reminded them that I was the lady who had been in earlier that morning. "Uhmm we got home with the new car and found a kitten in the boot?" The line went dead for a few seconds whilst I guess the Receptionist tried to work out if I was a hoax caller.

"Do you have any feral cats at the garage, do you know who he belongs to?" I continued. Unsurprisingly she made a few enquiries and came back with a negative reply, nobody knew how the little kitten had got there.....but I suddenly felt like fate had dealt me a guiding hand that day. I was meant to buy that car....to save this little lad's life. We named him Halshaw after the garage he came from.

Emaciated, less than 6 weeks old and totally black, we set about building him up and getting his health back on track, he was the most gorgeous little soul and had a lovely character. It was as a result of this event that I started to tentatively wonder about my existence in life....why did such strange and peculiar things always seem to happen to me?

A short while after this event Byron took me to a cat show in Newport, I never actually got to see the show as the very first trade stand inside the entrance door was one for Cats Protection League. It displayed a huge board advertising the homeless cats that needed help and I immediately fell in love with a brother/two sisters trio of ginger and white moggies (cross breeds) that needed an urgent home. Byron took one look at my face and said "your call!" I applied to adopt them but one of the girls had already been taken, so the remaining boy and girl were left but split from their sibling. If only I had acted faster by twenty minutes all three could have remained as a family because I would have taken them all. As it was, and after a visit from the Society to assess our suitability....Rupert and Verity (Vitty so nick named) came to live with us at Cherry Tree Cottage, my 'Cat Woman down the lane' years had started!

Renovations at the Cottage continued along with both our jobs, Byron was getting busier and busier and so was I at the Studio. I continued to 'network' with Mrs S attending one of her events, a hair/ fashion show modelling several of my designs. Mrs S needed a 'finale' of a finish and so Adrienne and I set about creating a 'Mystical' wedding gown. It consisted of a full skirt in heavy Duchess Satin lifted by many layers of tulle and wiring so that it billowed out around the Models legs, there was no 'train' because the Jacket was to be the 'drop your mouth open' icing on the cake. I designed a severely nipped in waistline, one lapelled heavily adorned with crystal and jewels jacket that flared into rolling folds of fabric below the waistline which then fell away at the back draping down as a 'V' shaped over skirt mock 'train.' The jacket was inter sectioned with panels of gold lame and the single fastening button at the waistline in the front was fashioned from a single 'rock' of a Swarovski crystal around the size of a small hen's egg, leaving the cleavage area tantalisingly suggestive. The one lapel swept from this central waist fastening up around the back of the neck ending at the start of the opposite shoulder and was inter-sectioned gold lame, satin, gold lame, satin giving the impression of a zebra crossing. I also used stiff card interfacing to force the collar to stand proud of the neck as it encircled it giving the impression of a Peacock throwing up its display behind. I visited the local electrical repair store where the man helped me to put together a sequential series of fairy lights that we entwined through a bound together bunch of Beech Tree branches that the Model could hand hold, they started short trailing into much longer branches until they reached her feet. The Model was a beauty of a girl around five feet, eight inches tall with long brunette tresses that Mrs S piled as high as she could in a 'mass of tumbling curls' cascading wildly down around her face and shoulders adding height and sexuality to the vision. I placed a simple head band within the mound of piled high hair that held a single, enormous Swarovski Crystal once again about the size of a large Hen's egg. Her entire appearance was one of glamour, glitz, gold, sparkle and twinkle of the most mythical, Hollywood style.

The plan was that and my business would end the fashion show on a huge adrenalin high. At the appointed time after the penultimate demonstration the lights would be suddenly and totally switched off in the massive sports centre hall, 500 plus spectators would be plunged into darkness whilst one single spot light would be immediately angled onto centre stage. I was to mount the podium secretly so that I could announce across the sound system, in the pitch black, to the audience in a calm, secretive voice "Do not worry my mortals, the light will come and with it a vision of the future.....of exquisite Bridal beauty!"

The accompanying catwalk music was Donna Summer's legendry and epic 'Love to Love You Baby' Soundtrack it was to start quietly in the background and build to a crescendo as dry ice was released on stage giving the impression of magical mystery. At the split second the track hit its peak, two more stage lights beamed forth onto our model as she stepped from the ghostly mist with her fairy light 'bouquet' sparkling and twinkling in the sub light. As the music gathered pace and the whole effect started taking place the auditorium took off...I recall people doing a standing ovation, some were actually weeping, the applause was deafening along with the wolf whistles and whoops of admiration....I knew I had to 'talk' her down the catwalk but I had a lump in my throat the size of a house brick and was actually weeping myself in disbelief that this monumental audience could be so appreciative of my work. Our Model did me proud, she paced her walk with dignity and poise, she gave the whole appearance of that of a mystical Queen surveying her kingdom, she flashed quizzical and superior glaring looks at them as if to say "how dare you cast eyes on your Queen in this manner!" The audience loved it, Donna Summer pounded out at a volume to rock the building and people were on their feet clapping and crying for more, more, more. I can still feel the sense of achievement this day, people burst forward to shake my hand and congratulate me on my performance....but you see, I only gave the true performer the props to work with...the true Star of the Show was my Model and to this day I respect her for the way she threw herself theatrically into 'living the part.' Her sole walk down stage that evening brought me £30,000+ worth of orders for bridal attire within three months. It might sound big money but in actual fact two thirds of this was cost of sale but in any event £10K of gross profit was good for my tiny business.

A year or so after buying the Sierra Saloon car I decided I'd had enough of it and couldn't tolerate its under performance any longer. Maturity nowadays tells me how daft this was because I only travelled short distances around the locale but I never felt comfortable in it and above all I never felt safe in it. It felt like an aluminium sardine can on wheels. This is perhaps my most stupid of statements as we are none of us 'safe' in any automobile but the solidity and security SEPY gave me was perhaps as much psychological as physical. A big car, powerful and wrapped around me like a safety harness. Feelings I had lacked in my life.

- Chapter 13 -

- Until death us do part and may NO Man'child put asunder -

I use the term 'Man' lightly, as he was nothing but an immature boy frustrated by what he could never begin to understand or have!

It was mid 1995; the banking needed doing so I left Adrienne at the Studio to visit the local town, Talbot Green to visit the Bank and pick up some groceries. Gardening at the cottage had supplied me with a healthy glow of a suntan, my long dark hair was pulled up in a sloppy, Bohemian twisted ponytail and I wore cream denim jeans with a chocolate brown 'V' neck vest style top, a large plaited designer leather belt sporting a buckle you could anchor a cruise liner with adorned my 'then' slim waistline, ethnic bead jewellery and heels added to my 'casual but expensive, fashion look.'
It was hot and I was thirsty so I grabbed a bottle of water in the supermarket beside the bank and donned my Versace sun shades against the bright sunlight as I made my way back to my car. On passing the local garage showroom I saw a bright red Honda Coupe on their second hand forecourt, my curiosity got the better of me as I ambled over to take a look at the car and price displayed on the front screen. I knocked my shades on top of my head as I peered through the drivers window to view the car interior....."Would you like me to unlock it?" I heard a voice from behind me....the view this salesman must have had was my ass clad in tight jeans up tilted whilst I bobbed about trying to see inside the car. I always used a body cream with gold sparkle in it giving my skin a healthy glow. As I stood up to address the guy he simply said "WOW...your skin?" I looked at him as if he was in need of therapy...."Pardon me, my skin...what do you mean?" I replied. He was around 6 feet tall, shirt and tie smart Salesman dress code, blue/grey eyes, tawny brown hair and handsome in a sort of 'final college year' boyish good looks." He could see I was offended by his comment, "No you misunderstand, I've never seen a woman's skin glow like yours, Wow I'm sorry but you are gorgeous!" His remark took me totally off guard....strangers do not

speak to each other like this surely? I just looked at him as if he'd spoken in god knows what language. He continued..... "I'm sorry that was so unprofessional of me, are you still interested in the car?" By now I had stepped back from the car and HIM, like most women I don't object to a bit of admiring but his attention was too full on given the situation for my liking. I immediately chalked him up in my brain as a cocky young buck trying to 'flatter' himself some sales commission.

"The Honda, what's its history?" I enquired. He stepped forward holding out his hand, "Paul Davies and you are?" I looked him in the eye before replying "someone maybe interested in the Honda!" He smirked as if he saw this as some sort of game, I was simply trying to protect my identity from this 'full of his underpants' idiot. He stepped into full blown sales patter as we walked about the car and discussed its saleability. I was interested, the price was good with part ex of my Sierra and I could afford the monthly repayments easily...I just wasn't happy with the mileage clock reading which for the year of the car didn't stack up?

"Tell you what, I said, I'm not convinced with this one, why don't I leave you my number and if anything comes in you think I might be interested in, you call me yeah?" I wrote down my details and handed them to him before stepping to the door of his office to leave .He looked at my scribbled note "You're MARRIED?" His comment was quite vocal and in disbelief...I looked back at him before asking quite sarcastically "Yes? Is that a pre-requisite for buying here?" He stared at me long and hard before replying "No, but it's never stopped me before!" I laughed a sardonic laugh as I walked out his door noting to myself what a pathetic excuse for a male full of his own bullshit he was!

Shortly after another incident transpired. Byron and I were always leaving little 'notes' for each other so knowing he was working in my area that day I left him a little note tucked under my windscreen wiper...it read, "You are a gorgeous man, I want to spend my life with you, tell me how to make you happy?" It was no surprise the following day when I walked to my car in the local car park to drive home, I could see the paper tucked under the windscreen wiper... the exact wording "I think about you night and day, I dream about you in my arms and I will do anything to make you happy....just tell me what?"

I laughed out loud standing in the car park reading the note thinking to myself oh bless him, ok I'll play the romantic game.

I said nothing when I got home that night....neither did he.

The following day I left for work and as I parked up, I tucked my reply note under my windscreen wiper anticipating Byron finding it sometime that day, he so knew how to court a girl in those days even if we were married! My note read "I look at you everyday Darling, I lust after you and you will feel much better between my legs than my arms! If you really want to make me happy...I'll meet you at the *Castle Mynach (local pub)* where you can buy me Dinner before I put a smile on your face! Xx" I giggled as I walked away from the car park imagining his reaction to my response. Sometime early evening the same day I emerged from the Studio tired and looking forward to actually getting home before 9pm for a change. I smiled as I saw a note still pinned to my windscreen and peeled it from beneath the wiper. It said:- " You have got to be joking yes? Please say you are not...I cannot believe you feel the same way about me and just say the day and time at the Castle Mynach, I'll be there." I read the note twice as it didn't really make sense coming from Byron? Something didn't stack up right here....I glanced around the car park curiously before embarking for home. As we sat eating dinner that evening I commented on Byron's response note....he looked at me stupid? "What ARE you talking about woman?" I explained further about all the notes and their content, Byron just looked at me in total disbelief.

Hope you can keep up with this because this is what REALLY happened. I left my initial note telling Byron he was gorgeous....Byron's response note was picked up by me....my reply note telling him I wanted him between my legs and dinner at the Mynach was plucked from my screen by a complete STRANGER who had been 'watching me' each day I arrived at work from his Bed & Breakfast window across from the car park....I thought I was conversing with Byron, the stranger thought I was conversing with HIM.... oh dear lord what a mess!!!

Between us Byron and I worked out what had happened and I became aware of a solitary figure watching my every arrival and departure from the car park from the adjacent Pub upper windows. I tried not to engage this individual but he continued to leave notes for me on my car that were bordering on harassment. As I arrived one morning dreading the walk from the car to the Model House I saw that this stranger was waiting on the doorway of the Pub. I braced myself and walked up to him...."Hello" he held out his hand to shake mine "Name's Rob, I can't tell you how hap..." I cut him short. "Rob, I am flattered at your attention but you've got the wrong end of the stick...I left those messages for my husband...I don't know how you came to pick them up but my comments are not directed at you, end of. I'm sorry for this utter mess but I'm not interested OK?" He looked hurt and another facial expression that I couldn't quite read into? I walked away leaving him no chance to respond.

Two days passed and I had not seen the 'face at the window' as I walked to my car so assumed the whole silly incident was at an end.
Wrong!
It was a sunny Tuesday evening as I left the studio and headed for the car park....my car bonnet was festooned with flowers of every description. I stood irritated, just staring before looking up at the pub window...the blinds twitched and I knew he was watching. I walked up to my car and swiped all the flowers on to the floor knowing he was watching my every action, I felt violated.

Several days of similar gestures continued before I'd had a guts full, this guy wasn't getting the message so I called the Police, only to be laughed off the phone. The Officer commented "Oh dear, so this man is harassing you daily by doing what, tell me again? Oh yes, leaving you bunches of flowers on your car.... yes I can see how annoying that would be!" I was angry beyond belief FUCK OFF you idiot... this is how women get assaulted and raped for Christ sake! I said nothing to Byron because he always thinks I am making a mountain out of a mole hill about anything!

The following evening I asked the Model House Caretaker if he would go to the car park and get my car, drive it further down the Village and park it up. I couldn't face the 'window watching' and this guy's unwanted attention. The Caretaker was only to happy to comply feeling the hero of the hour and reported back that my bonnet had once again been smothered in flowers which on my instruction he had thrown on the floor of the car park before driving off.

That evening I was so anxious I asked Byron to go and have a word with this guy at the pub. Byron drove off in a huff about having to deal with matters that he felt as a grown woman I should be able to handle myself.

Apparently there was some face to face confrontation in the Pub between he and Byron, words were exchanged and the guy was told to back off! As ever I will never know what was actually said because like most men, Byron refuses to reiterate conversation verbatim, all he told me was that I wouldn't be bothered again...and I wasn't!

I sat in my Studio one lunch time a day or so later with my large sash window on the third floor of this building wide open. The views were spectacular as it afforded a vantage point to see across the roof tops of the tiny stone cottages way below and over the Churchyard toward the Billy Wynt. At the Town's highest point is the remains of a 13th Century windmill, a stone tower known as the Billy Wynt. By early 19th Century the tower was in ruin and in 1893 restored to a Folly. *(Historically as referenced on Wikipedia)*

I popped the kettle on for a coffee when I suddenly heard an almighty scuffle of what sounded like a pack of dogs fighting. Running to the window and peering out to my right I could see a pack of four or five dogs in full hunt mode baying and snarling, fighting off each other to get behind some large commercial green dustbins, I assumed they had seen a rat until I saw a tiny scrap of a tabby kitten flee for it's life from behind the bin scaling the nearest wooden garden fence to the top, some 10 feet above road level. I gasped in horror, the kitten couldn't have been much more than ten or twelve weeks old.

I rushed from the studio down 3 flights of stairs, out the front doors of the building doing a handbrake turn to my right on my 3 inch high black heels and raced as best I could up the narrow cobbled lane leading to the back of the Model House building. The kitten was nowhere to be seen, the dogs had moved on.

To my left was a row of small two up two down Cottages with the nearest one to me being the end of terrace. Its front stable door opened directly onto the street and its top half was open, I could hear voices inside so I peered over the door knocking politely. A middle aged couple were sitting eating their lunch on a tray on their lap's, there was no way they would not have heard the commotion being just ten or so feet from their door? "Hi, I proceeded, sorry to interrupt your lunch. Just wondering if you know who owns the little Tabby kitten that's running around here only I just saw it getti......" before I could end my sentence their answer floored me. "Uhh yeah luv, 'e's ours!" My face must have been a picture because he continued, "'e'll be OK, 'e knows how to look after 'imself." I was furious internally, "but he's going to get killed by those dogs and he's only weeks old...." I continued. The man looked up from his fork full of baked beans on toast and stared me down hard, "I SAID, 'e'll be alright OK!"

My cue to push off then.....I walked away dismayed resolving to try and keep an eye from the window on this poor little mite which had probably fled in fear forever by now. Later that same day, early evening I sat waiting for a Bride to arrive for her gown fitting, my window was still partially cracked open and I heard tiny little mews coming from below. Peering out the window I could see the little kitten huddled up against the stable door crying to be let in, the lights were on, I could see movement within but nobody was answering the little lad and he looked utterly exhausted.

For the second time that day I raced from the building, no wonder I was thin in those days (laughs) but this time I kicked off my heels and did it barefoot for speed advantage, I had spare hosiery in the studio so could change laddered stockings later. As I rounded the building I slowed up not to scare him off and approached up the cobbled hill quietly, nobody was about and he was still mewing away cwtching up tight to the door on the street. Suddenly a car pulled into the lane at the top heading towards us, although it wasn't going fast in this narrowest of lanes there was no way it would see such a tiny bundle on a doorstep as its wheels passed within inches and I DO mean inches.

I flung my arms up to signal to the car stop but as I did the kitten panicked and ran in front of the wheels narrowly missing being squashed beneath, heading for his favourite life saving dustbins!! I screamed and covered my eyes and the car passed me looking at me as if I was some flailing drunk who'd just fallen out of the pub door in her bare feet...yeah I guess he had a point come to think of how I must have looked.

I ran to the dustbins but the kitten was gone. Now I was angry, I was in no mood to be fobbed off as I banged hard on the stable door of the adjacent cottage.

The man opened the door unshaven, in a tee shirt and his underpants with a cigarette dangling from his mouth which he made no attempt to remove whilst he spoke with me. "Thought you'd want to know your kitten is back but nearly got run over just now, shall I give you hand to find it?" He looked at me with a very irritated look, "Look luv, iss a cat, 'e knows how to fend for 'imself GOT IT?" With this final spit of ash and saliva he made to close the door. I pushed it back open hard which somewhat took him by surprise, further annoyed he shouted at me "Piss off luv will you!"

"Please yourself, I responded, I'll be calling the RSPCA first thing tomorrow!" I strode off as defiantly and imposingly, as much as anyone could in bare feet and laddered stockings. In those days I believed the RSPCA were there to help poor animals and would come charging to the kittens rescue as soon as I rang.....oh how I've learned in coming decades what a waste of space this ridiculous charity is, show them a TV screen with their name in all glory being advertised and you have their full attention.....an animal in distress is of no interest to them whatsoever, I despise the RSPCA for the unprofessional, uncaring, useless bunch of bastards that they are!

Arriving back in my studio there was a very angry note slipped under my door. My bride had arrived for her fitting but I was nowhere to be found, she was bitterly disappointed and would be calling me the very next day! I should have been professionally concerned about this and called her straight away to apologise but her £4,000 wedding gown was not high on my priority list I am ashamed to say....a tiny kitten was!

No point in getting changed now, I'll just lock up and head for home I thought. As I went to slam the window shut, there it was again, a pathetic little mewing. I peered out the slit in the window and there he was aloft his life saving wooden fence at the back of the pub, in the dark, all alone and shivering. RIGHT THAT'S IT I decided there and then he was coming home with me. Grabbing the phone I called Byron at home, "Get up 'ere NOW can you please, soon as!"

Byron had been relaxing at home watching TV awaiting my homecoming...."What's wrong, what's happened?" he asked with a sudden tone of worry. "We've got a kitten to catch and save, come via the back lane down the cobbles and I'll meet you there, be quiet or you'll scare him off!" I cracked out my orders replacing the receiver whilst Byron was still spluttering "M...M? It's 9.30 at night wha............." I waited patiently at the bottom of the hill keeping a close eye on the little one's movements.....then it started to rain! For Christ sake, I muttered under my breath. Gentle spots at first started to fall in heavier plops and I could see the kitten getting soggy and uncomfortable, he was just making moves to clamber down from his fence when Byron appeared feet away from him with a handful of cat food. I smiled in pride knowing my man would have thought a plan out on his way here. He called gently to the kitten tossing a bit of food up on to the wall. It was much to delicious an aroma for the rain to put off this hungry little mite, Byron edged closer to him but he started backing away grabbing morsels of food as he went. I crept up onto the lower end of the stone wall and edged my way toward the kitten from behind, he had no idea I was there, I was just feet from him as I lowered myself to my hands on knees on this 10 inch wide wall. Suddenly there was a loud rip as my very expensive black skirt gave way at the split at the back. It's fair to say I had not designed and manufactured this Armani skirt with the intention of scaling 6 foot stone walls in it!! The kitten jumped suddenly alerted to my presence and I knew it was shit or bust! I made one almighty lunge forward grasping his back leg and tail before I fell off the wall clutching him to my breast. As we didn't want to alert anyone in the street to our stealth attack on rescuing a resident kitten, all this was done in total silence. I gritted my teeth as I landed on my side on the cobbles before Byron scooped me up and wrapped his coat around me hissing between his teeth.... "What the hell are you doing woman! Who's cat is this, look at you, you alright, you broken anything....fuckin' hell M!"

"He's not a cat, I hissed back, he's a baby and he's terrified!"

Byron was in there quick as a flash with his smart mouthed reply as ever..."So would I be if some mental bitch was chasing me along a wall at this time of night in the rain!"

"Right now where does it live, I'll take it and explain!"

I stopped dead in the street, "TAKE him, he's not going anywhere, he's coming home with us right now!" I spat the words out at volume, we looked at each other realising I may have been overheard and legged it as fast as I could run in bare feet to our cars in the car park, starting to laugh as we ran at our insane collusion to apprehend a kitten from the Village, in the dark, in the rain at 10 O'clock at night, we felt like a pair of hooded villains (laughing.)

We both have spare car keys on our rings for each other's vehicle in case of breakdown etc and so Byron and I drove our cars home leaving my studio unlocked and with all the lights on, my shoes in the corridor and my keys on the desk. As soon as I got home I called the onsite Caretaker to lock up for me telling him I'd had to rush home, job done.

We placed the kitten on the Couch and towelled him dry, more food and some milk....he started whirring like a clock work toy, his purr resonated from his very soul and his body quivered the louder it got. He beamed a little blue eyed expression up at us. Like proud parents we cwtched him and sat with him for an hour, removed whatever the thing around his neck was because it sure as hell wasn't a collar, a red band which even buckled up was no bigger than a coin. I reiterated the whole days events to Byron who was as ever totally non shocked by his mad wenches antics....the boy was learning at long last that a quiet life with me was never going to be! I rummaged together a bed for him, dug out an old cat litter tray with newspaper and feed/water bowls placing everything in the kitchen ready for his bedtime.

"What shall we call him?" I asked Byron....."Oh I dunno, you name him, you found him" he answered stroking the kitten who was vibrating from head to tail.

I looked at him, remembering Chester and Max....I wanted a strong name, like they had been, a strong name for one so little who had survived so much.... "Benson! Let's call him Benson" I announced. And so little Benson had arrived in a country home, full of love, warmth and his most favourite thing in all the world....food!

We switched off the lights downstairs and made our way to bed, it was now gone Midnight and had been a very long and eventful day. As we stood in the bedroom Byron looked at me and started laughing..."What? What...? I asked bemused.

"Take a look at yourself" he opened the wardrobe door with a full length mirror. I started laughing....my toes had come straight through my stockings, the remainder of the legs had more ladders than a builders yard. My gorgeous skirt was split right up the back baring my ass to the world, I'd ripped a hole in the shoulder of my jacket and there was green moss stains on the front of my jumper...I had muck off the wall on my face and my hair looked like a birds nest.... "by the way, where's your bloody shoes?" he stared down at my dirty feet. "I kicked 'em off because I can't run in them." It was a matter of fact reply which reduced us both further to hysterics...."Of course you did, stupid me for even asking, it's what one does running barefoot around a Village late at night with no shoes on!" Again we dissolved into laughter with him calling me all the mad bitches under the sun.

We climbed into bed exhausted, closing our eyes to relax, I could feel myself being pulled down into the depths of sleepiness.

"Byron?"

Grunt....

"Byronnnn?"

A very sleepy "Whaaaa, whaa now?"

"There's something on the bed, I heard something..."

Just as Byron muttered "For fucks sake M, give it up will you.." there it was again, but this time a very distinct vibration also.

Sitting up with the lamp on.....Benson was curled up at the bottom of the bed.....
"Hmmph, so much for his bed in the kitchen then....now G'NITE!" With that Byron flung
himself over in bed and we all slept.

Chapter 14

- Her Highness Queen R of the Abergavenny Empire -

Work continued and business ticked over, there was always room for increase in revenue but there's just some money that any business alive doesn't need. It was this source of money that found me one sunny afternoon.

I had taken a day off to catch up with some things at the Cottage, in particular I wanted to paint strip the Bay window back to the wood so I could treat it and varnish stain it. Curled up on my knees in the window space scraping away my newly acquired mobile phone rang. It could hardly be called mobile as at the time it was the size of a small block of ice cream and weighed about the same, but to me it was state of the art technology and I felt quite good about being contactable via mobile means.

I answered in my usual business efficient secretarial manner.

"May I speak with the owner of the business?" I heard. No introduction of the caller or indeed good manners enough to say please.

"That's myself, I'm Maria how can I help?" I enquired.

The voice was eloquent, smooth as glycerine and professionally no nonsense, she stated the following as if I should have already known and been suitably impressed.

"My name is Mrs R please tell me more about your services as I wish to come to see you with a view to engaging you as my Designer."

Silence.

I smiled to myself at her obvious pompousness.

"I see, I commenced, would that be an offer of employment as your designer or simply that you wish to order bespoke clothing from me?"

I heard a well rehearsed theatrical laugh much as a wicked Queen of the Shires would give.

"Ahhhh Maria, I do like your attitude already my dear, it is the latter I require my Darling!"

My eyebrow rose as I listened to this over dramatic woman attempting to impress me with her superiority, and by the way I thought to myself, you haven't experienced my 'attitude' yet lady nor am I your Darling, I don't even know you!" My guard was up well and truly.

We entered into dialogue and she requested a Consultation with me for which I advised there was no charge and could be arranged in my diary for the following week at my Studios in Llantrisant.

"Oh no, no, no my Darling, she continued, I simply do not frequent commercial premises to do any of my business. I will come to your home next Tuesday at 3pm where we can discuss my requirements privately, I wish to know more about you before I give you any of my money!" She laughed lightly as if amused at her own comment.

At this statement I was utterly quizzical, who WAS this woman with her airs and graces. Could I be on the cusp of meeting a very affluent client who would be a regular and highly influential contact for my small business. Best tread carefully so I agreed the appointment although it didn't suit my already scheduled appointments but what the hell, I was not in a financial position yet to argue with such 'upper class' as this woman appeared to be.

The following Tuesday I arranged to be at home and pottered around the Cottage awaiting some prestigious vehicle and well heeled woman to arrive at the gate. Dressed for business but wearing my large white fluffy rabbit slippers from Asda, £6.99 on offer...I had my heels ready to slip into as soon as I heard her car.

WRONG!

I heard her before I saw her. The wind got up and the trees fluttered, leaves and foliage blew around the garden as I heard a noise above toward the back of the cottage. Curious I wandered to the window overlooking the farmers field at the back of our gardens. A light aircraft, a Helicopter to be precise was landing some 80 feet away in the middle of the field. I watched wondering what the farmer was up to before the rotor blades slowed and a man got out. He walked around to the passenger side of the 'Copter holding up his hand to help a very smartly dressed older woman alight from within. That's no bloody farmer I thought as my head tried to rationalise that this woman was probably my client for her consultation, Mrs R!

He helped her stumble her way across the grass to my garden, there was only a country stile as entrance and I watched as she wobbled her way over it, raising her legs in an awkward and ungainly fashion. The man made his way back to the helicopter as she waved her hand in dismissal. I felt polarised to the spot and forgot all about my fluffy slippers as I padded out the back door to meet her.
She was a mature woman probably in her late 40's early 50's at the time, well coiffed and attired, she positively reeked of money and she knew just the effect she had achieved in impressing me by her imposing arrival transportation. I was indeed dumb struck and fumbled to gain my normal composure.

"Mrs R?" I enquired to her as she walked toward me. Well let's be honest dull ass thing to ask as who else was I expecting that afternoon in the middle or rural'ity?
"Maria, ahhhh Darling, yes 'tis I" she extended her arm and hand to me. For a moment I thought she wanted me to kiss the back of her hand whilst down on one knee!!!
I took her hand and helped her down the steps in her glamorous heels, escorting her further through the door.
Once in my country kitchen she peered around as if she'd arrived in the servants quarters and tongue in cheek complimented me on my' pretty little cottage' the emphasis on little. I immediately offered her a coffee which she declined and commented on her spectacular entrance. She laughed, "Oh Darling, that's just the day

car so to speak. I cannot be asked to drive these bumpy little lanes, I like to travel in style you see." Again she laughed lightly and gently as if enacting some royal part in a TV film.

"And these my Darling, are they your pets?" She cast a disdained look down at my feet to my rabbit slippers. I could feel myself blushing with embarrassment at forgetting to pop my heels on. I laughed and tried a back handed explanation but she was neither interested or listening preferring to stare around the interior of my home quite rudely I thought.

None the less I swung into business mode and we sat chatting about her WANTS, never mind my suggestions, her EXPECTATIONS....never mind my advice for her figure, her DEMANDS as regards prices, to hell with whether that would cripple any profit margin for me! Hmmm, I was starting to read this woman like a book. Used to getting her own way in life, a business woman self made, ruthless, no harm in any of that unless of course you are trampling on the little guys in business....and that was me!

"I like your ideas Maria, she declared with poised finger to mouth action. Yes I think we should meet again for you to sketch these designs and present them to me for consideration."

This woman had already invaded one entire afternoon for me already.

"Well that's the idea of today's Consultation Mrs R, which of these ideas do you prefer and I'll sketch it out now, and which colour would you prefer the Burgundy or Sapphire?" Never ask a closed question in Sales, never give a buyer the chance to say yes or no!

She positively purred at this reply, it was language she understood and liked to play cat and mouse with.

"Oh that's good Maria, yes, yes...I like that in you, good salesmanship, hmmm you could be very useful to me" again she laughed her genteel false laugh and rose to leave. No doubt about it we were playing her ball game all the way.

"I'll have my girl call you next week to make arrangements for you come to the Manor and we'll choose designs my Darling, yes, that's what we WILL do!" She flicked the back of her hand at me as if I was dismissed. This is the 1990's lady not the bloody 18th Century I thought, I wasn't happy at all but this woman had the ability to play with your mind, she was either going to be one of my most influential clients and benefactors opening doors I could only fight for....or a complete Bitch?

Byron arrived home that night and I couldn't wait to tell him eagerly all about my mysterious and impressive client. In a split second his face told me everything...."Mrs R....? Watch your back and I'm warning you!" My face crumpled...."Why?"
Seems Mrs R had made her money from managing Care Homes for the Elderly, she was vindictive, ruthless and cut throat in her dealings with any trade or service provider to her many businesses. OK well, she's a business woman I thought, no harm in being sharp. But Byron went on to explain how she could be totally unreasonable in her dealings with industry, his own company had fallen foul of her mouth and delayed payment for commercial equipment they had designed and installed in her various establishments....she was a business Piranha, she took no prisoners and stamped roughshod over everybody with her pompous, false airs and graces. She made her money by ensuring anybody she dealt with didn't get paid via unjustified complaints or was paid at some point in time that suited her....irrelevant of the traders terms and conditions. Some would admire her...most who cross her path detest her for what she is, a two faced user of those less fortunate than she, a manipulator full of her own self importance and also arrogant.

Over the next six months Mrs R was a prominent character in my life. She did indeed become a main stay client ordering many thousands of pounds worth of garments. I tried hard to stay one step ahead of her but on times, she ran me around in circles. I lost track of the amount of times she 'ordered' me to go to London for the day sourcing Catwalk fabrics from suppliers for her next desired garment. I begged her to work from sample swatches but no....she HAD to have the entire bolt of fabric to swathe around herself to see if it met with her approval. I spent many long and tiring days trudging the streets and tubes of London, supplier to supplier negotiating in person, dragging the goods back home and meeting with her Majesty at her 'Manor' in Abergavenny.

More often than not I would foot the bill for the fabrics up front, my business to small to interest these global suppliers in the Smoke for an account. I would invoice Mrs R and wait...and wait, and wait for my money. There was always a sprat to catch a mackerel ..."Oh Darling this fabric is just what I want, just not quite a dark enough red....add it to my bill and we'll sort it out later anyway I've gone off that design now!" I used to pull my hair out with her....but just when I decided to kick her in to touch each and every month, she'd make a payment of some description on account....just enough to keep me from not wanting to regret burning any bridges. Clever lady...selfish lady!

My weeks became occupied with my frequent visits to Abergavenny a beautiful Historic Town roughly 70 mile round trip from my home in Llantrisant. Indeed, Queen R occupied a Manor House on the outskirts of Town, in a lovely setting with acres of ground, the Helicopter parked on the front lawn as one does!! Their cars were prestigious and there was nothing to suggest their finances were anything but solid. I would arrive at the door with her gowns in carriers in my arms, my workbox, necessary bits and bobs only for her husband Colin to fling open the massive arched, oak studded door and fling his arms around me in an effusive welcome...trouble was he was TOO effusive often sliding his hand along my breast or across my bottom for a damned good feel, he'd kiss me on both cheeks with a finale of a full mouth slobber often pushing his tongue in my mouth....I could do nothing with my arms laden down. But I got wise to him and would barge past him as soon as he opened the door....he was a complete letch of the first order...and she knew it, they lived an estranged relationship, well matched if you ask me!

I was ALWAYS asked to wait in an anti room for Her Majesty. I called it her servants greeting room....it was a vacuous space, wood panelled walls all very country house style, large paintings adorned the walls, a Parquet wooden floor well trodden and polished. A large extended oak table...no chairs? An Abbusson Rug of massive size graced the floor.....I dread to think how many thousands it cost, and right there in the middle of the room were the only two seating provisions just in front of a massive casement window adorned by enormous velvet drapes in the deepest shade of bottle green. An imposing high wing back chair in studded oak colour leather was strategically placed centre stage immediately in front of which was a dining style chair with a padded seat around the size you'd place in a child's bedroom, in fact one of the seven dwarfs would have fitted it perfectly!

Mrs R would ensure she kept me waiting sufficiently long enough so that I recognised my place in life, that being sub servant to her, then she would waft through the great door in a blaze of 'here I am, so sorry Darling,' Mwah Mwah to each cheek. She knew exactly how wearing this ignorant and inconsiderate practice was so much so that I couldn't wait to take her instructions and get from there no matter how much it cost me...and it usually did!

She would usher me to sit...guess where? On the dinky little servants chair at her feet whilst she languished on the high back throne, I would sketch away and produce samples from my bags and cost out designs....she would choose many and I would write out her quotation with the deposit terms at the bottom....the minute it came to handing over money she would jump to her feet, "Oh is that the time, Darling I didn't realise I really must fly, meetings you understand. I'll get my girl to mail you the cheque...see yourself out won't you!" And she'd be gone in a rustle of designer garments and perfume...Poof!

I started to get sick to death of the charade each time but played along as I knew at some point the money would materialise excuse the pun, but she grated on my nerves in every way. I needed her business more than she needed me and she played me like a puppet.

Then came the day she called to invite Byron and I to Dinner at the Miskin Manor Hotel. Her intention was to offer me an all paid for premises in Cardiff City Centre as a high brow fashion shop downstairs with the bespoke manufacturing sewing room upstairs. We would work things out legally and I would be employed as her Fashion Designer and Manager. At last I thought to myself, a reason for putting up with her which is worth the trouble she is. I could put up with this woman because I could go home from her....I pity those trapped working with her.

We met one evening enjoying a fabulous Dinner at the Miskin Manor, Byron and Colin debated the business side whilst I conversed with her Ladyship about interior design, fixtures and fittings. The premises had been chosen in the historic St David's Arcade in Cardiff City Centre...prestigious beyond belief. For a few days I floated around concentrating half on my business and dreaming the other half of what was coming....life seemed so fulfilled, I was carving a path in life for myself at last.

It was a Tuesday afternoon when the phone rang at the Studio..."Darlink, darlink it's me. I'm throwing a fancy dress party at the Manor this weekend...you will come my Darlink, I want all my business friends to meet you!" It wasn't so much an invite but an order, typical of her style. The carrot dangled of course to meet her connections, how could I refuse. The following reiteration of events remains planted in my memory like a video on loop, I will never, ever forget it.

I sourced a decent costumiers and decided I would go as Carmen Miranda with Byron as my Toreador. The costumes were a bit 'worn' but impressive none the less and we set off early Saturday evening heading for her party. As we pulled up in the long driveway to her home, cars of all makes and models littered the approach to the house, it came as no surprise to me that Mr and Mrs R had parked the Helicopter and their personal prestige motors nearest the house so that the guests couldn't fail to observe their wealth and status. I laughed as we walked past and flicked an insolent finger at the chopper.

Guests were milling around everywhere, the Manor was beautiful and had it's own banquet hall complete with dance floor, it was here that many of the guests were congregating. Liveried Waiters breezed about with trays of champagne, canapés and a Quartet played in the corner on the elevated podium. Huge displays of lilies and foliage adorned the sides of the room with one full wall length of the room given over to the buffet layout. There was nothing missing from caviar to champagne fountain. Byron felt completely uncomfortable, mind you his bull fighter trousers were a bit snug. I felt quite glamorous with a shopping trolley's amount of fruit piled on my head, there were pineapples, grapes, exotics, cherries, lemons you name it. The head dress was roughly 2 feet in height, quite light to wear as it was all plastic but very impressive visually. The blousy top was ruche'd and low scoop necked, I had tanned up accordingly and flamenco skirt was sexy and sultry with a bit of a train and a massively deep centre front split to my crotch. I had the legs and heels to do it full justice at that time and felt quite a show stopper.

There was no sign of the Hosts...I guessed she was milling around in other rooms but no, she was upstairs in her Boudoir awaiting sufficient numbers of her minions to assemble before she would descend her grand balcony staircase as showpiece of the night....Queen of her Realm and all who bestowed vision on her Majesty. Mrs R had chosen to come as Marie Antoinette....well there's a surprise (laughing my socks off.) Colin meanwhile had been despatched to the cellar to bring up more beer, know your place in life my son.

God knows how she got word to them but the quartet suddenly stopped before launching into a musical crescendo that clearly announced the arrival of something or someone. Everyone stopped chatting and the buzz around the rooms and corridors quelled as we all looked around for the reason for the music?

Oh my god...here she came, Madam Marie Antoinette in all her splendour. She had indeed sourced her costume well from the world renowned 'Angel's The Costumiers' of Shaftsbury Avenue, London suppliers to TV & Film Sets. Her outfit was incredible and as a fashion designer I feasted on every fold, pleat, tuck, ruche and drape. I take nothing from her she looked spectacular, a magnificent vision in multi shades of cream and black and she knew it....she stood for a few moments at the top of the staircase whilst wolf whistles and lengthy clapping ensued. She bowed a graceful, royal head bob to her audience, revelling in her dramatic entrance to her evening affair, and I suppose why not? Had it been anyone other than Mrs R who had thrown this magnificent evening I would have been thrilled for them and their choreography, but madam was so up her own arse and supercilious I couldn't benefit her with the praise she should have deserved.

Mrs R wafted her fan delicately to her face whilst clutching at her voluminous skirts to descend the stairs...unfortunately she wafted a bit too hard and blew her large black beauty spot off her face. A few people laughed but she was oblivious to this and unknowing of their source of hilarity. Well trained was our Colin the Puppet as he alighted to staircase in 'let me throw my cloak before you my Majesty' grand gesture. He took her half arm gloved hand and one by painful embarrassing one, she made her way slowly down the stairs to the Butler waiting at the foot of them with his silver tray and single flute of champagne. Queen R HAD arrived....and didn't we all know it.

The crowd settled a little and she weaved a deliberate pathway through those that were most important to her first, ignoring anyone outside this 'pack' who acknowledged her. She smiled and I noticed she had mock diamonds stuck to her teeth....oh puleeeeze, I was expecting a film crew to leap out from the under stairs cupboard at any moment. Her pathway was leading to Byron and I muttered 'stand by your beds' to Byron who laughed as she approached.

What happened next remains a family memory never to be forgotten and one that still renders me on my knees with tears streaming.

Her skirts were massive and fully hoop'ed taking up a good five feet of width as she walked. Queen R meandered her way through and I swear to god I saw one woman mock curtsey to her on greeting...for pity's sake don't pander to her I thought, and then there she was right in front of me.

"Ahhhh Maaaaaria, she drew out my name in a feigned loving vocal drawl, sooo glad you could make it my Darling, (I was ordered to remember I thought) OH...let me say how delicious you look !" laughing at her own joke at my fruit bowl aloft. In true Fashionista style greeting I dipped forward to peck my hostess on each cheek, in MWAH, MWAH gesture. Being 5 feet 7 inches tall opposed to Leah's 5 feet 1 inch tall I had the advantage. Her stunningly curly, piled high beehive of a wig studded with diamante tipped toward me and my fruit bowl head dress reciprocated.....unfortunately for me, one of my pineapples got ensnared in her wig and suddenly we found ourselves locked head to head like two rutting stags battling. She couldn't stand up and as I did, I dislodged her wig....she made a grab for her locks spluttering and squeaking in embarrassment hissing through her teeth for me to stand still whilst Colin and Byron dived in to try and untangle us....she and I sort of did a quickstep waltz, whilst locked horns together within a 3 square meter space before Byron was able to release her from her humiliation. All around us guests were in hysterics, her face said it all I had trashed her night! I was history.......and did I care (laughing to split my sides.) For the remainder of the night she avoided me like bubonic plague and Byron was highly embarrassed but I just couldn't help seeing the funny side of it all and even now I am so happy to have been the one to have knocked her off her high horse that night.

No surprises that a week or so later came the call to say she had changed her mind about the shop in Cardiff and that she wouldn't be ordering any more clothing for a while. THANK GOD for that I thought as I realised how lightly I had escaped the clutches of Cruella R!

Chapter 15

- Bitter Lemon's .... sweet and sour! -

At some point over the next few days, the phone rang at work, I recognised his voice immediately. "Hi it's Paul at Ford's, got a motor just come in that is YOU!" He emphasised the 'you' bit. We discussed what model it was and engine size, a few other specifications before I agreed to view it that afternoon. I was keen to change my Sierra and given Paul had hyped up this new arrival, I was curious?

Byron always taught me never to look too keen and so I deployed several typical sales tricks in order to throw Paul off the scent if I did indeed like the car I was about to view. It's always easier to barter and negotiate with a salesman if he thinks you are really not sure about a purchase and show no positive body language. I donned my Versace Shades so no eye contact could give me away....I made a point of wandering around the forecourt looking at other models so he'd assume I was still very much open minded, I took a phone call as he approached stating to the non existent caller "Yes I'm still interested, what happened to the other buyer? Oh really, oh OK..." I could see Paul twitching, standing politely back just enough to look as if he was not listening to my conversation, but he could hear every word. He was watching me like a hawk for some indication of what?

I ended my call...not sure what I would have done if the phone had actually rung whilst I was talking to thin air but thankfully that didn't happen.

"Hey Babes, you're looking fantastic!" He was straight in there with his sales patter and over familiarity....I will not deny I loved the attraction he clearly had for me, but it was not reciprocal. If anything he was so irritating I played him along like the Muppet he was! Paul knew he was a good looking guy, he dressed expensively, he was always tanned and smelled of top notch aftershave brands, but he was basically a stuffed shirt full of himself and would notch any number of women on his bed posts if they were stupid enough to fall for his sexy chat ups, he made me laugh but overall he got on my nerves most of the time.

I ignored his compliment for what it was 'lip service.'

"Where's this motor you are dying for me to see then?" I asked.

He tossed his head indicating for me to follow him to his right into one of the inner garages. Chuckling to himself in a manner that suggested he felt he had this sale in the bag, he commented "You're going to wet your knickers as much as I could make you when you see this baby...." he laughed again at the sexual innuendo of his remark whilst staring directly at me. Fortunately my shades hid my eyes and I forced my mouth to stay firmly straight and expressionless, I neither spoke or acknowledged him in any way. As I followed him through a doorway he started punching the air with his fist whilst stating....."what d'ya think, done deal, I'm right ain't I."

Dear lord above. Thank goodness I DID have my shades on because there in front of me was a magnificent fluorescent neon lemon sports car, it was to die for, I didn't need to take a step further...I WANTED this car!

Paul was watching my every move, I still didn't speak, he was getting irritated at my lack of any outward signs of interest. "Take you're 'Bans (Rayban) off, you can't see the colour properly" he declared.

"Their not 'Bans...Versace's Darling you obviously can't recognise class which goes for this as well" I poked a flippant finger at the car. "Bit loud isn't it, what the hell colour is that?" I asked curling up my nose in distaste. I was of course IN LOVE with the car and it's colour.

"You're having a laugh, no way wouldn't you like this....look at it man....it's a beauty! I can see your gorgeous ass in there and you know it." He started dancing around the car. "Look....look, look there's plenty of room in the back, but we'd have to be careful about not staining those velour seats!" Again he burst out laughing at his innuendo. This time I peeled off my glasses very slowly and deliberately staring hard at him. "I'm here to look at a car Paul, not listen to your crap, I'm not comfortable with you is there anyone else I can have a chat to about the vehicle?" With that I opened the drivers door to peer inside. The outside appearance of this motor was only surpassed by it's interior. Deep padded plush navy blue seats dotted with tiny squares in the

156

same neon lemon as the paintwork. Sporty racing bucket front seats, smaller racing style steering wheel, dashboard in deep mock walnut with all controls in the same colour navy as the seats but with bling white numerals, colour coordinated knobs and switches, even the seatbelts had been designed with the same seating colour/pattern. The car was heart stopping to say the least.

Paul had been taken off guard with my comment, he looked like I'd slapped him in the face but he recovered swiftly and fairly professionally. "Oh I'm sorry if I've offended you, it's my way you understand, especially around gorgeous women. I'd rather be the one to help you choose the correct vehicle," he stuttered searching for his next words, "I mean, if you really don't like it, I find that hard to believe, but if you don't well I can keep searching for you?" His face was a picture of disbelief and indignation that I could have thwarted him on both counts...his choice of car and his attraction to me! Smiling inwardly I knew I had him on the back foot.... "I didn't say I'm not interested, I might be? I just find the colour extreme," again to confirm my distaste I screwed up my nose, "and it looks expensive to run, I mean look at the size of those low Pro's." I pointed to the beautiful low profile wheels hugging the bodywork, there couldn't have been more than an inch of rubber between the hub and road!!

Paul seized the chance to get back into a potential sale, he could see his commission sliding away. I will confirm to readers at this point there was never any doubt I wanted this car...I just didn't want to make it an easy sale for Mr Arrogance and I wanted to ensure he couldn't command best price.

"Yes but you're in the fashion game, it's the perfect motor for you to look the part!"

I looked at him quizzically, "I'm already 'the part' as you put it, I'm in the fashion business, I don't need to try and look as if I am...I AM!"

I could see by his expression he had realised he'd said the wrong thing again. Frustration started creeping into his voice..."No, I didn't mean that, Ughh...look do you want to take it for a run, see how it drives?"

Did I? OF COURSE I did!!!

"Well, I suppose there's no harm in trying it out..." I commented flat as a pancake but secretly feeling sorry for him he was so, so, so oblivious to my desire for this motor.

He climbed in alongside me and buckled up....he was going to need to wink, wink.

I drove calmly and sedately from the garage heading for the nearby Motorway, not the manner a car like this should be handled as it was pure racing machine.

Typical of a man passenger he was fidgety and impatient. "You can go a bit faster if you like, there are no speed cameras here." I smiled and edged up to 40 miles per hour in a 60 zone.

Byron has taught me so much in life, to handle a car and drive responsibly was his living as a Sales Director. He covered 2000 miles a week and has even been complimented by Police as to his driving skills. I'm no lily livered woman behind the wheel. I cruised around the roundabout entering the slip lane to the M4, Paul was chatting about warranty and servicing. I didn't need to as there was plenty of oomph under the bonnet, it was a 2Ltr Turbo engine, but just to shock or impress I didn't care which, I doubled the clutch and dropped into 3rd gear before flooring the accelerator. I knew exactly what stretch of road I could 'try her out' on. I entered the motorway at 85mph with Paul pulling G Force in his seat, trying to remain composed but clearly thinking what the hell? I indicated, glided out into the middle lane, indicated and asked for further power as I pulled into the fast lane. This motor was a flying machine, responsive, light on the wheel, purring easily and with plenty more to give....I'd hit 120mph before running out of safe road, so eased back on the throttle, leaving the motorway at the next exit. Paul was muttering something about not much fuel in the tank and then turned to me with the most stunned look on his face. "Bloody hell, who taught you to drive, the Ferrari Team?" I laughed but could see an element of respect in his face....I was no nervous woman who needed a Ford Fiesta 1.2Ltr!!

Arriving back at the showroom, we entered into negotiations about price, warranty, servicing and the usual. I feigned dislike of certain things, moaned about aesthetics and complained about fuel prices. The car was a Ford Mondeo Turbo Sports, 2 Litre with factory fitted low Fairings making the car look as if it was an inch above ground and with a full set of Pirelli Low Profile Tyres costing a minimum £2,000 alone. Paul wanted £15,500 for the deal. As a small business and budgets to work to I offered him £11,500, he came back with £14,500...I persisted, £12,250, he rallied with £14,000.

I took an educated gamble and stood up from my chair, "tell you what, maybe I'm rushing into this, I'll go home have a chat to Byron and call you tomorrow with a decision." As I walked to the door he called after me, "Hang on, it's obvious I've shown you a car you can't afford." Ooof bad answer professionally! OK, I'll give him that one I noted to myself. "What's your maximum?" he asked. A question no good salesman will ever ask!

I turned to look at him, " No it's Ok Paul, I wasn't fussed on it from the minute I saw it anyway, don't worry."

He wasn't going to lose this sale. "No, no go on what's affordable for you?"

"£12K tops, it doesn't interest me enough beyond that" I answered.

"£12,500 and she's yours" he pushed on.

I was more than happy with a £3,000 saving but I remembered my rules...never look that keen. "I'll call you in an hour, I just need time to myself without you pushing me along OK to work out if this is best for me."

He looked utterly frustrated. "OK, an hour, but after that it goes on the forecourt!"

"Fine, I understand." I replied.

I drove around the corner in my dinky toy Sierra, bought a coffee and counted down the minutes. Three minutes past the hour I called him to confirm my purchase.

"Oh good, I knew you'd go for it" he stated triumphantly. "It's only 4pm, why don't you pop back down and sign the papers before you change your mind, a woman's prerogative which we men have to suffer."

Oh Paul you will never learn the art of true salesmanship I thought to myself.

"OK, if that's what you want" I answered...he had played right into my hands as I so wanted this deal signed and sealed.

As I entered the garage for the second time that day, he strode out to meet me like a Stag having won his Hind. Paul could never keep his arrogance under control for long. He popped his arm around my shoulder, dropping the keys to the vehicle in my hand like he was doing me some huge favour whilst waiving his payslip of all things in my face! "See that?" he stated "a nice fat £2K going on there this month, knew I'd win you over, bet you've never earned that type of money in your life have you?" He laughed sarcastically.

I smiled demurely before looking him in the eye. "Depends on what you consider 'winning' Paul, could have been much more so it seems because I actually adored the car the second I saw it...but a good SalesWOMAN knows how to work a deal!" I winked sexily at him and laughed as I strode toward the car punching the air.

Paul was gutted, his very body language spoke volumes. Striding after me he spluttered that he'd only done me a favour in dropping the price because he felt sorry for me because I fancied him!!

"You deceitful cow!" was his last comment as I sniggered whilst signing the contract. Absolutely perfect Paul, your Customer Relations skills are to be deplored!!

I left my old Sierra behind and sailed out into the sunset in this stunning motor. On arrival home Byron's face was a classic for the family album. We both appreciate nice cars but wouldn't say we are 'Motor heads' by any means, but no matter where we went in that Mondeo, heads turned and eyes goggled, we loved it (laughing.)

A few days passed before Paul called to ask how I was getting on with the new motor, was I finding it too much for me to cope with? Oh you just had to laugh at this guy's front.

"No, I'm loving the thrill of it Paul" I answered honestly.

"That's not a thrill Babe, only I could do that for you!"

Here we go again, I sighed heavily down the phone.

"Paul, you are married with a young baby. I am happily married with no desire to hook up with you so give it a rest will you, please?" It was a genuine request from me as he was wearing me down.

"I'm in an open marriage he declared, she don't care what I get up to."

It was at that point I made a fatal mistake, I tried to soothe his bruised, rejected feathers, just like I had with Dillwyn and Rafael.

160

"Paul, you're a lovely guy, I can't help but like you're sassy attitude and yes I find you very attractive but I'm not on the menu OK!"

I may as well have handed him a green for go card.

"Well if you're attracted to me, let's do it Babe...I imagine you in my bed at night, you know you want me!"

"For Christ sake Paul, I yelled down the phone, what bit of NO can't you understand?"

He just laughed and hung up.

In the weeks that followed, he called a few times asking if I could alter clothing for his wife and child. I did so because I bore no grudge but each time he came to the Studio he was hard work, touchy feely and I had to put him in his place more than once.

And then he totally jeopardised my marriage!

It was a Friday night.

Byron and I always met up on a Friday evening after work to go for a meal at a local pub and blow away the week's work cobwebs. A chat and catch up with each other was important to us. We had agreed that I would meet Byron at a favourite pub at 6pm that night.

The girls packed up their machines and left just after 5pm, I had a few phone calls to make before calling it a day and was just finishing up when who should breeze through the door but Paul.

I smiled professionally thinking he'd brought more alteration work but thinking to myself oh for pity's sake NOT now!

His cheery smile, beautiful white teeth (enhanced) beamed at me.

"Hey gorgeous, have you missed me?"

"What do you want Paul, I'm just about done for the day?"

He produced a skirt from his wife's wardrobe and some children's wear asking if I could shorten the length on them by an inch.

I agreed and we chatted some more about the Mondeo before he left. It was now 5.50pm and I was meeting Byron at 6pm.

I rushed to the mirror to repair my days make up and brush my hair, Byron has always complimented me and I didn't want to look 'work weary' when I got to the pub.

Unbeknown to me, Byron had decided to come to the Studio and surprise me by picking me up, leaving my car at work so that I could have a few glasses of wine.

He had arrived on the top floor of the Model House to hear voices in my Studio and assumed it was a client, so he sat and waited in the cafe area in case my client was undressed for a fitting or whatever.

When Paul left my studio he strode past Byron and smiled.......

Byron looked in through my doorway to see me hurriedly repairing my make up and hair.

What was my husband to think but the worst?

Byron left as silently as he had arrived and drove to our designated meeting place.

I arrived shortly after 6pm and kissed him on the cheek. He was like a dead fish toward me. We ordered and he got me a drink and I could see he was rigid with ....what? Temper, anxiety, the need to tell me something?

"Been busy have you, that why you're late?"

It was almost through gritted teeth this comment?

I explained a client had popped in which in fairness was what Paul was, he'd brought me an order for work. But what I should have said was that Paul had dropped by.

I had no idea at this time that Byron had been sitting a few yards from my Studio and knew exactly who had been there. Even so I had nothing to hide?

Eventually Byron challenged me about Paul having been there, it came out as to his presence and that he'd witnessed Paul leaving then me rushing to tidy myself up.

I could see immediately what he was getting at but NO, no, no, no this was NOT how it was! I tried to reason with Byron but he was livid, we abandoned the meal and drove home.

The evening was an emotional and tearful argumentative affair with me trying to justify my innocence and Byron disbelieving me, it culminated in us sleeping in separate bedrooms and trying to find some level ground with each other. I was damned well not going to back down when I'd done nothing wrong....but my husband didn't believe me? I hurt more than words could describe.

I was angry with Paul, and when I get angry, worlds fall apart!

The following morning I'd just got off the phone to one of our Bridal clients when the phone rang almost instantly.

Paul was in a flat out panic on the other end of the line stating how Byron had been sitting outside the Studio the night before, that he was worried sick all morning waiting for Byron to pitch up at his office to 'smack' him...had I set it up to frighten him off?

Dear god man get a life will you was all I could think....he ranted on about how he couldn't get me out of his head, he couldn't just walk away, how was he going to see me now that there was no need for me to go to the garage?? I listened for a while and then gently replaced the receiver.

Byron and I were frostily cool with each other, I didn't know what the hell to do next to be truthful.

But event's took a turn which meant life changed forever once again.

Chapter 16

- Don't take your love to Town -

In the words of the famous singer Kenny Rogers. My next adventures entailed me taking my love for my fashion business, to town!

We had grown into adjacent studios at the Model House and *Labello Angelina Couture* was now their largest Tennant occupying three studios of various Square Footage sizes alongside one another. The interconnecting doors made it easy for me to open up the whole area into a massive working environment. We had the Sewing Work Room, The Client Fitting Room and Retail Area, my Main Office and Consulting Room. I should have been satisfied with my lot but I am never one to sit back and languish. My main gripe with the Model House was that the Studios were open roofed. They were sectioned off areas with their own entrance doors but no actual enclosure. I could hear exactly what was taking place in the opposite Business Studios as they could hear mine. Phone calls were far from private, we couldn't play any music as it was audible to all other businesses on the top floor, any problematic clients were entertainment to all other businesses who listened in. I was chastised for the noise of my printer, asked to get a quieter kettle that didn't whistle when boiled and it all became TOO much!

As always my spontaneity, being a 'do'er' not a 'thinker' overtook me one morning as I popped down the mountain to our local Town, Talbot Green to do the banking.
A stone fronted, two storey shop with bay windows lay empty with its 'To Let' sign pinned to the wall. Formerly our local Art Supplies Shop I had known the Proprietors and felt sad for their loss of premises, I'd heard they'd gone bust falling on hard times. I peeped through the window, I imagined, I dreamed and I rationalised in my head but by the time I had arrived back at the Studios my decision was made, we were MOVING!

Adrienne had long since got used to my proactive mannerisms. If I said I was 'thinking' of doing something in the business, it generally happened within a few weeks or a blink of the eye!

I consulted with her about my find....."Can we afford it?" she sensibly asked.

I reasoned that it gave us the chance to have a retail shop downstairs and the Atelier manufacture upstairs, a chance to increase turnover, a prestigious presence in the trade and we'd have room for more staff.

I consulted Byron who was understandably concerned and played the devil's advocate to such a move. What if's abounded, but as ever in my head strong and newly found abilities to be something in my life at last, I could find sensible answers to all that was thrown at me. I spoke to our business bank who positively encouraged growth and employment, well of course they would!

Within days I had spoken to the Landlord and negotiated a Tenancy at £8000 a year and this was 1995, irrelevant of any other utility costs. It meant I needed to take £300 a day from the minute the shop door opened just to pay my rent, staff wages, draw a wage for myself and cover stock purchases... I was confident given the Wedding Fayres we were attending, orders coming in but there's nothing so fragile as a house built of straw!

I had the dreams, the ability, the motivation and the drive....but I wasn't in control was I? The customers were!

And so our move from the Model House in Llantrisant to the Shop in Talbot Green was underway. One small problem was the condition of its interior and after much deliberation by me and Byron we agreed the refurbishment was too big a job for us, we needed a shop fitters to come in.

At this particular time I had a new bride to be on my books called Cath whose partner owned his own building company in Town. I approached her and 'about to be' husband

165

Colin came to give us quotes for the job. My design as a typical French Atelier layout was sophisticated in style giving Ye Olde World image of traditional Workrooms as per The House Of Elliot TV programme. Black highly polished wooden floors, silk embossed wallpaper coverings with decadent inlay panel sections of contrast wall paper. An £800 crystal chandelier hung sparkling from the highly decorative ceiling rose. Expensive drapes adorned the front shop window offering a glimpse into a fashion emporium previously unknown to Talbot Green. A flagged frontage to the shop with Bay trees and potted plants gave an impression of luxury and grandeur....just like Mrs S...we were ahead of our time, local residents were more in tune with buying from Tesco and Asda and the local bargain shops! Customers were quite literally wary of using the handle to the big glossy Black No.10 Downing Street style front door.

In dealing with Colin it had been agreed the cost of refurbishments would amount to approximately £8,500 I agreed the quote and notified our Accountants of the amount. In fairness the job was achieved on time, the Shop was stunning! Subsequent conversations saw Colin and his Business Partner David offering to reduce their invoice for a 'share' in the business that they saw as being successful and solvent. As businessmen I took them at their word, I made a few legal enquiries but by now we had all become friends and Cath was due to marry Colin, my bubble seemed complete. After many, many conversations I agreed along with Byron to go Limited and sell them minority shares in the business, I would always retain major shareholder status. I felt like I was going somewhere in life for the first time. A businesswoman in my own right, the support of a wonderful husband and staff and now the support of Shareholders in the business.

How wrong can one be?

The move from the Model House was not without difficulties as we needed to keep production operational, meet wedding deadlines and encountered problems that any

166

business would in uprooting its HQ to a different location. We battled on, dealing with each crisis as it arose.

Finally we were fully ensconced in the new establishment and our Opening Evening Event was being planned.

VIP invites were sent out to around fifty guests, I don't think the building could have housed more than that. For the Ladies it was evening gown attire and for the Gents full Dinner Suit. Arfon Haines Davies, a local TV celebrity was to open the evening with fees for his time donated to the Ty Hafren Charity. It ran like clock work!

I organised a Serviced Buffet with Wine Waiter and Waitresses in full Livery, we even had a Master of Ceremonies to announce each of the guests as they arrived. A flood lit shop frontage and some very prestigious motors rolling up outside saw the sleepy little town of Talbot Green turned into The Oscar's Ceremony for the night. The shop glistened and twinkled, the comments, congratulations and praise we received for the entire proceedings was awesome. I floated around in a gown of my own design and manufacture, a cream velvet butterfly bodice encompassing wing sleeves ending at the empire line before flowing into a column gown of chocolate knife pleats flaring slightly at the hemline to create a small puddle train which I ingeniously tapered into a 'V' shape so that it looked like a snake slithering along behind me, a deep centre split allowed me to show off my tanned legs up to the mid thigh in a seductive manner. I felt like the Queen of my empire. Our TV Celebrity arrived bringing ME a huge bouquet of flowers and similarly one of our German Suppliers arrived bearing framed fashion shots of their clothing line as stocked by Labello Angelina Couture.....it took pride of place above my office desk. Speeches were made, lots of champagne was drunk and the evening was an entire success.

To end the evening I had introduced our two new Director Shareholders, Colin M and David J, they looked every inch the Entrepreneurs in their 007 Bond Dinner Tuxedo's.

In the days that followed, we were the talk of the Town, shopper's peered through the big bay window, some ventured in.

Being only a stone's throw from his workplace, Paul became a pest of a visitor several times a week.

We were moving into Winter and the evenings were pitch black at 4pm, thus one evening as the staff left for the day I locked the heavy front door behind them to prevent anyone wandering into the shop whilst I was out in the back office.
I had no sooner sat down at my computer when I heard the big brass door knocker go. Cursing because I wanted to get on with designs and pattern cutting, I opened the door to Paul. He must have read my body language because he asked if he was holding me up? Always politely professional I assured him that he wasn't but how could I help. Seems it was his wedding anniversary in two days and he didn't know what to buy his wife, could he have a look around.
We had some extremely expensive Swarovski Crystal jewellery in stock, beautiful Italian leather handbags and some exceptionally realistic and stunning MOCK fur coats, they were divine and over £300 a piece.

I started showing him around the rails and the jewellery cabinet but each time he invaded my personal space pushing his body up close to mine or touching my arms as I handed him things to view. I sighed heavily attempting to indicate to him I wanted none of it but he knew what he was doing, as I bent down to pick up a handbag to show him he reached out to push my hair from my cheek...ENOUGH! I threw the bag on the floor and walked into my office stating if he wasn't really interested in looking then there was no point in me showing him anything. He followed hastily behind me laughing saying "I'm getting to you though aren't I." This guy was so up his own arse full of his underpants and self proclaiming of his fantastic body and looks....I just wanted right at that minute to punch him! As it was I suddenly heard a key in the front door but as I'd dead locked it from the inside the door wouldn't open. There was only one other person with entry keys to the shop.....Byron.

My heart sank as I realised how this whole fiasco would look to my husband. Me locked in my own shop, after hours with many of the lights switched off...alone with Paul. Great, just fucking great, thanks a bunch Paul I really need a divorce right now was streaming through my head as I rushed to unlock the door to Byron.

His face was like stone as he weighed up the scene before him, he nodded a curt acknowledgement to Paul before demanding to know why the door was locked? Paul instantly looked nervous and I don't know why because absolutely nothing had or was ever going to happen. I tried to explain that Paul had popped in to find something for his wife on his way home, the door was locked simply out of habit, I was after all alone in the shop it was dark and I didn't want anyone wandering in after hours.....I could see it was falling on deaf ears with Byron. In temper I flounced out to the shop floor, grabbed a fur coat off the rail and bundled it in a large luxury carrier telling Paul to take it home on trial, if his wife liked it and it fitted, pay me later! He took the bag and made a hasty exit from the shop. Byron was in no mood to talk and stormed off home. I locked up and wearily made my way after him. Hence to say another very ugly evening ensued whilst I tried hard to get Byron to believe me that nothing was going on with Paul, yes I found him attractive but the idiot man drove me insane with his pathetic arrogance. I retired to bed in tears and once again we were in separate rooms.

The following morning we each left for work without speaking to the other and my temper at being wrongly accused, hung, drawn and quartered was at nuclear explosion point.

I arrived at work to find two of the machinists squabbling over an incorrectly cut pattern piece, a delivery left dumped in the middle of the shop floor to be unpacked and my shop Manageress was no where in sight, the till hadn't be opened up and the phone was ringing persistently. That moment when you feel you could scream at the top of your lungs flooded over me in sheer frustration. I grabbed the phone snapping down the line "Labello Angelina, Maria speaking."

A deep laugh before I heard "Hello Gorgeous, fuck me that was close last night wasn't it, old man jealous now is he, he's not enough for you Babe and you know it!"

I don't know if I felt it before I saw it but an intense 'red mist' flooded my brain, I'd lost control and my temper was raging through my body. I hurled the phone at the window, grabbed my keys and stormed from the shop heading for Paul's workplace 100 yards down the road. I must have looked like a crazed bull as I crashed down the pavement. Arriving at his exterior Porta Cabin office I damn near ripped the door off the hinge, his head shot up and he had a customer with him. Taking one look at my face he realised I was about to create a terrible scene, taking his customer by the elbow he ushered him past me stating he would call him shortly, he needed to speak with this lady very urgently (me)... and propelled the man out the door.

Ever the arrogant bastard he turned smiling from ear to ear " Temper, temper....calm down, come 'ere let me kiss it better" with which he chuckled at his self amusement.

I was huffing and puffing for breath having military marched my way down the High Street, pointing my finger in his face just inches from his nose my voice rose in an angry snarl....."Enough of this insanity, you hear me? I've had it with you and your childish stupidity! Who the hell do you think you are, what is it with you, you getting off on busting up my marriage huh...huh??" By now I was screaming in his face, he tried to dodge my invasive pointing finger and thrusting of my face in his, he looked uncomfortable both at my anger and the amount of noise I was creating which clearly could be heard on the forecourt by customers and his fellow colleagues.

"You started it" he lamely muttered as if seeking for a good reason why he had no sensible answer.

I was positively spitting saliva, "I WHAT! You arrogant piece of shit! You've hassled me since I tried to view the Honda with your stupid chat up lines and...and..." I was out of breath and seething angry. With that I wrenched off my high heeled shoe and aimed it at him, he instinctively ducked but I hadn't planned on throwing it, "see this, THIS!

I waved the 3 inch heel at him...come near me or my shop OR my husband again and I swear I'll shove it so far up your arse you'll never fuck anything again!"

I swung around one shoe on and one shoe off making for the door before I heard him say "....Yeah, yeah well you'll fucking think twice before you try and tuck me up again you stupid cow!"

I stopped dead in my tracks.

"what did you just say.....tuck you up?"

"yeah you heard, tuck me up. I took a hit on my targets over that, you cocky mare thought you were clever didn't you... his voice took on a mocking babyish gibber... I don't like it Paul, it's the wrong colour Paul" his eyes were angry and his face screwed up in temper.

I stood looking at him for a moment before the sudden realisation hit me that he'd been trying to get his own back at me for me tricking him about the Mondeo and knocking him down hard on price, I was dumb struck at the mental age and idiocy of this man.

I started laughing, whether out of shock, disbelief or relief I don't know but my reaction enflamed his temper further. I sauntered off across the Petrol Forecourt throwing my head back laughing as much at my own stupidity as his, I should have seen what game he was up to many weeks before, the last time I heard from god's gift to women he was yelling behind me from his office door...." and don't bother buying yur fuckin' petrol here no more either!" His door slammed shut and I never heard from him or saw him again, the fiasco situation was over!

Life was about to change again.

Chapter 17

- To rob a dying child.... may you Spina in HELL! -

Labello Angelina trundled on with business steady but not great. I attended many and regular Wedding Fayres never failing to book at least £15,000 worth of wedding orders and as much as £25,000 on well organised events. As always two thirds of these sums would be cost of sale so gross profit was never fabulous but good. The retail shop downstairs struggled from day one, we were ahead of our time, the stock too Paris/Milan/New York for the inhabitants of the Towns and Villages....the local Supermarkets were more their style and of course small retail parks started popping up around the area bringing unwanted competition.

Before long the design and bespoke manufacturing side of the business was carrying the retail and I should have realised and accepted that first loss is best loss, but I didn't want to lose the shop that I was so proud of. It gave out a huge success image for the Design business, Brides suitably impressed as they entered the building to consult with 'their Fashion Designer,' it actually helped secure many orders over the few years we were there. Stocking the shelves was becoming more and more difficult, in the retail world you buy your summer stock in winter and your winter stock in summer so at critical cash flow times of the year, we were always fully extended and eating into our business overdraft yet again. But we battled on and new clients started to seek us out from further afar, more Suit and Gown work arrived via the 'ladies who lunch' bunch. But I was still very innocently trusting of these type of people, unwise to their tricks and antics, I was now around 36 years old and reasonably worldly wise but you truly cannot believe some of the stunts people pull, people who appear in every sense to be successful, reliable, responsible and above all 'nice' people. It is very often these same people/business people who do not have two pennies to rub together and acquire everything they possess by foul means rather than fair!

By now we were starting to get somewhere with the Cottage refurbishments, it was taking on the country cottage style and look I so wanted and loved. I had moved into a stage of my life and business where clients were 'courted' via Dinner at mine, or a meal at a chic restaurant in the City. I would cook lavish meals and bake sweets and puddings, I actually loved to cook and taught myself all I know. We were moving in a social circle that involved much entertaining. My wardrobe stepped up a gear, mostly all my own design and make, I was forced to enact my profession in life with the Chanel Suits and Jimmy Choo footwear, long red painted fingernails made for difficult gardening but on a weekend whenever I got one to myself I would be in rags of jeans and tee's covered in mud from the garden or paint from the cottage and I was never more happy in my sloppy jo's....I am a down to earth woman. I loved helping Byron to create our gardens, to be decorating the cottage and making my nest, but by weekday I was the queen of fashion and my little empire in Talbot Green Town.

Our little family had grown considerably.... Halshaw, Rupert, Verity and Benson were as happy as country bumpkins, we'd saved some kittens from a fate worse than...from our next door neighbours. Being farming folk their general attitude is that if the animal hasn't got a worthy job to do, despatch it! We were now mummy and daddy to Thomas the Tabby, Basil the Black/White, Emily all Black, Fat Barry the Black/White, Macey the Blackie and little Millie the Albino all bar a tabby ear tip. All had found our door tired and hungry or been rescued from less than savoury living conditions, some were feral but they all bumped along nicely together and life was busy with their everyday needs and wants. I became known as the mad cat woman down the lane, strangers would ring me asking If I could take their kitten/cat off their hands for various reasons, some which angered me immensely. I did all I could to find homes for these and at one point on a boiling hot Sunday afternoon I went to deposit something in my wheelie bin to find a small, on deaths doorstep ginger tom thrown in there!! I was horrified and rushed him to the vet...I have no idea how long he'd been in there as the bin had been emptied the previous mid week.....he was dehydrated and emaciated, he died two days later at the vets and I despaired of how anyone could drive down my lane and dump a defenceless animal in a hot plastic bin that it had no chance of escape from....I hope whoever it was boils in hell.

I was rarely home from the shop before 8.30/9pm but on this particular occasion I had been blown out on a fitting appointment as the client was ill. I seized the chance to high tail it home for a well earned early evening. Byron and I sat chatting over the dinner table before clearing away. With a glass of wine each we relaxed in the Lounge to watch some TV. I had switched the lights off in the kitchen and dining room so the rear of our cottage was in darkness.

Some time later I popped out for a refill when I heard the most unearthly noise from beneath the dining table as I walked past. I bashed on the kitchen light dreading whatever it was I was going to see with Byron calling from the Lounge "What? What is it...?" Well blow me down with a feather, my mouth dropped open wider than a train tunnel entrance.

Who should be peering out from under the table, jammed right back in the corner of the room........was MAXWELL!!!!! He stared me in the eye snarling and spitting, Byron was speechless and I was overcome with emotion, my boy had come home. He would have been around 8/9 years old now, he looked three times that and was covered in battle scars. he was positively monstrous in size I have never seen a larger cat since....he had lost one eye which has sealed itself up and the end of his tail was missing. I clasped my hand to my mouth stifling a cry of pity for him....I tried to approach but he was having none of it lashing out viciously if we got too close....but he stared at me in a way I can't describe. His expression was one of deep distrust but not fear, a longing for something he seemed to remember but had learned to live without. I spoke his name gently and his ear twitched twice, in that split second I knew he remembered us, my boy had come home to say his final farewell, to let us know he was still around but now it was time to go, to once again visit the home and people he had loved so much. We placed food and milk down and left him in peace in the corner he had always slept in as a kitten, he wouldn't let me get close enough to put down a blanket. The next morning he was gone, vanished back through the cat flap from whence he had appeared, his last meal devoured no doubt with gratitude. He had finally gone for good and I know in my heart it was to meet with his angel this time. I don't know why he came back that night after all those years but I'm glad he did to ease the ache I carried having never known what happened to him, thank you my beautiful Maxwell, RIP and god bless your little paws for honouring us with your final visit.

As I picked over the company accounts one morning I knew serious action was needed, we needed another revenue stream. It couldn't be more bespoke work which was time consuming, it needed to be fast turn around work, bread and butter money. There was only one route to take and that was CMT work (Cut, Make & Trim.) Your typical mass produced factory production line type of work that could be filtered in around the Bespoke order book. I set about searching the Industry publications and adverts, calling around my London contacts and eventually I saw an advert for a workroom and services required for CMT of luxury bath robes. I contacted the people direct on the number given and was answered by a man called Peter, I subsequently met his wife but for the life of me cannot recall her name. We agreed a meeting and they travelled to us the following week. Immediately they arrived I could see they were so utterly impressed with our premises and work ethos, our staff were a great bunch of girls four in total including the shop floor manageress. Their project was to make pure silk designer bathrobes to be sold as boxed gifts on board flights to the well heeled and first class jet setters. These were no ordinary bathrobes which were to be sold at £750-£1000 each!!! Relatively plain in design from my point of view it was the 'finishing' touches that captured the eye and of course the main fabric itself which was the worlds finest satin finished raw silk in its purest form. The packaging was simply exquisite with delicate tissue paper threaded with silver or gold strands, colour coordinated ribbon in generous ties around the outside of the box plus a Certificate of Authenticity bearing the Garment Design name, it's colour way and it's Production Number. I realised immediately I had found myself what was effectively exactly what I was already doing 'Bespoke' work....this wasn't what I had planned. This work was going to be intricate and incredibly difficult to manufacture. Anyone who has worked with silk will attest to the huge amount of problems that can arise. My work tables would need 'damage limitation to fabric' surfaces when cutting, machines would need changing over to silk /ball headed sewing needles, staff would need to wear white handling gloves to work with, the smallest snag or thread pull to any pattern piece rendered it bin fodder! None the less I needed a capital injection to the finances and I set about costing the work involved. It took me an entire weekend to break it all down and set it out on a formal quotation and it bottom lined at around £16,000.

Peter and his wife lived in Hertfordshire in a typical rural country house, they were upper class individuals dabbling with starting up a fashion business via this project now that Peter had retired, his wife was much younger than he and she wanted a little 'something' to do from home. We were invited up for the weekend to present my quote for acceptance/refusal, I couldn't for the life of me see that he would accept as the cost of materials was so high there was little left in it for them let alone pay the fees I was asking to manufacture, they had simply set their sights on a garment that was too expensive to actually make selling at the price they had set. Either they needed to increase their retail price or opt for less expensive materials....Peter was reluctant to do either, his chosen market price was what he felt he could ask for, I couldn't reduce my manufacturing costs knowing that our own company bespoke work would have to be cut back to afford the extra time to work on such garments. What I really should have stuck out for was simple CMT...babies bibs, kids shorts, ladies tee-shirts that type of throw it together in minutes and get paid work!

Peter accepted my quote that evening and wrote out a cheque for £10,000 as a retainer for our business services. With my business account back in the black as of right that moment we left for home with a car load of materials, boxes, ribbons and whatever. The girls at work had been consulted throughout but when they actually saw the work involved in front of them plus what was already on our order book for the year, mutterings of increased wages and bonus pay outs started to whisper around the workroom.

For a few months we got stuck in and despite some teething problems, we seemed to be hitting the mark with what was required from Peter and his wife and just short of 100 of these deluxe garments had been made, boxed and returned to Hertfordshire but none sold from their side as yet? I found that quite strange as they were now sitting on a minimum £750,000 worth of retail stock....was bewildering to me to say the least, I wanted to say to them get out there and start selling but none of my business. And so we plodded on our minimum weekly target was 25 of these garments to be made up and the total original order had been for 300, so keep going.

As we crept into early 1998 I became involved with the Ascot crowd being asked for dress and hat designs and so I teamed up with a couple of local Welsh Milliners, one in Abergavenny and the other in West Wales who worked with me on my designs to produce coordinating hats to the outfits. My clients were delighted, Labello Angelina was becoming a one stop shop and although still not financially raking it in, we were trading in and out of the black as the cash flow deemed.

Our big black door swung open one sunny afternoon and a miniature version of Goldie Hawn but with rich strawberry blond locks swaggered in. Perfectly groomed, carrying a £15K Channel Sac Bag and dressed head to toe in Yves St Laurent. As there was no formal door on my back office I heard her introduce herself to my shop manageress who then came through to me, "There's a Mrs Liz S asking for you." I left it a minute before going through, never look too keen remember.
Barely scraping 5 feet tall she was an attractive woman no doubt, her wealth emanated from her like a Designer fragrance.
After brief introductions we sat in my office discussing her Ascot requirements and so she became a client of Labello Angelina. She had a great figure to dress and she loved to show it off so I was able to pull out all the stops with my designs....she loved them. Weeks passed by with Liz back and forth the shop regularly, on any one visit she would ring up a minimum £300 in the retail till, any bespoke orders placed which became a 'roll on' order, start another design just as we finished the last, saw deposits

of maybe £600-1000 a time on the bespoke side of the business. Liz was the style of client I needed and many more like her. We got friendly despite my common sense of never mix business with pleasure but I still didn't know much about her or her husband Mr G the Italian Stallion as he liked to think of himself. Seems they were both some bigwigs in a Charity Organisation.

"Can I ask you a favour" Liz asked me one afternoon as we sketched away in my office.

"Sure, go for it!"

"We need a temporary third signatory for the Charity Account whilst our current guy is in hospital, he's seriously ill so it could become a permanent signatory who knows, but it must be a business person or GP or somebody in a position of authority, would you help us out?"

"Yeah, don't see why not, what does it involve?" I asked this whilst still scrawling away at her design on my board.

Liz produced a large brown envelope from her bag, seems she took it as read that I would agree.

"Just being the third authorising signature on any finances or legal documents, a neutral party so to speak as it can't just be me and G being married and all that, here you go, here's the papers for you to read over if you have any doubts." She pushed the papers toward me. Liz knew I rolled from client to client around the clock and had no time to stop to read reams of official papers.

"Ok, cheers I'll take them home, have a look tonight" I carried on sketching.

Liz looked perturbed "Oh, I was hoping you could do it now, we have a 'chaired' meeting tonight and I promised I'd get this sorted. Mr G will give me hell if we can't sort out some of the backlog at the meeting tonight" she looked genuinely disappointed, "...having said that, don't worry. I realise you have to be careful, read what your signing, build a bit of trust in me!"

She made to withdraw the envelope as I grasped at it, here I was making a client who had spent in excess of £30,000 in my business these past few months feel like I didn't trust her.....WHAT THE HELL was I thinking off.

"Hang on, let me just finish this jacket line and I'll sign it."

Liz was exuberant, utterly grateful and whisked the document from the envelope.

Duly signed and her design secured with it's deposit payment, Liz left and work carried on. I saw her a week later for Dinner at theirs, she was back at the shop ten days later choosing the most expensive of the jewellery cabinet items and a pair of £250 sling back heels. Then she and G were away on holiday for a month so all was quiet, Liz certainly commanded the shop whenever she visited with her screechy over polished laugh and Barbie doll antics. I never knew whether she was upper class trying to be 'one of the crowd' or just a plain good old fashioned slapper on times.

I was in the middle of a phone call to suppliers one Thursday afternoon when the front door opened and four very burly, officials walked in asking for me.

I immediately came out to the shop floor with a quizzical look on my face.

The first in line of these gents spoke first, "Mrs Maria Parnell?" I nodded.

"DI Williams, CID is there an office we can have a chat in please?"

I must have looked bewildered because he felt the need to reinforce his introduction with "...we're from the CID Mrs Parnell."

"Yes, yes I realise that, what is the problem?" I then showed them through to my small back office. The four tall gentlemen filled the room with a very dark presence declining my invitation to sit, so I did in my office chair making them seem even more overbearing.

He went on to explain they were investigating a case of Fraudulent use of Charitable Funds held by a Charity for Children who are terminally ill. This was one of several charities providing funds to take children on dream holidays or other such luxuries as a dying wish come true.

I absorbed all this still shaking my head in non comprehension of what any of it had to do with me and my business?

"Do you recognise this?" He handed me a slip of paper which I recognised as one of our till receipts.

"Yes, its a receipt from our till..." I was immediately concerned at this point, what the hell was going on?

"....And this?" He handed me a card terminal receipt also from our shop. "Yes, yes from our card terminal." I confirmed.

"Look what is all this about and why have you got our sales receipts" I asked bluntly and worriedly.

He completely ignored my question as one of the other gents stepped forward, "Could you look at this picture Mrs Parnell please, do you recognise this lady?"

Oh my god it was Liz S!!

"Yes of course I do, she's a good client of mine." My brain was coursing, had they found Liz dead on holiday, had there been an accident and they were trying to identify her...oh dear god, poor Liz.

"...and her name, Mrs Parnell, what name do you know her by please?"

"Mrs Liz S, and I know her husband G as well, oh my god are they both OK, you're worrying me now."

The two men at the back of the room muttered something but I didn't catch it.

"Could I ask you when was the last time you saw Mrs S and where?" he pressed on dismissing any of my questions.

"She was here about three weeks ago to buy some holiday clothing, they went on holiday after that" I answered honestly.

He then held up a document, "Could you confirm that is your signature Mrs Parnell please, and do you recall signing this document?"

Well of course I did and I could suddenly hear pennies falling into place, oh no, oh no, no, no, no please?

"Yes it is and yes I do" I answered again my voice dropping off as I was starting to realise what I was thinking I didn't want to believe.

"Mrs Parnell we have reason to believe Mr and Mrs S are embezzling funds from the Charity Account, they came under suspicion several months ago via other charity workers. Mr S was asked to stand down as Trustee of the Charity and a neutral professional, non relative or charity involved signatory/TRUSTEE found. This appears to be you according to this document?"

My knees were shaking, I felt sick and so very angry as I realised she had duped me into signing as a Trustee for the Charity and thus responsible for decisions and actions regarding its funds. They could tell by my face I was in total shock and disbelief, calling on Charlotte our manageress to fetch me a glass of water.

"Are you arresting me" I asked.

"We need to take a statement from you Mrs Parnell at the moment, we will be back in touch after that."

Yet again he had avoided my question.

I explained how I met her, her visits, her shopping habits, what she'd bought that I could remember and handed over her Design Portfolio of ordered garments. They asked for dates from my diary when she had visited and generally wrapped up the interview.

It seems Liz had been draining money from the charity to fund her lavish lifestyle and fashion obsession spending a good deal of it in my shop then implicating me in proceedings by getting me to sign as a Trustee NOT a general signatory for affairs.

I called Byron who came to the shop immediately, we were completely shell shocked, and Byron was angry with me at being so stupid as to sign anything at all.

I worried myself sick for a few days wondering what was going to happen to me, I tried to get hold of Liz but surprise, surprise incommunicado! We received a call from CID to advise the S's had been arrested and charged and were awaiting a court hearing, I can't remember if that meant they were out on bail or just charged awaiting proceedings. None the less I was pleased to hear they were caught for their despicable and horrendous actions in stealing from children who were dying. We were told I may be called to give evidence and asked to be available as such.

It was the time of year for a fashion trade show so Byron and I decided to take a day out to visit the NEC in Birmingham to re-stock the shop.

The NEC (National Exhibition Centre) was it's usual heaving arena of trade stands and bodies elbow to elbow trying to manoeuvre up and down the aisles.

We'd been there a few hours when Byron popped off to get us some coffees whilst I waited against a wall in one of the Halls so he could easily find me again.

No sooner had I popped my jacket and bag on the floor to lean against the wall I see a face on the opposite side of the Aisle about 20 feet away....it was Mr G with his Charity collection box collecting funds as usual.....I was aghast that they could continue with their thieving activities and realised if he saw me, he'd make for the door so I ducked down grabbing my things and scuttled away from his sight.

I made for the nearest phone kiosk dialling 999 asking to be put through to any CID office urgently. Quickly explaining that I had just seen a man I believed to be under arrest for fraud who was at it again!!!

I was connected somewhere and explained the entire situation as fast as I could giving them the names of the Welsh CID Inspectors with whom I'd been dealing. They told me to stay put and keep G in my sight, I gave them the Hall number and the nearest Trade Stand and nearest entrance door plus my description.

As I made my way back to where I had seen G I could see Byron standing looking around for me.

Pouncing on him from behind, I babbled out "Quick, over here now, he mustn't see us, quick, quick!"

Byron with a coffee in each hand was naturally bewildered, "Who mustn't? What you doing....watch out your spilling the coffee!"

I propelled him to the side of a trade stand where I could still see G.

Once I had explained to Byron, we stood and watched. Byron was as astonished and angry as me that the S's could be such scum as to carry on as they were.

Roughly half an hour went past before I saw two men approach Mr G appearing to ask him questions, he looked shocked and worried....good enough for the bastard I thought. With that Byron and I made our way up the Aisle until we were stood in front of the trio. As they led him away he looked straight at us...his face was a picture of disbelief and temper.

I was never called to give evidence as I heard they pleaded guilty. I neither know or care what happened to them thereafter, but nor did I understand the proceedings in it all The Police seemed disinterested in me after I gave a full statement as to how I had come to sign the document, nor did they pursue any further enquiries however I was just grateful to have escaped any trouble!

Chapter 19

- Can I show you my brush? -

A short while after this my dearest and probably oldest friend, the gorgeous Carolyn Lee suggested we have a night out together to catch up...you know how us ladies do, a few hours debating the grief our 'worst halves' are causing, the price of food shopping and oh yes...SEX, or the lack of it whichever!
We decided on a night out in Cardiff City hitting the Bars and a Club maybe....not really my scene any longer but I was actually looking forward to it and was a great way to wind up another busy week at the Shop.

I think it may have been a Saturday evening, but could have been the Friday...memory remembers events not actual dates more accurately. Dressed as the Lady in Red, in crossover, tie front red dress, heels and the works as regards make up and jewellery, Byron dropped Carolyn and myself into the City Centre for a girls night on the razz!

As ever Carolyn was drop dead stunning in black with her magnificent long blonde locks glistening. This lady is awesome at around 6' tall or more, vivacious, glamorous, loving, witty, fun and entertaining....she brings so much to life itself....but life has dealt her nothing but heartache and misery! In the quarter century plus that I have known her, she has stood rock solid beside her wonderful Son, Harry and suffered many, many, setbacks in life.....none more harrowing than the loss of her new born son Edward. I will never forget that day...or his funeral in the weeks afterwards. My heart bled for you Carolyn.

We pitched up in a Bar City Centre who just happened to have 'Cocktail Hour' going on, buy one get the second free! Without a moments hesitation, Carolyn ordered 3 GLASSES of white wine each...thus 6 glasses each were delivered to our table. Rubbing her hands with glee Carolyn declares "we're good Babe for the next two hours!!" I bow to her fast thinking and money saving prowess......but I hadn't eaten all day and these were not wine glasses.....they were goldfish bowls on stems. At a conservative estimate I am guessing we had 4 bottles of wine in glasses in front of us! After downing the first one in less than minutes Carolyn was on a roll...and I was right there alongside. "I think I need something to eat, I declared, how about one of these steak sandwiches off the menu?"

Duly ordered we ploughed into our respective second glasses whilst awaiting food service.....service was slow!

I was at the end of my third 'gold fish bowl' when I realised a needed a 'bathroom' moment but this involved stairs and as I wound my way up them I felt like my feet were strangely divorced from my body?

Carolyn was totally compos mentus and chatting away assuming intelligent comprehension behind my glazed over eyeballs.

I recall thinking she must have hollow legs and arms sopping up this much booze and given that she was taller than me, must have more capacity to sponge up the liquor?

Around 9.30pm we decided a nightclub was on the cards...at least I think I decided....who knows? I would have agreed to Red Sky at Night means the Zombies are coming!!!

I DO however recall trying the descend the very.....VERY....long sweeping curved staircase from the upstairs bar in this building. I had to strain to focus on every foot tread and I felt like I was on a helter skelter ride. It was a relief to hit the fresh air of the main High Street and....Breeeeeeeeeathe!

Fortunately there was a Nightclub just across the main street and at this time of the evening the nightlife of Cardiff City was starting to kick off. Carolyn strolled, I tottered my way across the pedestrian'ised street to the Club.

Talk about throwing my senses to the wind....the Bar had been storeys UP....the Club was in a BASEMENT, I felt nauseas as my body's gravity field tried to keep pace!

There was a long queue in front of us down the stairwell buying their entrance tickets....

I commented to Carolyn that we appeared to be 'the oldest Hippies in Town' as I kid you not this queue looked like they should be outside the school Tuck Shop not a Night Club in a bustling Capital City??

As I approached the window to buy my ticket....I asked if I could have a Cloakroom Ticket for my coat?

"What?...What did I say....WHAT????"

The Kiosk Attendant looked at me stupid as several kids....AND CAROLYN....fell about laughing.....seems I was a 'throwback Thursday' right that moment to the 'dark ages' of a night on the town!!

Well all I can say, is thank god for Carolyn who was well aversed to club nightlife because as we hit the bar and dance floor, I wondered if they had forgotten to pay the electric bill? I couldn't see my hand in front of my face exacerbated by the steam coming off the dance floor...oh sorry, dry ice? You must remember I have led a sheltered life and did none of this 'clubbing' as a teenager given my circumstances. *(Volume I - The Pre-Dog Year.)*

There was no doubt about it we were both around a decade too old for this Club....but what the hell we got stuck in and wriggled our 'tushes' around the dance floor and before too long a couple of young whipper snappers thought they were 'Buck' enough for the job! In my days you 'jigged' apart unless it was a Waltz....this guy was straight in there with his arms around me in a 'how big are your tits and what's your arse feel like' embrace before I could ask his name?

My face must have said it all as I could see Carolyn looking at me laughing.......

"Gerrof, you cocky little sod" wandered through my mind at the same time as I found myself very grateful to have something to lean on the keep me vertical!

I was so, so, so, so bladdered in every sense.....I couldn't function. Six Gallons of white wine (as it felt at the time) had rendered me almost mute, dysfunctional and yearning for my bed.

The school boy I had been dancing with was most enamoured at his ability to 'pull' a Grannie but conversation was stilted and I struggled to join up any words let alone talk to him...about what for Pete's sake. How were his grades doing? Had he reached puberty as it was hard to tell...? Did his MOTHER know he was OUT???

And so I launched into 'learning mode,' if you can't debate....educate!!!!

Wandering back to where Carolyn was standing with her juvenile dance partner I asked mine..."Would you like to see my brush?"

His face along with Carolyn's crumpled into hysteria....they fell about laughing. What?.....whattttt was so funny?

I had just bought a new Babyliss Hair Brush...a little round gadget that contained a pop up hair brush and a make up mirror....I thought it was very clever and had offered to show him.....this remains a topic of hilarity between Carolyn and I 17 years later!!!!

Suddenly a couple in the corner of the Club caught my eye....Oh my God, were they doing what I think they were doing? Oh yes indeedy they were! No shame....my mouth was wide open...."Carolyn" I spluttered...."Are they...? She smiled and patted me on the shoulder...."of course Hun" and threw back her head laughing, her eyes sparkling and totally amused at my ignorant innocence.

As the night drew to an end and the club started to evacuate, we made our way back up the Helter Skelter staircase to the exit where we hoped we could find a Taxi home. Was going to be no cheap trip as we both lived some 15 miles outside of the City but what the hell, it was a night out together.

The usual piranha attack on the lined up Taxi Rank ensued until finally we acquired a less than happy driver to see two drunk, giggling women who lived so FAR AWAY he'd lose more revenue in one night on one long haul journey than six short hops around the City!!

We clambered in and gave directions to home...go James, go!

The journey was some 45 minutes long during which I engaged the driver in professional business dialogue as to how he could 'grow' his taxi business, he accommodated my ramblings in a gentlemanly manner.

Being the more sober of the both of us, Carolyn decided I was to be dropped home first....I live in the middle of rural 'nowhere' so the driver was already pissed off! Pulling up outside the Cottage I paid my fair and responsibly alerted him to the fact he needed to get his cab roof fixed....he looked at me quizzically for a split second before clamping his hand to his forehead. "Your woof iz leaking!" I defiantly announced as he realised I had pee'd myself on the way home without even realising it!!!!!

Waving them off with a limp wrist and a dribbling smile I made my way to the front door.... I couldn't even find the bloody key on the key ring let alone the key hole! There are NO street lights where I live....I could barely see my hand in front of me. NO CORRECTION...I couldn't see bugger all in front of me! When suddenly the door flew open and I fell in my knees in the hallway!

Byron was less than happy!

"Ahhhh Jesus M, you're pissed!" he declared.

How observant my man, I thought but could never have said same as my lips appeared not to be working?

He propelled me up another 'helter skelter staircase' I felt like I was going up and down like a bloody yo-yo, and dumped me in frustration on the bathroom floor. "If you are going to puke...do it in the bath, can you hear me?" He tapped me on the head....it sounded like a bomb went off!

"I'll go lock up!"

As I sat on the floor feeling rather wet around the nether regions who should come wandering up the stairs but my beloved Rupert cat. In a split second I decided he looked dirty...no problemo!!!

I filled the Bidet with water and in very jerky actions deposited him for a scrub.....he was such a docile little soul, staring at me as if to ask "Why I do be needing this watery treatment at 2am in the morning Mummy?"

The next thing I heard was Byron thundering up the stairs "For fucks sake M....!" He grabbed Rupert who was never so glad than to see his Dad and belted for the cat flap! Oblivious to my wrong doings I sat cross legged on the floor....in frustration Byron threw a quilt over me and left me there to sober up. I have never felt so ill in all my life as I did in the four days that ensued.

Life carried on that year much as normal at the shop and as ever I battled to balance cash flow, income and expenditure. Christmas loomed and I made plans for our festive period shutdown.

We had a fabulous restaurant right next door to the shop, we had dined there often with one of my favourite deserts on their menu being their luxury Brandy Custard Bread & Butter Pudding. I asked if the Chef would make me a catering tray size of this so I could have it for our Christmas desert at home, freezing down the remainder.

Our last day in work was the 23rd December with Byron's office party that same afternoon, I agreed to close up around 4pm, collect him from his staff party and collect my restaurant pudding on the way home.

As I pulled up outside the pub I could see Byron waiting in the doorway trying to keep dry as the weather had turned bitterly cold, wind and heavy rain. He pottered out toward the car and I instantly knew he was wrecked in every sense, happy, drunk and in high spirits....in more ways than one as the Vodka shots hadn't helped!

I sighed heavily, happy that he had enjoyed a good time but I was tired, trying to get everything done before Christmas Day, silly really but it's a time of year I love and I like everything just so.

Plopping through the door into the passenger seat, his eyes were heavy as is usual when one is bladdered...grinning from ear to ear he bent forward to kiss me muttering "G,me kiss, I loves you....I dooo" and then in an attempt to appear sober he engaged in suspect coherent dialogue!!! "Iss bin offul day hasn't it? Have you been wet Babee, I don't wants you to be wet in all thus rain, you lissnin'?

Yup I'm listening to all this drivel Hun, I smiled at him.

"Uss good in we, we're good in we babe?"

Again I confirmed Yup, we're good babe, promise.

"Thass good in it? Cuz I dun no where I'd be wivout you...you are my world, you know you iz my world don't you....you lissnin?"

I had travelled some 10 miles by now, mentally planning when to make the stuffing for the bird and should I keep Byron out in the driveway for ten minutes to give him time to puke up and save the carpets??

Yup...I'm listening Hun, I confirmed once again.

"Now YOU need to listen OK....Byron....Byron?"

"Whaa Babe, I lissnin...."

" I'm just stopping by the shop OK, I need to pick something up, you stay in the car and wait...YES!" It wasn't so much a request but a demand in my voice.

"Woff we gotta get Babe....?"

"Never you mind, it's a surprise BUT don't get out of the car OK?"

"Hokay, I wait in the car ...?"

"YES!"

"Hokay, I wull!"

Knowing full well he wouldn't have a clue which door I'd gone through I headed into the Restaurant and collected what looked like a 20 inch long catering tray of pudding FRESH from the oven!!!!

Back at the car I opened the passenger door to a nodding, sleepy Byron.

"Here Hun, can you hold this CAREFULLY on your lap whilst we drive home...please?"

"Woss it?"

"It's our Christmas day special pudding, and it's still a bit warm so put this towel on your lap and hold the handles with some of the towel, keep the tin straight...yes?"

"Hokay..."

I duly placed the cargo on his lap and we headed for home.

100 yards from the Restaurant I turned left.....so did Byron and the pudding!

A quarter mile on I took the third exit right off the roundabout.....so did Byron and the pudding!!

The best was to come.

As I entered our winding three miles of country lane with it's pot holes and sharp bends I witnessed copious amounts of my pudding slopping down his legs, into the foot well of the car and into the door pocket......my lovely pudding had about a bowl full left in the tin! I had paid £38 for this pudding....I had a retail portion at £5.95 left!!!

Less than happy I arrive home the rain is bucketing down the wind is howling a gale, it's around 6.30pm and pitch black in the lanes at the Cottage.

"WAIT THERE, do not move whilst I go put some lights on in the house" I instructed.

"My legs are warm....?" he muttered sleepily.

As my top lip curled, be grateful it's just your legs I thought to myself unkindly.

At the time we had no exterior lighting installed at home and the driveway to the Cottage was an uneven surface plus down some steps to the kitchen entrance. I navigated in the dark on auto pilot soaked by the rain as I put my key in the door.

Flicking the light switch on in the kitchen I was alerted immediately to the fact we had a 'power out' electricity was off no doubt due to the high winds. I recall the kitchen stank when I opened the door and I could hear my cats scrabbling around....more concerned for Byron I headed back to the car to drag him out!

By now he was chin on chest snoring with the pudding hanging down the side of his leg. I grabbed the tray and a fist full of his clothing easing him out of the seat.

"Hold this and hang on to me, we've got no power so I'll get you into the house OK and then I'll sort it out."

Byron stumbled alongside me to the kitchen, pudding in hand.

I made a grab for the flashlight we keep on the shelf as we entered....

"Phooooooo, woss that stink?" Byron declared.

"I don't know Hun, look pick your foot up...that's it, up the step, you OK?"

As I switched on the powerful flash light I was speechless, horrified and aghast all in one hit!

My kitchen looked like a cesspit had been emptied into it....my cats were all clamouring up high on shelves and work surfaces......whilst a fighting ferret careered around my kitchen having shit and pee'd EVERYWHERE in it's hunt for my cats!!!

HOW THE FUCK did a ferret get in my kitchen?????

I dropped Byron who sank like a brick falling into what was left of the Christmas Pudding! Oh my god, what to do next, I couldn't see much other than the light of the torch.....have you ever tried to catch a Ferret single handed in the dark?
I did.

I was covered in it's excrement and urine by the time I had grappled around the kitchen floor but caught the little beggar in a large towel and bundled it into a laundry basket holding it down hard with my hand.

I left Byron where he was, made my way to the shed and grabbed the cat box, again in the dark I plunged the poor ferret into the carrier and slammed the door.

OK I thought, one problem down back to the Cottage....I dragged Byron up who by now was fast asleep on the kitchen floor, plonked him in the chair and cleaned up the mess in the kitchen, bleaching everything in sight. By the time I had fed the cats and checked them all over for any ferret injury it was 10pm. I put the ferret in the car and headed for the emergency vet some 20 miles away who thankfully agreed to take the creature which was in fact a 'Gill' and pregnant!!! Wouldn't you just know it.....as my life goes.

Back home and by now it was 12.30am I was absolutely dropping on my feet and starving. I flopped into bed and collapsed listening to Byron's dulcet snoring.

- Chapter 20 -

- *A Holiday like no other.... crash landing and BOOM!* -

We decided we were well overdue for a much needed holiday so I started making plans for 10 days in Cyprus, I couldn't wait to get away from all the strains of business and the trouble that seems to follow me through my life.

Once I had organised for suitable home sitting for the fur babes, I started to unwind a bit looking forward to the imminent holiday. We arrived in Paphos self catering and the Apartment was average, nothing to dislike for what we'd paid and all amenities on hand. We were both looking forward to a damned good rest and warm our bones.
As ever the first few days were spent sussing out our surroundings and locating beaches which were close by.....but the nights were a bit of a problem!
It seemed we had moved in alongside Mr Shifter himself because bang on 2am every morning, the guy in the next door apartment which was owner occupied, would move all his furniture around, dragging tables and chairs across tiled floors so you can imagine the cacophony. We never saw him or indeed knew if that was what he was doing but it certainly sounded like it. It interrupted our sleep every night and I took to catching extra Z's on the beach by day to recover my rest.

Cyprus was an old haunt of Byron's having been stationed in Nicosia when in the RAF so he wanted naturally to visit a few old memories and I thoroughly enjoyed being shown places where my man had stood and walked years before me. Cyprus was also where Byron encouraged me to cash in my life insurance if I had any when he insisted I'd love to paraglide!

The sand was too hot to stand on, I was toasting a lovely shade of golden brown when the boy came along the beach selling rides. "Shall I?" I looked at Byron. I'd been watching the other people taking off and it looked fairly easy and quite exhilarating.

"Why not, he said, you should always try something new in life and you've always wanted to go up in a hot air balloon."

"Yeah I know but I'd be standing in something, what if I fall out of the harness, their miles out look, I can't swim."

"You're not going to fall out of the harness, they wouldn't do it if it wasn't safe" he replied from under his sun hat.

We duly bought a ride and turned up for my turn.....yeah safe, my arse!!!!

A rather good looking young man strapped me into a multi harness, yanking it between my legs rather intimately I felt, he laughed when I squeaked. Chest buckles tightened and a brief explanation in Cypriot as too pull on this and yank on that when we shout were given....I think? I didn't understand a bloody word..... I was encouraged to take a few steps along the beach so that the boat could take up the line slack and gently pull me up into the air when the lines tightened.

The speed boat pulled off, I'd barely walked three steps when I was violently yanked into the water feeling like my chest had been ripped from my body.....I screamed as my feet dunked up and down in the sea as the wind started to elevate my chute.....I rose higher and higher.....the beach was far away on the horizon with pin head people running along it. Then I started dropping fast as the wind dropped, the boat took off even faster to gain wind speed under the chute....I rose up and up and up and up until I was virtually vertical above the boat. The experience was awesome, it was silent but for the rush of the wind, the sensation of floating through the air was incredible, to be at such height when I'm terrified of them was unbelievable. All to soon the ride was over and the boat headed for shore. I looked down at the man on the boat who was yelling to me and demonstrating something I needed to do with my arms...he pointed to the beach shouting and gesticulating "pull, pull" with his right arm....then the same again with his left arm. I figured out he was trying to tell me when we get to the beach pull on the cords.....why? OK I thought...here we go.

As the boat slowed and killed it's engine I floated over the beach speeding toward where I could see Byron and the original guy who strapped me in....they were jumping up and down yelling something. I pulled on the line with my right arm and dropped abruptly by many feet instantly, as well as veering violently to the right, it frightened the crap out of me....they were getting closer and closer, I yanked hard on the left line and dropped like a brick again slewing to the left, I felt like a rag doll suspended on puppet strings. Now suspended about 20 feet above the beach and heading straight for Byron who was by now looking as worried as the Ride Owner I heard voices on the wind...."Pull.....pull....Maria puuuuuulllll" I yanked hard again on both lines assuming this would at least keep me heading straight.....I plummeted to the sand hitting it running faster than the terrain would allow, trying to keep my balance as I stumbled on several feet dragging the chute which two guys had caught and were running along with behind me. I finally stopped as I hit the Ride owner who caught me in his arms. I was hyperventilating, spluttering and shaking like a leaf.....they were all laughing, Byron jogged over, "you Ok was that fun" he asked beaming a grin....had he been within arms reach whilst I fought like a Tigress to get out of the Harness I would have smacked his fucking lights out!! I spent the rest of the day rearranging my nervous system and it's tattered remnants back in place vowing never to try anything new ever again.

The holiday was lovely in all other respects and we enjoyed favourite Bars and restaurants, I faxed home twice asking Charlotte if all was Ok at the Shop, were the cats OK, she assured me they were. We finished up the holiday and made our way home feeling much more relaxed and ready to face work again.

Two weeks back my newly formed Directors, Colin and David delivered their Invoice for the work refurbishing the Shop. Although we'd been there quite a while they hadn't rushed to issue their bill and briefly mentioned it at quarterly meetings that were held, no urgency they said....we know where you are.

I opened it expecting to see just over the original £8,500 they quoted as I'd asked for a few extras. What I saw typed on the final balance line caused me to jump up from my chair....no way.....no damned way could it be that! I stared at the invoice like it had burned my fingers....£37,629 and some odd pence!!! I sat down, then stood back up I couldn't take it in....there must be some mistake surely....they'd invoiced the wrong bill to me obviously, I grabbed the phone to call Colin.

"Colin, what's this invoice Hun, you've billed me by mistake for some other job yes?" I queried trying to keep my voice level.

"No Maria, that's our charge for the work" he replied calm as a cucumber.

My brain was reeling...."No way Colin, you quoted £8.5K remember..?" I was utterly confused.

He continued to confirm it was the correct invoice for works and asked when we could pay.

"Pay, pay? You're joking aren't you, I spluttered, you know from the last quarterly meeting what the books look like...what's your game Colin what's going on?" I demanded.

He was a cool cookie on the end of the phone calling for another meeting to discuss the invoice, I agreed for the following lunchtime and slammed the phone down.

I called Byron who was dumbstruck, he came straight to the shop and between Adrienne, my Production Director by then, and myself we sat down to try and work out what the hell was being charged for. The invoice was for total work, Byron said we needed to demand a breakdown for each and every service, item and materials this being the only way we could get to the bottom of how they had inflated their original quote that we accepted in good faith.

The following day was a horrible experience as we arrived at Colin's premises. He and David had laid out their office in such a seating fashion that Adrienne, Byron and I were seated in front of their office desk on hardback chairs with them sitting behind their desk in joint leather seats...we were very much the naughty kids before the headmaster status, what happened to around a meeting table as equals, it was tactical to make us feel bad.

I was furious inwardly that they could treat us in such a manner....I opened the meeting presenting their invoice on the desk asking them to explain what had gone wrong and where this extortionate figure came from. They stood their ground before David piped up. David was a clone of Ian McShane (the TV character Lovejoy) to look at but nowhere near as nice in character.

"I hear you've been on holiday to Cyprus" he spat out, then glancing at Byron's wrist watch which looked expensive but was a 40th birthday present from his parents and Sister, he continued "....and that looks expensive doesn't it, so how come you can't pay our invoice?"

We were speechless, Byron tried to lead the meeting sensibly and maturely on a business level but they wanted none of it, although Colin kept quiet most of the time permitting David to be the mouthpiece, they wanted an argument and as my temper got the better of me they got one.

We ranted and raved back and forth until it was clear to me we were being ripped off somehow, they refused to notate every whip stitch on the bill declaring I couldn't possibly have believed all that work would have taken £8,500. I rallied that we would have expected to be advised at each stage of extra costs and the extras COULD never have cost that much. It was futile, we were bashing our head in a brick wall as they declared they would sue us for non payment if not settled in 30 days.

A lady told me once that you are only ever 30 days from bankruptcy if you cannot pay your bills in business...and she's right. Any Invoice that a trading business cannot pay on demand renders them insolvent.... I was going under, stitched up by two people I had taken into the business in good faith as investors. I tried again....surely most of this Invoice could be deemed their investment and permit me to pay off the balance but again this was refused.

The real truth of the matter was, unbeknown to us, that their own business was going under and they needed to make their outstanding invoices figure owed to their business as high as possible to reduce their liability in the eyes of the Official Receiver, I was but a pawn in their crooked business.

With nothing in writing to prove I hadn't agreed to extra costs it was their word against mine, I had been gullible and learned a very hard lesson based on being too trusting. And so we had crash landed back from Holiday quite literally..... Labello Angelina was officially dead in the water....BOOM, just like that!!

Chapter 21

- *Never burn your bridges, past* -

We left Colin and David's office that day in a mental state of despair. I couldn't believe I had been so stupid as to trust this pair of wasters and that there was nothing I could do legally to disprove their claims as to their final Invoice. Of course there were extras, there always are in any refurb' or re-build, hidden costs, unseen problems that need repairing along the way but I sure as hell knew that mine had not amounted to such a huge amount of money. I had learned my lesson the hard way, document, notate and put absolutely everything in writing, it was now too late as Colin's company was in the hands of Companies House, I was simply part of his 'car wreck!'

As if I didn't have enough to cope with a week later the Bank called to say they were not prepared to facilitate our business overdraft further unless we could make an immediate and significant credit against it. If I couldn't they would call in their overdraft, this meant pay on demand or go bust!

I remember asking the Bank Manager to give me the afternoon to evaluate what could be done but in my heart I knew immediately I was finished in business. I had made some stupid and innocent mistakes along the pathway of making a career for myself, I had trusted people who were not worthy of the spit off my tongue, but I had made those decisions and I had to live with them. I needed to stand and fight or roll over and die. I wasn't ready to die........

I called Byron at work and simply said "It's over, we're finished!" Any other husband may have crumbled alongside me but not Byron. He was at the shop within the hour as I switched off the lights and locked the door to any day's trading ever again.
I mounted the staircase to the sewing workroom with my heart in pieces, these ladies had given their best and all to me and now I was about to tell them they were

unemployed as of right this minute with no pay off or compensation. Their faces haunt me as I explained what had gone wrong and why and as such we were insolvent. They packed up their personal belongings and filed past me to leave for good, half in pity the other half in anger for their own survival. I understood but could do or say nothing....I felt less than shit beneath their shoes, I had let them down.

With the building empty and quiet I could finally think straight and I knew that to enter Labello Angelina into Liquidation was the only way forward for the moment. As such I picked up the phone to Peter, I knew that his stock and work in progress CMT would be seized by the Liquidators if I didn't act fast. My actions were less than legal at that point but I didn't want to drag him and his wife into my pit of misery. If I could get his remaining stock out of the building he wouldn't lose anywhere near as much as I was about to.

I dialled his number with tears rolling down my face and explained as best I could what had happened and why. Amazingly he wasn't angry but understandably frantic to save his investment of stock already manufactured, fabrics and pattern blocks. He told me he would be with me that afternoon to collect his goods.....then he thanked me for alerting him and saving his loss before I spoke to legal bodies. At 3pm that day Peter arrived with a large white van and cleared his goods....he was calm and sympathetic but I was in pieces.

Liquidation is a soulless, heartless and dignity stripping procedure, difficult to live through and stressful to the point of nervous breakdown, at least for me it was.

Meetings with our company solicitor and accountants provided much needed advice and guidance. As a result of one of these meetings I decided I wasn't ready to die in business and my true Scorpio character and strength surfaced, I couldn't live with so many Brides and clients being let down and suffering financial losses as a result of my gullibility and lack of business acumen. I was NOT going to let these people down no matter what I had to do if it were within my power.

I made an offer of £20 to the Official Receiver for my own Order Book, I would buy back my own work in progress and continue with this work, sewing from home in my front bedroom.....exactly where I'd started many years before!

I would have to establish myself under a different name to trade and would need to contact all the people/clients involved.....the latter proved painful and very humiliating.

The processes of going into Liquidation are extremely traumatic if you have any sense of decency about you. I DO....and so I suffered painfully as white vans turned up to strip my beautiful shop of it's fixtures and fittings, throwing expensive garments into black bin liners and generally annihilating my business. Friends and close clients came to help support me and Byron, some couldn't see the big picture and eagerly looked to cash in on my misfortune...I'm sorry but that's how it felt as they asked to buy goods from the shop at knocked down prices, I maintained an emotional professionalism but wanted to physically throw them out for their lack of respect and compassion under the circumstances. The shop was closed and stripped within three days flat...Labello Angelina no longer existed.

Once all legal confirmations were agreed I sat at my dining table at home one evening within days of our crash with the telephone in front of me and a good number of client portfolios. Calling these customers and speaking with both them or their parents was one of the most difficult things I have ever had to do in my life. Explaining what had happened, advising our business had gone bust generally left them screaming abuse and offensive comments BEFORE I could even begin to explain I had no intention of letting them down or letting them lose their money. Eventually and painfully slowly I contacted our entire order book and organised a way forward out of this mess ensuring they would not lose their wedding gowns/or other garments or indeed their money providing they could stay calm and trust me to stand by my word. It was tough going but I never failed any single one of them.

In the weeks shortly after, and once I had calmed my clients sufficiently to move forward with me I set about establishing a means of manufacturing our order book.

I have nothing but utmost respect and pride in Adrienne, my previous Production Director who stood by my side throughout. She was a matter of fact type of character and I will always be deeply indebted to her for storing tens of bolts of fabrics at her home, working from her dining table as did I and attending home fittings with clients alongside me. Together we completed every single order that was on my order book at the time we went bust....on time!

Once the initial panic was over, life settled down a little although my pride and emotions had taken a Tsunami battering. I was drained, exhausted and suffering from depression although at that time I did not know this.

Day after day Adrienne and I battled on, either at her home or in my front bedroom and attending each client at their home for fittings and deliveries in the absence of a business premises.

It was in my front bedroom one morning as we were about to start sewing that I opened my mail from the previous day. Adrienne was busy working on a Basque bodice for a wedding gown as I casually flipped open invoices from suppliers, junk mail and then....a letter addressed simply to 'Maria' at my home address.

I cocked an eyebrow as I ripped open the envelope expecting to see an enquiry or something from someone who didn't know my surname? It read...

"ask your husband about Sue in Trustmark Ltd, think you're happily married do you, ask him about last Wednesday?"

In one sweep of the letter's contents my blood drained from my body...I felt nauseas and started to shake, what the hell was this about? Was Byron having an affair and worst still with a woman I knew in the Village? I bought stationery from the shop regularly. Adrienne caught sight of my face, "what, what's wrong?" she asked. I handed her the letter to read as I sank into a nearby chair.

As ever Adrienne was in practical mode whilst I mentally agonised over Byron and 'Sue!'

"Don't be so stupid, Adrienne yelled across the room, he wouldn't, not after all you've been through!"

My brain was whirling, was this payback? My just deserves for what he thought had gone on between me and that idiot Paul? Who the fuck sent the letter....why now amidst all this heartache and stress of losing the business.

BINGO!! As my brain stepped up a cog, but that's exactly why isn't it, drive the knife in harder, score maximum pain....but was it true? I felt ripped apart and raw.

I knew Byron was at his Office in Newport 35 miles away that day, I looked at Adrienne and she nodded...."Go, do what you have to BUT you're wrong I warn you. He wouldn't, I really don't think he would..." her words echoed in my brain as I hit the motorway gliding off the slip road at 80mph in the lemon peril!

I arrived at his offices shaking and tearful, I had a lump in my throat that I couldn't breath past let alone swallow. Entering the oh so familiar showroom doors from years before when I'd worked there, a young Receptionist enquired if she could help. "I'm Byron Parnell's wife, he's upstairs, yes?" I flung the comment at her like a grenade. Stomping up the old 'family staircase' I made my way to the sales office. Nothing had changed in all the years I'd been gone....my eyes were burning with the need to cry....but I needed to see his face on presentation of the letter, I knew I would know instinctively by his expression. We always told each other from day one....if ever there's someone else, just tell me, do the right thing by one another, never lie!
This was his moment to speak the truth....or lie!

I burst though his office door, he was chatting to Andrew and Keith. He looked shocked to see me and immediately saw my distressed manner. I stepped back and made my way to the smaller office that was empty and Byron followed. As he entered the room he spoke "They've come for the Cottage, right?" It was always a probability that the Liquidator could come after any assets and this is what Byron thought had happened.

I handed him the letter. Bemused he opened it and started reading.

His face was blank, he'd make a world class poker player if he was screwing with me I thought.

"Who's Sue? You don't believe this surely?" He looked at me with utter bewilderment. "I don't know what to believe" I spluttered as finally my emotions gave way to a flood gate of tears.

I positively shook from head to toe, I couldn't gain control of my emotions or composure, this was the LAST thing on earth I needed to have to cope with. Byron didn't attempt to embrace me or comfort me, I think he realised I would have recoiled in self preservation or punched him...."it's not true M, I don't know what this is about I promise!" I stared hard into his eyes and I believed...oh god I so needed to believe. He made me a coffee, just as he did all those years before after the 'Phil attack,' I calmed down sufficiently to drive home. I couldn't believe how some sad imbecile out there wanted to add to the pain and trauma I had suffered in the past weeks by making false accusations against my husband....at least I prayed that's what they were? Byron struggled to give me the benefit of the doubt over Paul and I was innocent....was Byron?

To this day we still don't know who sent the letter, we moved on, trusting in each other to survive all that was being thrown at us.

I contacted the Model House in Llantrisant, it felt like going backwards but sometimes you have to re-group to move forward. I was immediately accepted for a Studio and promptly set about moving my business back to a premises away from home. Studio 13 had been my original but Studio 12 was available....it felt very weird moving into the room next door!

Once again up and running with Adrienne continuing to work from home this time which suited her and the children better, I renamed the business 'Amara M Couture' something I dreamed up at the time?

Within six months of the Liquidation I had the order book back up to £80,000 turnover and on target to finish the accounting year around £100K....and that was with much lower overheads and just me and Adrienne back to back.

Life was as busy as ever and I worked to live....not lived to work! I was never home before 9pm at night and trebled up on evening gown fitting appointments for Brides after work. Byron kept our home running and we barely saw each other.

It was 1999, I was 39 years old and finally I felt in control of my destiny, older, wiser and so much more experienced in business.

WRONG!

Chapter 22

- *'Insuring'....it will be the end!* -

With a fairly healthy order book and having honoured all my orders throughout the devastation of losing the shop, life in the Fashion Designer trade carried on pretty much as normal. Adrienne was my pillar of support and I will never deny her this accolade...wherever in the world she resides nowadays.

We liaised at the Studio in the Model House, Llantrisant two maybe three times a week to update and progress the orders. A couple of months on the Potter's Studio on the opposite side of the same floor in the Model House became available. It was much larger and a little more in rent....but I went for it and we moved across the corridor. The new space gave me chance to incorporate a fitting room, an office and self contained kitchen....it was just perfect.

Wedding Fayre's abounded, orders flourished and generally the business found solid ground and was growing, I was never at home....always working but we were back on even ground financially. I regretted my past mistakes but what was done was history....time to move on!

A lovely Bride called Heather came my way and her fittings were a delight as she was so appreciative and understanding of the amount of work it takes to produce a 'Bespoke Wedding Gown.' Ultimately I hand sewed 1800 individual Swarovski Crystals onto the bodice of her gown. Her husband to be was Mark...he was Nigerian and a real handsome dude!
Heather arrived for her final fitting and all was going well until she realised she had left her bridal shoes in the car...."give me the keys, I'll go get them" I offered as I needed an accurate hemline. "No it's OK, Mark is waiting for me...I'll call him and he can bring the shoes up" Heather advised. Great, off we go then I thought. Heather called Mark

on his mobile giving strict instructions he was NOT to enter the Studio as she was in her bridal attire. We both awaited his knock at the door which came less than five minutes later.

I opened the Studio door and was confronted with a towering figure of a man, black and probably 6 feet 5 inches tall....he wore the most vibrant violet coloured shirt beneath his two piece suit...I was knocked out with the colour and commented accordingly......but it came out all wrong!!!

"Ahhh shoes.....Oh Mark, your... my gosh what a fabulous colour!" The colour of the shirt took my breath away.

He looked at me for a second deciding whether I was racist or stupid.

"Thanks....I was born this colour, good to know you approve?"

His answer decked me where I stood...I spluttered my explanation but he was much too much of a gentleman and forgave me instantly all faux pas.

Business soldiered on.....life was calm for a moment and then the 26th May 2000 at 6.22am arrived!

Our home landline was ringing? Nobody ever called us at this time of the morning??

I rushed from bed wondering if it was Byron's children in trouble or his parents, or what?

All I heard as I answered was Jenny's voice, the Manager of the Model House.

"Maria, I'm sorry but your studio is flooded, come as quick as you can."

She hung up leaving me reeling at the thought of the consequences, I had bolts of expensive fabric scattered around the Studio and above all at least 3 computerised sewing machines stored on the floor under the front cutting bench....oh my god....Noooooooooo!!!

I rushed from the cottage in my nightwear and headed for the Model House hoping her voice had not conveyed the true levity of the problem.

As I pulled into Llantrisant Village I could see the neon flashing blue lights of the Fire Appliances in attendance...all 3 of them! My heart sank as I realised the seriousness of the situation. I tried to access the building via the stairwell but the water was cascading down, the lift/elevator was a no go zone!

Fire crew were everywhere as I finally made it to the third floor of the building and my Studio. My client sofa was floating in the corridor, the multi concertina doors to my Studio had been flung open in efforts to release the water, my sewing machines were six inches under water and bolts of fabric floated around the studio and corridor, work in progress gowns along with completed wedding gown orders had been flung into the water whilst the fire crew took control of the situation gaining access to doors .....I took one look at the devastation and in a split second realised I was FINISHED in the fashion business for good!

I broke down sobbing....too soon after the liquidation I knew I could never work fast enough to recover from this event. I heard and listened to the platitudes from fellow studio owners.....you can do it Maria, come on....you know this won't beat you....but it did!

The Model House for the want of a better description was Governed by a bunch of local Council crooks, in my personal opinion! Each Studio needed to have its own business insurance, which I had!

But the facts are that the main and decrepit water pipe to the building entering at 3rd floor level so I am led to believe had rotted....thus on the third floor I sustained the impossible....a flood! Three business went to the wall as a result of the Model House and local Rhondda Cynon Taff Council's cover up and denial that it was their buildings faulty plumbing. Thanks a bunch RCT Council, you killed me off entirely!

The following days were a blur as I contacted Brides and Mother of the Brides explaining we were in crisis management of their orders, please stay calm we will not let you down. I and Byron, Adrienne and her family moved everything we could salvage back to my cottage and her home to maintain production.....I felt numb that I could be once again thrust into such a desperate situation?

I called the insurers and all the usual wheels were set in motion for financial settlement of my claim for business losses. The Loss Adjustor arrived, did his bit and extended an immediate £5000 pay out to assist continued production, our business Bank were candyfloss sickeningly helpful...."How much do you need Maria? Of course we can treble the overdraft facility until you can settle with the insurers." Suppliers were similarly helpful extending lines of credit that would be settled by the insurers final settlement for damages. Except they weren't!

For the following eight months whilst Adrienne and I battled to re-fit the Studio whilst sewing around the clock to meet wedding deadlines and continue to attend Bridal Fayres to ensure new business orders came in, neither of us saw our bed at all in a 24 hour period on many occasions! Whilst Byron understood why and supported me all the way, Adrienne's husband and children became bitterly resentful of her involvement in this Titanic of a business that I supposedly ran. I can't say I blamed them but I also hadn't looked for the trouble that beset me and my business.

Deeply in debt to the bank by over £20,000 on the overdraft, unable to work fast enough to keep up with existing remake of orders and new orders arriving and also unable to afford to employ any new staff....we were paddling like a baby in a swimming pool to stay afloat!

Once again we completed all the existing order book on time for all weddings, by the skin of our teeth. We were working around the clock and seven days a week.

One poor bride had her wedding gown, that she hadn't seen since final fitting some weeks before, delivered to her on the wedding morning in the Vestry of the Church.

I will never be able to thank her enough for her faith and trust in me. Julia said "Maria, if you tell me it will be there on the morning, I know it will." With which she hugged and kissed me. How she must have felt leaving for the Church that morning praying I would be in the Vestry with her gown so she could marry in resplendent glory is beyond me. Her face lit up as she entered, we both had a weep and I promptly got her dressed and decked out in all her finery. Julia walked up the Aisle a stunningly beautiful bride pausing just once to look back to the Vestry door at me peeping out, she winked and blew me a kiss.

Invoices were piling in from suppliers, some of these top designer silks and fabrics costing £000's a metre. Rent was overdue by some five months on the Studio, utility bills wracking up. I started 'cash flowing' on my personal credit cards as you do when you are passionate about saving something. I was wrong to do so.

Before too long Amara M was some £90,000 in debt and STILL awaiting £65,000 in settlement from the Insurers who were questioning every aspect of the claim. I had an order book of £30,000, it was going to be tight but I could survive this catastrophe by just £5K if I was lucky.

The letter arrived on a Friday, I opened it that evening as most people do when they return from work. No chance over a weekend to be able to deal with the offices of the insurers who would be closed.....again it's a tactic of theirs. They know when they deliver bad news you will hit the 'phone line screaming, a weekend to cool your heels makes the Monday morning discussions less explosive, Banks operate on the same policy.

It read:-

"Dear Mrs Parnell
In reference to blah, blah...
We have now completed all our investigations with regard to the claim incident dated blah, blah. Regrettably this has been a lengthy enquiry due to the fact we have been dealing with your local Council Offices who have been less than prompt with their replies to our correspondence.

(Sure they have...like 8 months slow!!) I thought. The letter continued;

XYZ Insurers will issue payment direct to your bank in full and final settlement of this claim in the sum of £3,143.

Thank you for insuring your business through XYZ Insurance.

Yours blah, blah."

I looked at the figure twice, I re-read the letter what there was of it. NO, no, no, no, no, this cannot be? I was expecting in the region of at least £60,000. Oh my God ...NO!!!!!!
I could do nothing over the weekend, I felt like I had been shot at point blank range.
I said nothing to Byron who I knew could take no more....he quizzed me all weekend as to my mood and stress level accusing my monthly PMT symptoms....I wished!

On the Monday I rose with a heavy heart and an aching brain, I was desperate to hear some form of explanation on the telephone. I called the Insurers and this is what I discovered........
My sewing machines were £2,500 a piece and 3 of them had been written off.
Materials and stock to the tune of £37,000 or thereabouts was ruined, refurbishment of my water damaged studio had cost in the region of £6,000, loss of earnings amounted to the rest of my claim.
However!
In moving my business operation back to mine and Adrienne's home to maintain production across our dining tables so that we would not have to abort or renege on any of our existing orders at the time of the flood, I had breached my terms of agreement with the Insurers?
How so?
They declared that whilst they could understand that I did such in honourable manner so as not to let my clients down. I had in fact moved a commercial business covered by commercial insurance to a domestic premises thus null and voiding my contract!
They advised that under the terms of their agreement I should have sought 'like for

like' temporary premises from which to continue trading for which the insurers would have met the cost of rental.

I was completely and utterly devastated!

Nobody, not even the Loss Adjustor had advised me of this fact, I trawled through my Insurance Policy only to find many, many pages in there was a Clause legally and confusingly worded but indicating that any business suffering losses affecting it's production/services/products/trading terms should seek suitable means of servicing it's business/orders/products/trading terms...or words to that effect?

As far as I was concerned, I HAD! I moved the business to the most immediate means of a 'work place!' I thought I had acted responsibly and sensibly.

I broke the news to Byron who by now was simply punch drunk with it all. I felt like I had let him and our life down so badly.

Over the coming weeks I wrote letter after letter of appeal against their decision to no avail, I fought my corner valiantly, they conceded some points such as understanding in my panic and desperation to continue trading I may have misunderstood what I was advised....NO, I was NOT advised anything of the sort about moving production to a 'like for like' premises, end of! They increased their settlement figure marginally for the 'overlooked' loss of computer equipment that I had forgotten was stored under the work benches, but that was it, take it or leave it.

It was September 2000, it was a Thursday, I am a Thursday born child. Thursday's child has far to go......!

I awoke that morning knowing what fate lay ahead of me, I had ripped my brain apart all night fighting to find solid ground, a pathway forward, a means of rising from this catastrophic situation like a phoenix from the fire. But the truth kept circling around the hamster wheel in my head right back at me....YOU ARE FINISHED, accept it, deal with it, move on! My era in fashion was dead, I was petrified of what lay ahead, I had been out of the workplace for so long, we had no money in the bank other than Byron's salary and I knew I was facing the worst of all ultimatums....I had to declare myself personally Bankrupt.

- Chapter 23 -

- To Die a Death....... -

90,000 of them to be precise!

I didn't go to work that day, I sat down with Byron and we discussed what was about to happen. Neither of us fully comprehended what was looming but we tried to rationalise together if there was any stone unturned, any means of salvaging this disaster, we are not stupid people, gullible, trusting, work hard individuals maybe, but not stupid. We felt like our world was falling apart and our emotions in shreds.
To this day I will never know how Byron had the strength to go out every day to his job, meeting all his targets, managing his projects and looking as serene as a swan on the surface because believe me he was falling apart as much as me behind the scenes.

It's fair to say at this point in my life there was no humour, there was no enjoyment there was nothing whatsoever to be laughing about. I and Byron were back to back in survival battle daily.

With the weekend out of the way, much discussion, arguing, tears and tantrums I took myself off the local Courthouse in Pontypridd on the following Tuesday, I went alone.....a mistake really but Byron did need to be in work that day at an important meeting.
I sat and waited my ticket turn approaching the double glass fronted counter with my knees shaking and my insides feeling like water. I was emotional with a lump in my throat the size of a golf ball. In my lifetime, Bankruptcy was something to be abhorred, reviled, only the lowest of the low and crooks became such....I wasn't any of these...how did I get here?
She was slight in stature with her hair scraped back in a tight bun on the very top centre of her head....she reminded me of a Cottage Loaf!

Her glasses perched on the end of her nose and her elevated seating position behind the window meant she could stare down at me like a crow about to peck out my eyeballs.

"Yes?" She barked in a high pitched, my thong is killing me tone of voice, her one eye winced simultaneously. It was obvious to me her mannerisms had been cultivated to accommodate the many crooks, thieves and con artists she saw before her each day. She was cold and dismissive, sharp and abrasive in her vocabulary.

I felt hot, nauseas and unable to hold back the tears any longer, my voice cracked and didn't sound like me at all as I declared "I...huh, I need, uhm I have to declare myself Bankrupt...how do I do this please?" My hands clasped so tight in front of me on the counter meant my knuckles were white...I shook and the tears flowed without sound from me.

Her expression remained intact.

"You'll need to fill out this form, you can sit over there to do it, she gesticulated to a chair nearby, then come back to the counter."

I sat with the form and did my very best to keep my hand steady as I completed each of the question boxes.

There was only one other man in the room who kept staring at me as if I was odd in my distressed state and I waited for him to clear the counter before approaching her with the completed form.

She looked up from her work as if I was a bad smell invading her nostrils.

"Take a ticket and wait" she screeched, her eyes were wide in disbelief at my insolence in approaching her highness without a fucking ticket!!!!

"But there's nobody waiting" I replied with a hoarse, cracked, emotional voice.

"Ticket! I'll call you when I'm ready" she barked.

You power crazy, jobs worth, up your own arse cow, I thought as I took a ticket for the second time that day.

She consumed a mug of coffee, joked with her colleague and answered two telephone calls before clicking the button on the queue number monitor...."Number 23?" she

215

called out in a room less than 20 feet square with nobody else sitting in it other than ME! You heartless bitch whoever you were on that day in September 2000.

I stood before her and handed over my completed form. She tossed a Bible on the counter and pushed it under the window at me along with a card with a declaration typed on it. "Place your right hand on the Bible and read from the card please" she instructed. I started to shake again and the tears poured as I read whatever was on that blurred card in front of me, I felt like a total criminal.

In auto pilot manner, done this a dozen times a day manner, she snatched back the Bible and card, stamped the form and held out her hand ...."£375 please."

I looked at her stupid, "Pardon me?"

Her face was exasperated. "The fee? The fee to register your Bankruptcy...£375 please!" She extended her hand once again.

In floods of tears and my voice in tatters I tried to explain that I didn't have 375 pennies let alone pounds? I was going Bankrupt? If I had £375 to my name right now maybe I wouldn't need to....stupid thought really but I was astonished that I had to actually PAY to declare myself bankrupt...spend money I didn't have to destroy myself...what the fuck was this system about?

Suddenly she looked at me long and hard, "you really are upset aren't you?"

I stood before her positively quaking, totally broken down with stress and upset. What was your first clue I thought sarcastically.

"Would you like a glass of water?" Her voice softened slightly, I nodded and she rushed off returning with tissues and water.

"Ok let's go through this slowly shall we?" she continued.

"You sign here and pay the registration fee, didn't anyone tell you about that?"

I shook my head silently.

"OK well no harm done, can you get the fee? Do you have somebody who can loan it to you?" Her enquiries were booming in my head.

I agreed to leave and return with the registration document and fee when I could muster it.

I left the Court House.

Byron's parents had some spare cash in a tin and we dragged together every penny we could raise over the following two days. I returned to the Court House the same week....on the Thursday, Thursday's child has far to go!

I handed over the form, I swore on the Bible and I paid my fee.....this time I was numb, silent and white as a sheet throughout the entire procedure.

I was now a registered Bankrupt with Companies House investigations to face.

I would not be the first in history to go bankrupt, nor would I be the last but at this stage you must understand that this experience went against the grain of every moral and ounce of self respect I had learned in life. I felt no better than my father, I felt like a piece of shit, I felt worthless and good for nothing, my life in my eyes was ruined.

The initial weeks that followed were some of the toughest I have ever lived through. You can forget the stress of the previous business liquidation....Bankruptcy proceedings eclipsed this on every level of my life.

People arrived at the cottage and drove my car off the drive, seizing it against the bankruptcy. Similar bods arrived in the house with a clipboard evaluating our personal possessions and carted them off in a big white van to auction. Anything that I owned that could be seized and offset against the amount I had gone bust for was fair game. Like any married couple we had bought goods together for our home, I tried to explain that the washing machine, TV, furniture was ours, mine and Byron's, not mine solely? Unless I could provide the receipt providing proof of my individual payment it was up for grabs. I watched as my home and car, life and soul was raped before my eyes.

This day was the day I shut down, my brain processed what was happening before me but I felt nothing, I watched as they carried stuff from my home, I stood in the middle of my lounge with one of our cats in my arms, I cuddled him for comfort and protection....of me, not him! Crazy!!!

I sat quietly whilst they busied themselves about my home and then suddenly as fast as they had arrived they were gone. I stood amidst what was left of the home I had lovingly created over the years, my beautiful country cottage, now almost empty of life and memories. All I could think is what next, this is not over by a long chalk!

From here on for a few weeks, life is blurred in my memory. I recall getting out of bed and sitting on the side of it with no where to go. I no longer had any job, no purpose in life, I was a dirty, filthy bankrupt, I owed money to people, my home was wrecked, my marriage under so much stress we barely spoke, I had no money, bills at home mounting up and about as much self respect left as a prostitute! What now, what next...?

The date arrived for the meeting with the Official Receiver at Companies House in Cardiff. The day when I would 'explain myself legally.' Declare how my business had got into such a mess and gone bankrupt. This was my chance to set the record straight surely.....WRONG!
By now we were about four weeks into this life crisis and Brides/clients were turning up for fittings and appointments with my Studio locked shut, panic was starting to mount. This time I REALLY couldn't do anything to save their losses, I couldn't honour my contracts with them, I couldn't hold my head up and survive the onslaught of events that had hit me like a tidal wave.

On a Wednesday morning in October 2000 we arrived at Companies House and were shown into a small room with tables laid out in 'interrogation' position. A camera in the top corner of the room declared that we were being watched by big brother and a panic button on the inside of the door lay testimony to how many people may just have attacked the little arsehole who grilled me and Byron within an inch of our lives!
His name is irrelevant, wiped from my brain with the disgust I felt for him, but I do remember he was around five feet tall, with neat greying hair, shirt and tie appearance and a smug look about his face that nowadays I would remove with one comment....but today I am older and much wiser!
"Ahhh come in, Mrs Parnell, Mr Parnell take a seat." He ushered us to the tables which were staggered, one slightly set back from the other so that we were not sitting side by side. I now realise this is so we couldn't 'kick an ankle' to alert the other when

answering, or touch hands in warning under the table, or indeed exchange sideways glances like perhaps most of the real crooks do?

For the next four hours....yes 4 HOURS....we were interrogated, there is no other word for it. Mr Job's Worth flitted between 'good man, bad man' routine even denying me a requested toilet break at one point whilst he acquired a document from the file and then as if by power status he declared, yes off you go, toilet is at the end of the corridor. You jumped up little bastard was all I could think.

I rushed to the Ladies room where I vomited in nerves and upset before returning composed to my interrogation cell.

"Ahh Mr Parnell, I see you drove up in a Mercedes, hmmm?" Job's worth stated with a supercilious look on his stupid little face.

Seems he had popped out of the room whilst I was in the bathroom to check what mode of transport we had arrived in.

Byron was ready for him and tossed his car keys on the desk at him "It's a company car with my job, here, take it!"

Knowing he couldn't legally, Job's Worth was momentarily deflated.

He soon rallied and came at me full force demanding days, dates, amounts and explanations for this that and the other that I simply couldn't correlate in my brain fast enough....."So in other words Mrs Parnell, you don't know, is that correct?"

NO it fucking well isn't I am trying to tell you what happened as it happened and you are not giving me chance you imbecile!

Again I tried to explain event by event but this was all too long winded for him, he wanted a quick death, another crook in the bag banged to rights!

After much paper pushing and signing and questioning he wore us both down....we didn't know what time of day it was let alone what day? Just as he could see we were both becoming utterly distressed he dismissed us...just like that!

"You can go now Mrs Parnell, I have all my facts!" he pranced out of the room leaving us to collect our shattered wits and depart.

Outside on the pavement in Cardiff City I clutched on to Byron's arm knowing if I let go I would fall to the gutter. We were both silent and in shock and bewilderment at what

219

just took place. I am sure others have breezed through such proceedings but for us it felt like total destruction of our good character, self respect and sense of decency...what the hell just happened? As Byron took my arm to help me across the road to the car I shook so violently my teeth chattered, I remember thinking to myself I will be 43 years old before my name is clear....clear...CLEAR?? Of what for pity's sake, I hadn't fucked up my business the insurance company did! My 40th Birthday was just day's away.

Just a decade plus back the stigma surrounding Bankruptcy in the UK was enormous, a period of 3 years penalty and with it came the generalised reputation of being a low life. Maria Parnell was now a Registered Bankrupt to the tune of £90,000......I felt less than sub human, I hated how I felt, I hated myself.....and I didn't know why? All I had ever tried to do was make a better life for myself, to keep the promise I made myself. I had been too trusting, ignorant, uneducated and gullible....I wished I had never been born at all.

Chapter 24

- *The Cave* -

In the weeks that followed our entire lives were tipped upside down. Our home came under question and was valued with a view to be re-possessed against the bankruptcy. Fortunately the property market was in decline at the time and our home had moved into a negative equity situation. No point in the Receiver taking it as it was worthless. My 40th birthday loomed and Byron did all he could to make it special....but it wasn't and could never have been, I didn't even want to breath any longer. Depression had set in hard although I didn't realise this at the time. I functioned on auto pilot, if it was morning I needed to clean my teeth and wash if I felt like it! If it was evening I sat in the chair with no lights on often in the pitch black until Byron came home. He often left for work with me in tears at 7am only to return at 7pm to find me still in tears. Life was non existent for us both. Throughout this my wonderful man kept his sanity and worked his job bringing in a salary albeit not enough to keep us going.

I had no purpose in life, I could see no reason why I should have been put on this earth...to do what? Hadn't I tried my very best? It had all gone so wrong.....why me? This was not self pity but a time in my life when I questioned my very existence, to what end, for what purpose. Byron was scared to go to work and leave me alone in fear of what I may do to myself whilst he was away. I duly saw the GP and was prescribed anti depressants for severe reactive depression. Byron kept the cottage and the cats and his job running....as I have said before he was and always will be my rock! What wasn't being addressed was the impact on his health and emotions this entire episode was taking. Byron likes to be in control, he will never admit to weakness of any description health or otherwise.

Each day I dreaded him leaving for work, as soon as he'd gone I felt cast adrift at mercy to the events the day would bring....and they often did!

By now we were about ten weeks into the Bankruptcy and much had already happened but little did I know what was still to come. The Official Receiver had by now written to all customers and suppliers alerting them to my business demise. Clients were in a state of panic as to imminent wedding dates and gowns by now long since abandoned and seized against the company debt. I keep using the word seized because that's exactly how it's done, they come, they take no questions asked, I had no say in the matter whatsoever!

It was mid morning when I heard a knock at the door, I had been up a few hours and Byron had left for work. I was at a loss what to do with myself for the day.

I opened the front door of the cottage to a TV camera thrust in my face and a woman with a microphone asking question after question about the closure of the business and did I have anything to comment regarding the dozens of brides who had lost their gowns and £0000's of pounds?? I was startled and panicked in one hit...this was my home. Was I not safe from all this pain even in my own home? I tried to slam the door but the camera man jammed his foot in it...I pushed and shouted for them to leave eventually managing to shut the door. I rushed to close the front window curtains and ran to the kitchen door to lock it, I felt utterly violated and attacked in my own home. With shaking hands I dialled Byron's number but he was in a meeting and his voicemail kicked in. I threw the phone across the room and raced to my only sanctuary, my bedroom where I crawled under the quilt and hid until Byron came home.

This and one other event was a massive turning point for me.

My illness, depression, was in full swing. I was registered long term sick and unemployable, I lived in a cave in my head. When breathing became too much, I retreated to the Cave in my head. I sat in the blackness that was safety, I peered at the cave opening in front of my eyes waiting, waiting, waiting for the next attack of whatever, pain, worry, stress attack. I had no real existence, I ate because that's what keeps you alive...did I want to be alive? Not really! I went days without washing or cleaning my teeth, I didn't care about anything, at all, any longer!

A knock at the door one evening just after Byron got home saw an entire family on my doorstep baying for blood! She was one of the Brides who had lost everything....her insurance company were asking for a signed letter from ME to confirm I had gone bankrupt. Insurance companies globally I spit on you for your lack of common sense! Parents and grandparents, brothers all shouting at once as to what a bitch I was and look at the house I lived in...no wonder they had been ripped off and her wedding was days away how could I live with my conscience? Byron stood in front of me bodily protecting me from the punch in the face that was coming....we tried to explain, they were hysterical initially, I was no more than a robbing bastard in their eyes.

Eventually they calmed down and left with a scribbled note from me as to what had happened and signed accordingly. She, at least, would recover her money if not her wedding gown.
I was sad for her, upset for myself, terrified to be alone in my own home and at my wits end. I couldn't go on like this....leave me alone, please, please, please god will you all leave me alone.

A few days after this incident my business collapse was recorded in a London newspaper for Insolvencies/Bankruptcy's and Financial Disclosures. I felt on show to the world for the piece of shit I was being accused of being....I had done nothing wrong.....why won't anyone listen...pleeeeeeeeeese, I'm begging you.

A month or so after this I left the safety of the Cottage one afternoon to go shopping for some underwear plus an hour out in the fresh air and normal everyday life that seemed to belong to everyone else.
I parked up at a well known Store, Marks and Spencer's at Culverhouse Cross in Cardiff. I wandered around the Store, shopping basket in hand feeling strangely 'spiritually elevated' from what I was doing....like I was above myself watching me walking around shopping. I stopped at an end of aisle gondola inspecting the items on offer when I felt a tap on my right shoulder, automatically I turned right but then felt a

tap on my left shoulder.....A mouth full of spit hit me in the face and I felt a hard thump in my chest where she pushed me. "You bitch, you robbing cow, all she ever wanted was that dress and you stitched her up, we want our money you hear me...you cow, you bitch!"

Stitch? Stitched her up ....what a relevant term of abuse I thought to myself as my brain tried to analyse what was happening. By now I had fallen into the Gondola and was trying to gain my balance and composure. I recognised the mother of the bride whilst trying to prevent myself retching at her spit all over my face, who was by now stomping away delighted with the results of her attack on me in public. The Store security guard and a shop assistant were bearing down on me and I felt panic struck like a hunted animal.

I explained briefly to the Guard why I thought I had been attacked, he raced off after the woman. The Store assistant was more comforting, she helped me to my feet and gathered up my fallen basket items whilst on lookers stared. She ushered me behind one of the shop counters asking if I was OK asking what could she do? Nothing lovely lady, nothing at all I thought staring at her through watery eyes. I am a target for revenge thanks to a well known insurance company and it's loophole cop outs!!

The Store wanted to call the Police but I vehemently refused, I wanted no more trouble on my plate than I already had. Making my way from the store I felt vulnerable, conspicuous, notorious even and emotionally broken down, I raced for home in my car slamming the gates shut and drawing all the curtains once inside.

That event changed everything in my world!

The 'Cave' got deeper, it got darker....and it felt safer than ever! I started erecting mental barriers at the entrance so that NOBODY could enter.......ever again.

- Chapter 25 -

- *Within these four walls, I grew!* -

The initial paperwork and administration finally settled down, my affairs were being conducted via the Bankruptcy official bodies so I was left to pick myself up and recover but that was proving more difficult than ever. I had never been without some form of a job in my life since I was 15 years old and I was now heading up to 41 years. Having always considered depression was some sort of invisible ailment that people 'leaned' on as an excuse to be ill I was actually discovering what a debilitating and destructive mental illness it truly is. Nothing matters any longer, there was no desire within me to lift one foot in front of the other, I lost masses of weight as I trimmed right down to a neat little 10 Stone, food was there, I ate but it was tasteless and of no interest. If anything needed doing around the Cottage, it would be there tomorrow if I felt like doing it. Inside my head I listened to myself telling myself how useless and stupid I was, I felt no emotions like love, happiness, only the desperate need to sleep or cry neither of which brought me any relief or comfort. I would sit for hours staring out the window without a single thought in my head, I was dead from the neck up. Byron would try to engage me in conversation but I would just stare at him and listen not really wanting him to speak to me at all, I wanted silence and peace, I didn't want to be asked to do anything, to go anywhere......don't make me have to do something, anything, I withdrew further and further into my brain Cave.

It was around this time I realised that I was avoiding life altogether. Refusing to leave the Cottage for so much as a loaf of bread. Byron took care of everything from the shopping to the housework. He had managed to buy me a little run around Jeep which sat week after week on the driveway. I wouldn't answer the telephone, wouldn't speak to anybody and if anyone visited I would hide away upstairs until Byron got rid of them. For almost 15 months I never left the safety of the Cottage.

His parents had their Golden Wedding Anniversary and a family lunch was organised at a local Restaurant....I refused to go. I couldn't and wouldn't cope with that amount of exposure to people and life! Letters addressed to me lay unopened as I removed myself further and further from people and life, in fact as far away from everything as I could get. Throughout all this I tended my cats, fed and cared for them but in a robotic manner, nothing reached me, not their purring, cwtches or love.

Byron would leave for work each day begging me to get dressed, go for a walk, eat something and to reassure him I wouldn't do anything stupid.

Stupid?

What type of stupid? Hadn't I done enough of 'stupid' already I thought?

My eyes were lifeless as I stared at him nodding my head that I would be OK for the day. His patience ran thin with me on so many occasions, nasty arguments and rows ensued, he couldn't understand why I couldn't just take the tablets and get better?

Make an effort he would scream at me, try and get a job, get off the sick pay and stop feeling sorry for yourself.

The Summer of 2001 was kind to the garden and I started to sit outside with a coffee once in a while, then I started pottering with bits and bobs in the garden. Byron had bought me what I had always wanted for my 40th Birthday, a big beautiful greenhouse but it had been stored in the garage all this time forgotten and abandoned in the melee of what had happened.

To make space in the garage he had erected it and it stood empty, unused at the bottom of the garden.

It was with a few packets of seed and some grow bags that I started getting up of a morning and heading down the greenhouse after he'd left for work. It was peaceful and quiet and there was nobody at all around. Within these four glass walls I found something that made me smile when the first shoots appeared, I felt a tiny surge of joy when I 'potted on' the larger of the plants.....the greenhouse began to fill up and Byron quietly encouraged and helped clear areas in the garden for me to plant out. Our beautiful cottage garden had become overgrown and neglected again having not had the time or inclination to get out there and maintain the upkeep.

Over the coming months I transformed the garden into a chocolate box cottage garden, it was a sight of pure beauty and a labour of love. Not one single inch of ground wasn't designed, planted up or being used for fresh fruit and vegetables. There was so much food being produced that it was becoming too much for us so Byron took some to work and a lady who used to ride her horses through the lane stopped me at the gate one afternoon, she had been watching me for weeks in the garden and asked if she could come inside to have a look at the 'beautiful gardens?' At first I was reluctant but invited her in, she was dumb struck as she walked around asking after names of plants and growing conditions. By now I was living my life inside gardening books and magazines and as with anything which captures my total attention in life, I was completely absorbed and obsessed with gardening and learning how to. I rattled off information and advice like I had been 'working the land' for a lifetime.

As we stopped near Potager one (I had two Potagers) she commented on the Asparagus and salad veg growing. "Do you sell at the gate?" she enquired. I didn't understand what she meant at first looking quizzically at her. "I don't get time to grown and I much prefer home grown, I could buy a Veg Box from you weekly if you'd like? The thought had never occurred to me to sell what I was growing but I agreed to put a small box together for her that weekend and Byron would drop it to her farm.

That afternoon I took my first step back to the life of the living. I felt something inside twitch, a sense of pride at my own efforts to grow food for us, after all I had no job and wasn't contributing to the household budget, this was my way of trying to help out. The fact that a person had shown interest in me and my efforts felt strangely pleasing, I couldn't wait to put a veg box together for her.....but if I was going to, I wanted to do it right and presentation was everything. The old business woman was still in there somewhere.....

When Byron came home I was quite excited to tell him about the day's events and the lady who wanted fruit and veg and he was genuinely happy to see me actually happy about something at long last.

I literally launched myself into full scale production and at one point even had sweet corn growing in a small bed, there was nothing you could buy in a supermarket that wasn't growing in our garden, I even had red and white grapevines!

My chest puffed up whenever I surveyed my handiwork from the bedroom window, I felt good at something once again, something to get up for each day that asked nothing of me, took nothing from me but gave me so much.

Over these months a number of our cats either wandered off, something we'd now become used to living rural, they would track around outlaying farms living off the land. All had been spayed or castrated so were not adding to a growing feral populace. Some passed away from old age and we were down to just four babes aging gracefully.

After sourcing suitable 'cottagey' looking cardboard boxes and tissue paper, I made up a small amount of veg/fruit boxes each week and ventured out from the cottage to find outlets. I had lost an enormous amount of confidence in myself so this first foray back to the land of the living was taking all I had. A couple of the local farms were regulars, the lady in the post office and one of my friends who had started out as a client and remained in touch occasionally.

We had lost a good deal of contact during my 'cave dwellers' months but she called up once afternoon by surprise and we sat talking over a coffee in the garden.

Jane was a high flyer in the 'Smoke' top of her game in Telecommunications, a high end five figure salary was 'norm' for her. She bought properties like they were gems to be collected and disposed of as one became bored with them. She drove a Mercedes SLK and dressed in nothing but the finest. I had designed and created many, many outfits, gowns and suits for her over the years. Jayne had been fascinated with our then late departed and gorgeous Princess Diana, ordering copies of whatever new gown Diana wore. Since my demise from the fashion business her wardrobe full of my bespoke creations had dwindled.

As we sat talking Jane asked how I was feeling nowadays and did I ever think I would get back into fashion design, I sensed instinctively what was coming next. She went on to explain how she had missed being able to work with 'her designer' (so impersonal, I have a name!) on creating her personal fashion and was planning her wedding to the new man she had met. Would I make her wedding gown?

It was something I didn't want to think about, somewhere I didn't ever want to go back to but for some reason I allowed her to talk me into it and I agreed.

Looking her in the eye I started to wonder if her 'chance visit' hadn't been so chance after all? Come to see how I was and the 'mwah, mawh' kisses, hugs my Darling I've missed you pretence more like.

I tested the water.... "When did you decide to get married?"

"Oh months ago Hunnie, he's super with me, knows exactly how to keep me on the reins" her head back laugh entertained only her.

"I just thought you might have told me sooner that's all, there's not much time left to get the gown done is there? But then I guess we haven't seen each other in best part of a year." I commented.

"Well Darling you were so poorly and you didn't want visitors..." she trailed off.

I couldn't deny this of course and she was absolutely right, but her next comment ended any friendship we had for good.

"....and besides I was splitting up with David and you know what he was like, he didn't want me to see you, get involved and all that!"

My head snapped up.

"What do you mean by that? Not see me, get involved, involved in what?"

Jayne shifted uncomfortably in her garden chair, staring out over the garden searching for her reply, I could see she wished she hadn't just said that.

"Come on Jayne, what do you mean?" I pressed her further.

"Well, you know, all the trouble..."

"You mean the Bankruptcy, say it Jayne the word won't hurt you as much as it did me!"

"Well yes, OK the Bankruptcy then...!" She was becoming agitated.

"AND?" I was in no mood for any further delays to the answer I wanted.

"Oh Maria, it doesn't matter now does it."

"YES, it DOES!" I want to know please, what did he mean, and why haven't you come to visit sooner?"

Jayne stared straight at me realising I wasn't going to let go of this bone... "David wouldn't let me come and visit OK? He was bothered, worried that I'd get involved being good friends. All the trouble you were going through.....he thought you'd probably ask us for money or something. Maria you know what he was like...?"

She pleaded now for some sort of forgiveness from me for what she'd just said.

I was appalled, insulted and hurt all in one sweep.

"Jayne, I've hit hard times, I'm on my arse and wiped out financially. I may be on sick benefit payments and have fuck all to call my own nowadays but I'm no beggar or scrounger and besides which I should never have NEEDED to ask, a true friend would have given unquestionably!"

She looked like I'd slapped her in the face..."Oh see, I knew you'd be upset, you know I would have helped if you'd asked." She tried again to justify her lack of friendship in my eyes.

"No, Jayne, I'm sorry...you're a big girl, a high flyer who makes multi million pound decisions everyday of her life, David has NEVER kept you in check in anything you've ever wanted to do so don't give me this crap that he stopped you being a friend....because that's all I needed, not your fucking money or anything else!"

I was livid and red faced and upset.

"Will you still do my wedding gown then?" She asked with a pained expression.

I burst out laughing at her sheer audacity and insensitivity.

"I said I would didn't I? We better take some measurements and get something on paper."

For all I have ever had and lost it has never been my word. I said I would do it and I did. Jayne married less than two months later in a gown with overlay cape train of my design and manufacture, we attended the wedding as guests.....and I never saw Jayne again.

As Autumn passed into Winter and I learned daily how to cope with my dreadful mood swings from the depression, it became obvious I needed to find some sort of employment for us to financially manage. My reclusive lifestyle had to cease and life needed to restart, I was not looking forward to it at all.

Initially I sought jobs in the vein of what I knew and my first real interview in decades was a disaster.

I walked into the Fashion Store in Cardiff Bay Docklands, now a vibrant and rejuvenated part of the Capital City of Wales. The Manageress interviewed me in a matter of fact manner, I guess she'd seen many hopeful youngsters wanting a foot on the fashion ladder.

British Law states that if asked the direct question "are you, or have you ever been, declared Bankrupt" and you avoid/deny or lie in your answer, this may be classified an criminal offence. That's what I was told by the Official Receivers and that is what I adhered to lawfully.

Whilst she did not ask the direct question, it became increasingly difficult to 'disguise' where I had been and how I'd earned a living these past 10 years.

"What experience have you got in this line of work?" she asked perfectly reasonably.

I explained I'd been in the fashion industry for a decade and was familiar with sales, marketing, profiling, administration, accounting, staff and employment laws blah, blah. She looked taken aback. "Oh, that's quite extensive, where have you worked then, a corporate retail store?"

"Uh no, I had my own business."

The first kiss of death was dealt. Self employed people are frowned upon when returning to the workplace in the UK, been your own boss for too long, won't take telling or instructing, think you know it all bigger and better, used to being in charge goes against you every time. The fact that I was more than willing and ready to be the one NOT in charge and would be THRILLED at somebody above me taking the rap for everything was irrelevant.

She pressed and pressed until I explained all and the sordid end ...Bankruptcy!

231

She thanked me for the interview and my time and I got the distinct impression I'd received the 'kiss off, don't call us we'll call you' routine.

Her call arrived less than a week later as she explained the job had been offered to another. I asked why I'd been overlooked, a reasonable question that could assist me in future interviews.

"Well, it wasn't my final decision you understand" she poked around for an answer.

"But the Management felt it would be awkward for you as you would be handling staff wages, being a registered Bankrupt as such.....soooory!"

My brain processed her reply and a grenade of temper exploded! "I beg your pardon, how dare you?" I demanded, but she promptly hung up.

I had been refused a job I was over qualified for on the basis I was a registered Bankrupt thus considered a crook, a con and a thief....good god how could I ever be expected to handle money and wages.....without doing a runner with a mask over my eyes and wearing a stripy tee shirt! I was so upset I rushed to the bathroom bawling my eyes out and feeling dirtier than ever.

A few weeks later I applied to the great and godly Tesco Superstores for a 'shelf stackers' job. It was a start....

I arrived for the interview in Talbot Green and was duly handed over to a shop floor assistant who would monitor my trial efforts at stacking salad bags in date order on the shelf in the vegetables department.

Task completed, neatly and in date order I returned to their offices with the Manager. Once again the 'past history' enquiries were raised. Once again I skirted around them as best I could until inevitably the truth was out.

"Thank you for your time, we'll be in touch!" He stood up shook my hand and I left.

Three weeks passed and I heard nothing so I called Tesco, to be told I had been 'rejected.' Not 'unsuccessful' or 'not suitable'......but god damned REJECTED! What the fuck was I a 'seconds in life'....comes complete without a box? Good packaging but no marbles inside! I was incensed as I realised I was becoming virtually unemployable.

Wrong side of 40 years, over qualified as a former self employed business person, a registered Bankrupt.....perhaps I should contract small pox as well just to be on the safe side!!! My re-entry into normal life was not going to be a soft landing that was for sure.

Christmas was looming and I felt anything but festive!

Chapter 27

- *Till death us do part* -

.....and god knows we so very nearly did!

As life wove it's pathway during 2001, early 2002 my depression was not subsiding, if anything it was becoming worse and I cannot explain why?
Financial worries were at the forefront of our daily life but we played 'tennis' with everything thrown at us. We juggled, robbed peter to pay poor and generally coped, as couples and families do.

To digress from this Chapter slightly, I document an event way back in 1999 when life was turbulent but liveable.

Byron had bought a motorbike, a magnificent machine. A Suzuki Intruder 1400cc.
I seem to recall reading somewhere it was 600lbs in weight which would not surprise me as she was a bitch to hold up! Gaining his Motorbike License was a momentous day and we celebrated his passing the test in style.
He called the Studio at the Model House declaring his achievement and I screamed in pride and pleasure down the phone "Oh my Babe, way to go you! I knew you could do it." That very same evening, swelled with pride at his day's achievements Byron asked me "where do you want to go for your first Pillion ride Gorgeous?"

"Uhmmmm...I thought about it for a split second....Ireland!" I declared.
His face was a picture...."what's the matter with Porthcawl?" he asked. A seaside town a few miles away. Do I look like a woman who does anything by half?

And so Ireland it was!

Just a week or so later, we headed for a long weekend on the Irish shores, Wexford, our original Honeymoon destination was to be our first stop and I booked ahead accommodation for our arrival.

Had I ever been pillion before...NEVER!
Had I been on the back of a motorbike before...NEVER!

We rapidly kitted ourselves out with leathers and head gear, ruck sacks and paraphernalia and booked the Ferry crossing. My first memory of this magical period in our lives was mounting such power and throb between my legs!! If you've never ridden a motor bike, you've missed an experience in life! The Intruder's pillion seat was slightly elevated so I sat a little higher than my man up front, I felt like a Queen and so FREE!

We organised care for our cats for our four day away trip and took to the highways. 'Born to be wild' singing in our ears as we thundered down the motorway heading for the Ferry. Byron had purchased a head set intercom much against his Hell's Angel attitude as this type of kit was normally associated with Honda Gold Wings...the armchair bikes!
"Right, now tell me when you need a pee or anything OK?" were his instructions as we left home.
The sheer freedom and vulnerability of riding a motorbike cannot be described truly. It awakens every sense of self survival, fragility and thrill seeking emotion any one person could ever want in a lifetimes experience. I was busting with pride for my man at having achieved his bike license and the fact I was experiencing something so unimaginable in life. We arrived at the ferry in Fishguard, West Wales for our disembarkation in Ireland. During the trip to West Wales, I had become restless on the back of the bike needing a 'bathroom call' but instead of alerting Byron through the headphones I clenched and wriggled and thought Fishguard couldn't be much further

COULD IT? As we hit the Pont Abraham Services on the link road I yelled to Byron to pull over........not the fist time he'd heard this instruction from me in our life together. As we purred into the Services car park I was rocking like a hobby horse on the pillion seat. No sooner the bike had come to a full stop I leapt off the back with my hand jammed between my legs trying to stop the inevitable. Problem was I didn't take into consideration we were still helmet to helmet connected on the intercom.

"Whoah WOMAN...for fucks sake hang on!" I heard Byron bellow as I ripped the wires from his headset whilst leaping from the bike.

The intercom was totally trashed, I raced to the Service Station toilet facilities and breathed a sigh of pleasure as I sat aloft the toilet seat still with my helmet on!!

I knew I was in for a yelling at when I returned to the bike but that bladder release was worth every mouthful!!

We eventually arrived in Ireland and enjoyed a fantastic four day break touring between towns and tourist attractions. We covered some 630 miles inclusive....not bad for a Biker who'd just passed his test, had never carried a Pillion, a Pillion who'd never been one before and together we travelled between shores by some 630 miles. Hmmm not your average FIRST trip but then we are the Parnell's!

The bike was to become, sadly, a weapon of war!

Our initial enjoyment as a couple of our new found hobby was awesome. We rode out on good weekends, I loved the attention the bike attracted and Byron was a superb Biker. A man in harmony with his machine....his bike was a part of him, you could see how much he was in tune with it, loved it and mastered it. I was so proud of him....

I don't actually remember when throughout this period he found a Biker's Club locally known as The Patriots. This Bike Club was just short of the Hell's Angels as a Chapter as far as I understand, correct me if I am wrong.

At first I was delighted Byron was putting his new found biking skills to good use. Joining a Club and venturing out on weekend tours, a club life to enjoy with his fellow Patriot's.

The rot set in very quickly. It seemed each and every weekend, bank Holiday and critical family time were demanded by this Club. To achieve Full Back Patch status the club members were expected to comply. Byron was by now a Company Director in his job, a man of some 52 years old intelligence and worldly wise experience...so I thought. But there is none so stupid as those who are led.......

Within a very short space of time Byron started excluding me from the enjoyment of the bike, I had tried to 'customise' it with ape hanger tassels and leather fuel tank cover, a skull and cross bones braking light. On hind sight it was Byron's bike...I had no right to interfere but I was ignorantly enjoying the pleasure and release the bike brought me. Byron fought me all the way, chastising the bike decor and accessories, his Club House becoming more and more dictating in their terms of membership.

'Missions' became part of Byron's initiation into the Club, a 700 mile round trip in 24 hours being one that I call ridiculously to mind. He was told to drive from A to B, deliver a package and return to A....and the package contains? None of your business, just deliver it! Byron's reward was a step further to attaining his full 'Back Patch,' a full club Brother! I think at this stage I must state that whilst I have no quibble with such Clubs and their rules and reg's, I do question and disagree with the common sense of it all.

The Club was starting to drive a wedge between us as Byron rejected my participation on the bike more and more. We did enjoy a few trips out whilst he was a member but it was clear to me, and my opinion, that the women folk of this Club were classified as the men's 'bitches' know your place and don't interfere. I helped out with a few Saturday night bar duties and trust me this place was a hell hole as far as I am concerned. On one particular night Byron was on bar duty so it made sense to sleep over in the Club House....in fairness Byron could sense my anxiousness as he led me to a large room with some 20 bunk beds in it...bitches and dogs slept together no matter who they were! I had men and women all about me in various sleep stages....clothed or not, I felt uncomfortable and on edge.... I'm no stupid little girl but I just felt disappointed that my husband was prepared to 'subject' me to this. I of course had the choice to go home but wanted to be with my man who quite frankly I was in competition with against the demands of this damned club.

I attended the club on another occasion and deliberately dressed in skirt, tee shirt and sandals, hair and make up......it was frowned upon as the dress code for the bitches was strictly 'Biker gear.' TOUGH! I will not be dictated to or conform was my attitude. Byron commented that I was unsuitably dressed for the club....REALLY? By who's judgement, certainly nobody I gave a damn about that's for sure!
Months passed and Byron was at the Club or away on a 'ride' whenever he was called upon, I was becoming truly sick to death of this 'cult' lifestyle. I never wanted him not to have his club enjoyment....what I couldn't accept was that he allowed it to impact our life together so much? I've heard of golf widows, cricket widows and wives in general who didn't give a damn if their husbands spent weeks away from home.....well I DID! Perhaps if I had not been suffering depression so badly, perhaps if Byron had been a lot more understanding we could have worked it through....but he fought me all the way defying my requests to stay at home, give it a miss this weekend please, please. He saw my protests as a means of trying to deny him a personal life, any enjoyment, he defended his club and 'Brothers' in a manner indicating they meant a lot more to him than I did during this time! I very quickly built up a hatred for this damned club and it's 'brain washing' methods of membership!

My anti depressant treatment was helping me cope with life in general but it was obvious our financial situation had to improve. I plucked up the courage to return to secretarial work, it galled me to do so but needs must and all that. I applied for 'temp' jobs and thankfully was assigned a month at local House Building Company's Head Office known as Persimmon Homes in Llantrisant. No questions were asked, I didn't have to declare the bankruptcy...to all intent I appeared a 'normal' human being!

It was a relief to fall out of bed and roll 2 miles down the lane to work, travel costs were negligible and I could pop home of a lunch hour if I wanted. I was to become Technical Department Secretary and threw myself into the role trying to be the best I could for my Department Manager, I held the job down despite all disruptions at home, the worry of the bankruptcy and marital issues.

For a few months longer we seemed to bumble on, arguing and fighting each other about the club's intervention in our life. The more I complained the harder Byron dug his heels in. I knew he needed something of his own but as far as I was concerned, he was handling it all wrong...badly! It seemed like every time he was away with the Club, something would happen at home and I would need to call him for his help. He saw this as almost manipulative, that I had instrumented these events to spoil his club time, nothing could have been further from the truth!

Things deteriorated one Friday night when he had returned from work to change and leave for a 2 night duty at the Club... I faced a long and lonely weekend yet again. We had words, a verbal fight and he left, without a circle of friends in my life I was as such alone without him.
I made myself some food and settled down for a Friday night TV watch, early bed and a Saturday of shopping and entertaining myself.
It was around 9.30pm when one of the cats came through the cat flap and I could suddenly smell a very strong odour of petrol? I grabbed Rupert sniffing him all over and he stank of fumes. Thinking he had slept beneath the vehicles on the drive I took the flash light and inspected around the cars for a petrol leak or something? Nothing was obvious so I returned to the Cottage but could smell fumes quite strongly on the air.... I became anxious wondering what was wrong...where was this odour coming from? As I neared the kitchen door the smell became pungent and powerful.....the only nearest origin was our central heating/cooker oil tank. Oh my god NOOOooooooo!!!

I rushed up the pathway leading to the steps up to the 2000 Gallon Tank....domestic oil was oozing out under pressure all over the upper patio and running down the steps in a mini waterfall draining into the garden and gravelled pathways.

I was horrified...I had no idea what to do....how to stop the discharge. I raced for next door calling on my only neighbour to help, Glyn being a farm manager was calm and controlled as he organised 50 Gallon Oil drums from a nearby farm and a pump to evacuate the tank, meanwhile I called the Fire Service who sent an Appliance to arrest the oil escape and wash down with detergent to reduce contaminate to the local agricultural land and water course. Throughout all this, with a blue light Fire Engine blocking the country lane where we live, Glyn charging around decanting oil and everyone trying hard to contain the toxin damage to the garden...I called Byron at the Club House.

"Hi, can you come home please, we've had an oil leak, the tank has split and it's everywhere. There's a fire crew here and Glyn......" Byron cut me dead in my tracks, "Oh for fucks sake, what now?? Every time I'm here something happens....for Christ sake M....what d'ya mean the oil tank is split?"

I listened to his temper outburst and something inside me switched off!

Byron arrived at the cottage within the hour as the fire crew were mopping up and what was left of our domestic oil had been pumped into drums...in the pitch black by flashlight and rigged up lighting via the fire appliance, cups of tea were served to the fire crew and Glyn thanked for his calm and speedy intervention....Byron then returned to the Club House, clearly a man torn between his loyalty to his so called 'Brothers' and his duty as a protective husband to me!

Shortly after this event another weekend 'meet' was called. We desperately needed to render the newly block built garage and I had hoped we could tackle this together on the approaching weekend.

"I'm at the Club this weekend." Byron announced.

"We need to do the garage and re-lay the front slabs to the Cottage" I rapped back.

"Well it'll have to wait"

Will it now I thought to myself as my blood boiled.

Without speaking to each other on the Saturday morning, Byron roared out of the driveway. I stared after him with pure hatred, I cannot lie or say different.

That weekend I called a colleague from Persimmon, one of the Site Managers. "How do you make render?" I asked.

He laughed..."What? What you doing you mad woman?"

"I'm going to render my garage" I stated as if advising of a shopping trip.

Again he burst out laughing..." ...you're having a laugh yes?"

"NO!"

Mike's tone of voice became serious..."...Uhhh OK well, you need this much sand and blah, blah, blah and this is how you mix...is it by mixer?"

"NO by hand" I replied.

Mike was further disconcerted...."Where's Byron then...?"

"Who the fuck cares anymore, thanks for the help!" I answered and hung up.

That weekend I mixed render by hand on my driveway and rendered my garage block walls, scoring the mix as I 'cake iced' it on to the walls with a nail imbedded in a stick as I had seen on so many DIY TV programmes. The labour nearly killed me as my joints screamed with pain and the sweat poured off me..... I then set about digging up the slabs at the front of the cottage ready for re-laying.

On the following Monday morning I was behind the bedroom curtain watching as Byron drew up on his motorbike....his face was priceless as he stared at the garage in utter disbelief. He entered the kitchen stating "How did we afford the garage render then?"

"We didn't..... I did it!" I stated without even looking at him....

Byron laughed a disbelieving laugh...."I have photo's to prove it!" I declared as I had self timed camera shots of me doing the work...I was intent on making him feel bad, end of! This shut him up and I believe my point had been made.

It was April 2001, we had booked the Easter Bank Holiday week off on holiday with plans to get stuck into the DIY on the cottage once again.

"...don't suppose you wanna hear this but there's a meet planned this weekend." Byron made his declaration over the kitchen sink with his back to me.

"But it's Easter Bank Holiday?" I answered wondering what had happened to our plans?

"Yeah, I know but the Club's got a ride organised, if I don't show up it'll go against my full patch" he replied as if this was sensible justification for wanting to yet again spend time away from us/home.

"You're not going though?" I questioned, knowing what I was about to hear.

"Awww for Christ sake don't start M, I have to .....I want to!" He protested whilst groaning at my comment.

I was consumed with rage, "Byron this bloody club is controlling you, can't you see that?" I screamed at him. No he couldn't, wouldn't, didn't want to....simple as! Something snapped within...."OK you go if you must...and if you do, don't come back and I mean it!" I spat the words out filled with more venom than a Cobra on strike attack!

Byron looked at me with disgust, "I'm going M and I'll be coming back as well!"

"I'm warning you Byron, I'll change the locks, you go...you DON'T come back I swear!" We were head to head in emotional battle...he laughed at me, a sarcastic and spiteful dismissal of my threat. "Yeah in your dreams!"

We both retired to bed in separate rooms.....what would Saturday morning bring?

Byron was up and dressed, the bike was packed with all the gear he needed and he awaited my rising for our final confrontation.

"So you're going then?" I asked matter of fact.

"Yup!"

"It's Easter Bank Holiday weekend Byron....what about me, what about time together?"

"It's part of my full patch initiation....can't you see that?" he yelled at me.

"Yes, yes I can, but every weekend, every public holiday....it's insane!" was all I could reply. "You have cut me off from the bike, you won't include me anymore...what happened to our 'hobby'....something for us in amongst all this shit that's happened?"

242

He just looked at me, I could see his torture...the need to escape ME and all THE SHIT....I didn't want to deny him this....but I needed him too.

He jammed his helmet on and made for the gates....... OK you BASTARD tore through my head we're finished.

Byron roared off in defiance up the country lane from our home and I could still hear the twin exhausts long after he had disappeared from view.

I was volcanically angry, I was intent on divorce, I wanted to hurt him as much as he was hurting me. Instead I departed to the local Tesco Superstore and bought some Country Home & Living Magazines, a bottle of wine, a ready meal for one and box of chocolates.....this evening was to be mine and then I would start my proceedings to end our marriage, the worm had turned well and true. I was intent on returning to my original self survival single mode of existence.

The phone rang around 4.45pm that afternoon.... I ignored it letting it go to answer 'phone massage. The caller hung up, I guessed it was Byron having cooled his heels now wanting to pave the way for a homecoming. FUCK OFF is all I could think!

I fed the cats, did a few things around the cottage and retired to bed after my ready meal that choked me as I wasn't in the mood to swallow! Around 7pm the phone rang again....I ignored it convinced Byron had by now arrived at his destination and was keen to expedite a remote 'patch up!' GO TO HELL was all I could think!

I switched on the TV in the bedroom and tried to relax but my temper was on full Scorpio revenge channel!

I drifted off to sleep exhausted by my own emotions and in need of shut down time.

In the depths of my sleep I was roused by the phone ringing, it was dark, I looked at the clock....10.10pm.

Had a few pints with the fucking Brother's now have you? Want to make your peace do you...had a good laugh at the bitch with your mates have you? surged through my brain. The answer' phone kicked in but still no message left? I smirked and turned over to wrap up my quilt of misery around me.

I tossed and turned, planned my departure, then drifted back off, woke again and got up for a pee! Zonked out again then jolted awake as the phone rang yet again at 05.20am. SUDDENLY I sat upright in bed, galvanised into reality. Byron WOULD NEVER call at this time of day no matter what had happened between us, I knew him, he wouldn't! I shot out of bed suddenly worrying for his safety and I was right to do so....to this day I bitterly regret not answering the previous calls alerting me to the fact my husband had been near fatally injured in a road traffic accident on his bike!

I grabbed the phone barely awake and trying to sound alert.
"Hello?"
"Hello is this Mrs Parnell?"
"Yes"
"Hello I am Sister Morris at the Royal Gwent Hospital in Newport, Mrs Parnell we've been trying to contact you since 4pm yesterday, is there anyone with you right now?"
"No, WHY?" I demanded.
"OK, can you come to the hospital immediately? Mr Parnell has been involved in an RTA (Road Traffic Accident) yesterday afternoon, he is stable at the moment in Intensive Care Unit but we couldn't make contact with you."
I cannot describe how my body felt at that split second hearing this....I went into shock trembling from top to toe, spluttering that I'd be there immediately and hung up. My blood felt like it was draining down through my feet as I tried to don bra, pants, clothing.....unbelievably (or not for me) I grabbed the phone and dialled next door...."Peggy, Byron is in intensive care, I have to go....feed the cats!" I screamed down the phone..... I heard her voice but don't recall her words.
Byron drove a Mercedes 200 E Class Series at the time...it was a beautiful motor and a flying machine. I made Newport in under 30 minutes....35 miles away!
As I entered the Hospital I was shaking uncontrollably. I checked the desk and was directed to his ward in ICU. On entering I felt cold and numb, a Nurse asked who I was looking for and then guided me through the ward doors......just in time to see five

people around Byron's bed all tending to his immediate medical needs... his blood pressure had apparently dropped like a brick, he was mildly convulsing, not good! My first sight of him was twitching in his bed, totally unconscious and with tubes in every orifice his body could offer. Saline drips, cardiac monitors, equipment pulsing and bleeping.....I was rooted to the spot at the doorway. Eventually he calmed and they stabilised him, I still didn't know the extent of his injuries, I feared the worst and felt abhorrent of myself for how we had parted, in despair of losing him at the sight before me.

Maybe, just maybe, Byron hadn't been concentrating, his mind on other 'things' as he took the bend on the Hereford Town road that Saturday. A lorry/tank overspill had deposited fuel on the road, Byron was riding in pack formation when they all took the bend in the road....Byron went into a front wheel skid, his bike careering out of control. The front wheel hit the kerbside at speed upending it throwing Byron to the road, the bike came down on top of him with the handle bars smashing into his stomach shattering his spleen and damaging his liver. His 'Brothers' picked him up off the floor, leaving the bike there and put Byron in a car that was a 'follower' transporting him many miles back to the Club House....have always thought men and common sense don't often meet!!
Arriving at the Club House Byron was a 'whiter shade of pale' and managed to step from the car before collapsing. How thoughtful that a Doctor's Surgery was in the same street, the Doctor was called on to assist who then called an ambulance...finally someone with a brain!!! Byron was rushed to surgery with a ruptured spleen and liver injury....the rest is as documented.

Byron's spleen was in a bucket somewhere in theatre, his liver was bruised and damaged, he was in Intensive Care Unit trying to recover....the road ahead wasn't on two wheels or even back to back on our knees as far as I was concerned...it was on mutual understanding of the others needs and if that at least couldn't be attained, end of!

I knew Byron was incapable of showing compassion or understanding as far as I was concerned, at this point in our life we had reached a stage where 'if it mattered to ME...it sure as hell wouldn't matter to him!'

Chapter 28

- *Destination? Unknown.....* -

Persimmon, my employers at the time granted me immediate 'compassionate leave' and as such my days were spent running back and forth the hospital in Newport, 35 miles away to be with Byron. His family had visited consisting of his parents and Sister....his children had been advised but didn't come. Practically my brain tells me that I guess young children at school and work commitments made it difficult but my heart tells me that if it were someone they loved, their FATHER!.....nothing would stop them! I reserve my comments........

Byron recovered slowly initially and was eventually moved to a main ward off ICU but to High Dependency Unit. Around eight other patients of varying ages and much older than Byron were all 'spending time' there either recovering or dying.
The ambience of this Ward was heavy with worry, stress, pain and hopelessness.
Byron soon tuned into this and his general demeanour sank like a stone.
I visited daily staying for as long as I could around our home commitments.

On one occasion the gentleman in the next bed to Byron was visibly upset....in his late 80's with no visitors family or otherwise, he had taken to chatting to himself in his mental isolation. Byron and I watched as he sat in a wheelchair abandoned by life, humanity and existence. I don't recall his name but he was calling for his 'secretary?' Unable to watch his distress any longer I approached him... "I'm here, I was at lunch sorry Sir" What do you want me to do?" I asked this in full view of the rest of the Ward. The gentleman's head snapped up, suddenly proud and alive...."I want to send a letter...." he declared.
"Let me just get my pad please" I responded.
He was suddenly alive and alert if only in the backwater of his memories.

"OK, I'm ready" I stated as I sat before him, with nothing but a paper tissue and a pen to feign my shorthand of his dictated letter.

He rattled of incoherent sentences and I read them back mostly from memory....he chuckled and smiled feeling 'somebody' again....then thanking me before dismissing me from the 'Office!' He nodded off into a deep sleep in the wheelchair and I returned to Byron's bedside, he looked at me with utter respect. I felt I had done something good in life....another of the patients started clapping his hands and thanking me for my compassion.... all I can say is that I did what I did from the heart not for any acknowledgement or gratitude. As the lovely old gentleman twitched in his sleep, his lap blanket slipped from his lap exposing his nakedness to the ward...the Nurses passed in and out ignoring his dignity....I gently tucked his blanket back around him and prayed that I would never suffer this humiliation myself in later years given that I had nobody left in my family to ensure otherwise.

Byron's Sister Barbara was a regular visitor, I detested her presence at any time. Barbara is Byron's sister some six years younger and a veritable pain in the arse of a woman. Divorced from her first husband she is a dominatrix, I take nothing from her ability and success in carving out a life for herself and caring for her two daughters but her attitude in general sucks! Superior, supercilious and a general know it all....when Byron was in Intensive Care she took over, taking advantage of my distressed weakness. The god damned Consultant talked to her explaining about MY Husbands injuries as if she were his Wife! She ignored me completely in this conversation. Other incidents during our 23 years of marriage have left me intolerable of Barbara the 'great I am!' Barbara could be a lovely lady in every sense in my opinion...if she could just 'get over herself!' But when Barbara enters a room...it's look out 'I am in the building...here I am, bow before me' atmosphere!

I have no doubt she and I face 'verbal wars' ahead.....whatever and whenever!

The future looked uncertain for Byron and I at this stage but we took his accident in our stride and 'worked' our life around it. After three weeks Byron was discharged to home and I recall the day I collected him from Hospital. Thrilled that he was coming home and so relieved for him I arrived at the hospital around Noon for his 2pm checkout.

I was shocked to see his bed empty on the ward? Byron had been moved to a singular side ward for discharge....my initial panic relieved I made my way to the side ward only to find Byron in tears sat in a chair by the window.....clearly suffering post operative shock! The Nurses padded in and out going about their duties whilst he sat shivering and weeping, ignoring him completely? I threw my bag/coat on the bed and rushed to his chair....he stared at me before cwtching into my arms..."I'm finished M..." he wept and shook. "No, no, no Baby you're not" I laughed to try and lighten the mood, "You're just sore and tired and a bit out of sorts that's all....you are not finished I promise!" I recognised his symptoms from those I had felt in years gone by after surgery. I cuddled him until he felt able to dress and we left the hospital to travel home. Byron's employers were great, permitting him whatever recovery time off work he needed, I returned to work at Persimmon and together we recovered from the trauma of it all.

Where life was going from here on was a mystery but at least we were together and ....and...and??

Chapter 29

- *It was going to be a Dog's life!..... -*

The following months into 2002 were a bit of a blur as I nursed Byron back to health, he returned to work and I sank deeper and deeper into depression, my job suffering as a result and life at home became more and more stressful.

It's obvious to me now that I developed OCD (Obsessive Compulsive Disorder) and to this day I work hard to keep it under control. If the tee towels in the kitchen were not folded identically and placed exactly the same distance apart on the rail I would dissolve into a hysterical rage!
Water splashes around the work surface of the kitchen sink would send me into blind fury.....
Any form of noise....TV too loud, a voice on TV that suddenly started kicking in as shrieking, music was an absolute no go! I felt fragile like a cracked glass waiting to shatter.
I coveted silence...as if my brain needed peace and rest, nothing to process.
Byron was unable to understand or indeed cope with my mood swings most of the time, many arguments ensued. I don't judge him for this or condemn him, it's a condition that NOBODY can truly appreciate unless they have suffered it... I slowly accepted that I suffer with a mental illness, brought about by life crisis and stress, nothing I could or can do about it other than work 'with myself a day at a time!'
Depression does NOT render a person a basket case or a maudling or attention seeking, for me it meant I had run out of steam, I couldn't cope with any more pressure or problems, I needed somewhere to hide and lick my wounds or someone's arms to hide in who would shield me from the life crap constantly raining down on me.
I became withdrawn, defensive, antagonistic, argumentative, hostile..... our marriage began to suffer accordingly.
Byron and I started to grow apart, our sex life dwindled and I for one didn't give a hoot!

It was all I could do to get up each day and keep going, hold my end up whatever worth that held nowadays. We argued over just about everything, and one evening in the middle of a heated conversation I seized up...as Byron ranted and raved at me from behind I calmly opened the third kitchen draw and took out a bottle of 1000mg Paracetamol that his mother had given us from her 'over' prescription.

As Byron ranted on in the background I slammed a fist full of tablets in my mouth...the journey out of this life hell was my intent!

Suddenly realising what I had in my hand Byron rushed forward yelling at me "Spit out you stupid cow...." He grabbed a fist full of my hair and slammed my face onto the kitchen work surface. I did indeed spit out the contents of my mouth more from shock and pain than desire...I had reached rock bottom, simple as, so I thought!

My face felt red hot and throbbing, Byron was angry, I crawled across the kitchen to the chair in the Dining Room. We both kept our distance, shaking and trying to rationalise what the hell was going on?

Eventually I took myself off to bed where I sat fully clothed sobbing, holding my face in my hands which by now was aching unbearably. Byron had the sense to keep his distance.

The following morning I awoke feeling like my face had been encapsulated in plaster of Paris....I had a job to move my lips let alone blink. One look in the mirror identified that the right side of my eye/face was black and blue bruised.

I met Byron on the landing between the bedroom and bathroom...he took one look at me before saying "Oh Jesus Christ M...I'm sorry." I ignored him and made my way to work where I barged into my Managing Directors office without invitation or agreement.... "I can't come to work for a while, I'm sorry but I have problems and I need to sort them out OK? My MD looked up utterly astounded by the sight of me.... and I'm going now before the rest of the office staff see me!" My comments were not so much advice to my employer but instruction! He tried to halt me in leaving, to ask after my injuries and problems but I wasn't in the mood for anything or anyone.... "Get out of my way John....or sack me, I don't care which!"

I left the building and drove home, head and face pounding in pain....I needed sleep and a future life plan...I didn't care which came first!

Byron and I led a 'distant' life for a few weeks whilst we came to terms with what each other had done to the other. Understandably we were both hurting and adrift in a sea of emotional pain and defiance and what's going to happen next anxiety.
Not long after I was diagnosed suffering from severe 'reactive' depression and pulled out of work for 3 months on sick leave, the isolation and seclusion at home gave me time to gather my thoughts and feelings. I felt utterly washed up as debris on the beach of life.

Chatting over a meal one evening we got on to the subject dog ownership.
"Did you ever have a dog when you were a kid?" Byron asked.
"No, but I did meet a dog in Woolworth's Store once when I was a kid and fell in love with it..." I answered wistfully, I went on to explain about the Black and Tan Teddy Bear that I'd bumped into and if ever I would have a dog, I would want one of these.
A light bulb was switching on for both of us during the conversation and before long we had somehow discussed and agreed we would get a dog....as you do!
The internet identified my childhood Teddy Bear dog as being an Airedale, King of The Terriers and so we went in search of one of these magnificent canines. After some investigations a Breeder in Berkshire was located, the wonderful Mac (Karl MacWilliams and his lovely wife Susannah and after a meeting at their home, our puppy was reserved....Dexter was to be my Baby in every sense of the word and I would adore him like the child I never had, he wasn't weaned so we needed to wait roughly five weeks and during this time I planned and nested and prepared like any new mother does....I simply couldn't wait for something in my life that wasn't tainted by all that had happened, a little life to love and protect.....a friend.
If you feel you can handle reading about what 'happens next' then you need to join us in my third Volume.... The Allbreeds Years.

DEXTER

Registered Kennel Club Name: Kingsacre Prince of Thieves

09.09.2002 - 07.03.2012

A truly magnificent, independent and beautiful character...always loved, never, EVER forgotten. God bless you my Baby Boy....

Me......Byron, Dexter, Hugo & Joshua

So much more to tell you in Volume III, meet Hugo and Joshua and join me in some bizarre and unbelievable adventures.....

CPSIA information can be obtained at www.ICGtesting.com
Printed in the USA
BVOW01s1316070714

358351BV00024B/854/P